AF556229

RURAL DEVELOPMENT THROUGH LITERACY CAMPAIGNS

By

Dr. G. Srinivasa Rao
M.A., M.A., M.A., B.Ed., M.Phil. Ph.D.
Programme Coordinator
State Resource Centre for Adult &
Continuing Education (SRC)
Visakhapatnam
(India)

DISCOVERY PUBLISHING HOUSE PVT. LTD.
NEW DELHI-110 002

Published by:

Tilak Wasan

DISCOVERY PUBLISHING HOUSE PVT. LTD.
4383/4B, Ansari Road, Darya Ganj
New Delhi-110 002 (India)
Phone : +91-11-23279245, 43596064-65
Fax : +91-11-23253475
E-mail : discoverypublishinghouse@gmail.com
sales@discoverypublishinggroup.com
parul.wasan@gmail.com
web : www.discoverypublishinggroup.com

***First Edition:* 2014**

ISBN: 978-93-5056-476-9

Rural Development Through Literacy Campaigns

Printed at:
Dynamic Printers
Delhi

IN LOVING MEMORY OF MY BELOVED BROTHER

G. Venkataramana

Preface

The knowledge of yesterday is inadequate to cope up with the complex and interrelated requirements of 'tomorrow' in the present Global scenario. The knowledge explosion in the context of scientific and technological advancements hasremained no option for the people to continue to learn throughout their lives. Life-long education provided people under the umbrella of Adult Education, Continuing Education, Extension Education, and so on. Continuing Education has been perceived as synonymous to the non-formal education, further education and even life-long education - it caters to the needs of all respects in the matters of age, sex, locality, occupation, language, education and socio-economic status.

In the contemporary world, no country can feel empowered unless all its citizens feel self-sufficient. In India, where majority of its citizens live in rural areas, it is the attention on rural development initiatives that assume greater importance in terms of empowering its people. Our country has unique nature, when compared to the other parts of the world. According to the census 2011, there are 63,8000 villages in India. Moreover, ignorance, illiteracy, social alienation and other factors contribute far reaching rural welfare schemes as per the expectations of the Government and planners. Further the previous initiatives like community development, rural development have no integrated approach towards the empowerment. The government has been implemented many programmes over the years for the developmental and infrastructural programmes/schemes on aiming individual welfare. But the impact of the programmes is not quite visible and effective due to the scattered nature of the distribution of the natural/human resources.

Continuing education centres are started at the grass root level and Preraks are appointed to carry out the activities of the centres. Neo-literates are the main cliental of the programme. The State Resource Centres happens to be the main agency to prepare and supply the post-literacy, continuing education and saakshar Bharat materials and to arrange for the training of Preraks to carry out the different activities like structured organisation of evening classes, library and reading rooms, charchamandal, short duration skill development programmes, recreational activities etc., at the centres.

Rural Development is mainly develops through increases the literacy and socio-economic empowerment of the rural community. In order to strengthen the socio-economic status of the people, Government of India implemented different schemes for rural welfare. These schemes are not fully been utilized by the individuals due to lack of awareness, participation and interest. There are research evidences that there some lapsesin implementation only due to the fact that the literacy rates of the rural area are not at satisfactory levels. Keeping in this view many Literacy campaigns organized by the governments are through field functionaries at various levels in a way to achieve the objectives set for improvement in quality of life. Functionaries at Adult Education Centers are strengthened through capacity building activities by 32 State Resource Centers established in the country. Continuing Education Centers are working as centers for information, reading, charchamandal, recreation activities and awareness generation. In fact, that the previous experiences explorations in the Rural Development is possible through literacy campaigns in a mission mode by the Adult Education centers. Sustainability of motivation among literacy educators, preraks, community members, N.G.Os and other voluntary bodies are to be given higher priority to take up these literacy campaigns in a mission mode.

It is hoped that the present book titled "**Rural Development Through Literacy Campaigns** will be useful to functionaries of the programme and implementing agencies in our nation. It also useful as a source book for National Literacy Mission Authority, voluntary organization, State Resource Centres, social workers, students, research scholars, teachers, Planners and all others who are involved theoretically and practically in continuing education programme.

Bringing out this book has been an exhausting-indeed an enervating task. Yet the encouragement of my research guides Prof. B.S.Vasudeva Rao and Prof. P.Ch.Lakshminarayana and my co-scholar Dr. P.Viswanadha Gupta shored up my confidence and helped me to complete this daunting assignment. I extend a note of special thanks to Discovery Publishing House Pvt. Ltd., New Delhi for publishing this book.

–Gedela Srinivasa Rao

Acknowledgements

I profusely express my deep sense of gratitude and indebtedness to my teachers and research directors Prof. B.S. Vasudeva Rao and Prof. P.Ch. Lakshminarayana, Andhra University, Visakhapatnam for their inspiring guidance with unstinted encouragement throughout the period of thesis work. With immense pleasure and profound sense of gratitude, I take this opportunity to express my heartfelt sincere thanks to them.

Dr. P. Viswanadha Gupta, Asst. Professor, Dept. of Adult and Continuing Education, University of Pune and Dr. P. Visweswara Rao, Scientist Retired, ICARI for their kind help during my study period.

I express hart felt thanks to Deputy Director, Zilla Saksharatha Samithi, Mandal Co-ordinators and other officials for permitting me to collect the data. I am thankful to respondents of my study for extending their cooperation during the process of data collection.

Many more people who helped me directly or indirectly during course of studies, if I don't list them all, it not for lack of gratitude, it is lack of space. To them all, I convey my best compliments and lot of thanks.

A lot of credit goes to my respectful and loving parents Sri. G. Kameswara Rao and Mrs. Suseela for all encouragement and support they have provided. I deserved to complement the services of Ms. Balamani. I thank my family members who have given me a lot of cooperative care in this endeavour.

–G. Srinivsa Rao

I sincerely convey my deep sense of gratitude and indebtedness to my esteemed research directors Prof. P. Vasudeva Rao and Dr. P. C. L. [illegible] Andhra University, who have [illegible] insight, guidance with unstinted encouragement throughout the period of these work. With a deep pleasure and profound sense of gratitude I take this opportunity to express my heartfelt sincere thanks to them.

Dr. [illegible] and [illegible] Department of [illegible] and Continuing Education, University of [illegible] [illegible] Retired, [illegible] for their kind help during my study period.

I express my heartfelt thanks to [illegible] Deputy Director [illegible] and [illegible] friends for permitting me to collect the data. I am thankful to the respondents of my study for extending their cooperation during the process of data collection.

Many more people who helped me directly or indirectly in the course of study [illegible] all of them could not be mentioned for lack of space. To them all I convey my best compliments and heartfelt thanks.

A special credit goes to my respected and loving parents Sri G. [illegible] and Mrs. [illegible] for all the encouragement and support they have provided. I heartily wish to compliment the services of Ms. Balamani. I thank the family members who have extended a lot of cooperation in this endeavour.

—G. Srinivasa Rao

Contents

Abbreviations

AE	Adult Education
BC	Backward Classes
BPL	Below Poverty Line
CABE	Central Advisory Board of Education
CBWE	Central Board for Workers Education
CDP	Community Development Programme
CE	Continuing Education
CEC	Continuing Education Centres
CEP	Continuing Education Programme
CMEY	Chief Minister's Empowerment of Youth
DRDA	District Rural Development Agency
DWCRA	Development of Women and Children in Rural Areas
FFLP	Farmers Functional Literacy Programme
GNP	Gross National Income
GOI	Government of India
GSM	Gram Shikshan Mohim
ICDS	Integrated Child Development Services
ICT	Information and communication technologies
IKP	Indira Kranthi Pathakam
INDIRAMMA	Integrated Development In Rural Areas and Model Municipal Areas
IRDP	Integrated Rural Development Programme

JCKs	Jana Chaitanya Kendras
JSNs	Jana Sikshana Nilayams
JSS	Jana Sikshana Samsthanams
LSK	Loka Siksha Kendra
MLOs	Mandal Literacy Organizers
MPDO	Mandal Parishad Development Officer
MPFL	Mass Programme for Functional Literacy
MRD	Ministry of Rural Development
MRO	Mandal Revenue Officer
MRP	Mandal Resource Persons
NABARD	National Bank for Agriculture and Rural Development
NAEP	National Adult Education Programmes
NBAE	National Board of Adult Education
NCEC	Nodal Continuing Education Centre
NFE	Non-Formal Education
NGO	Non Governmental Organisations
NLM	National Literacy Mission
NLMA	National Literacy Mission Authority
NPE	National Policy on Education
NREGA	National Rural Employment Guarantee Act
NSS	National Service Scheme
NYK	Nehru Yuva Kendras
OC	Other Caste
PLCs	Post-Literacy Campaigns
PLP	Post-Literacy Programme
PRA	Participatory Rural Appraisal
RFLP	Rural Functional Literacy Programme
SAEP	State Adult Education Programme
SC	Scheduled Castes

SEDS	Social Education and Development Society
SHG	Self Help Groups
SPSS	Statistical Package for Social Sciences
SRC	State Resource Centres
SRD	State Rural Development Department
ST	Scheduled Tribes
TLC	Total Literacy Campaigns
UGC	University Grants Commission
UNDP	United Nations Development Programme
UNICEF	United Nations International Children's Emergency Fund
VAO	Village Administrative Officer
VDO	Village Development Officers
VEC	Village Education Committees
VSS	Vana Samrakshana Samithis
ZSS	Zilla Saksharatha Samithi

CHAPTER 1 History of Adult Education Programmes

Society engages itself in many activities. Education is one of the manifold activities of the society. As such the aims and methods of education depend on the nature of society in which it is organised. For instance, in a predominantly agricultural society, agricultural education enjoys a privileged status. In an industrialized or industrialising society, technological education gains importance. In a democratic society, education is essentially organised for all sections of the society whereas in an oligarchic society, education is a privilege of the few. Further, all activities of a society require an education which may be either formal or non-formal or informal in nature. The type of education imparted depends upon the nature of information, knowledge, skills, attitudes, appreciations and values to be developed as well as the capabilities of the social institutions in that society. Every society attempts to sensitize its members to its norms, ways of life and set goals. A democratic society attempts to sensitise its members to democratic ways of life such as solving problems through discussion, negotiation and arbitration, open-mindedness for criticism, participation in group life, sharing of responsibilities, joint decision-making and so on. Any education given by a group tends to socialize its members, but the quality and value of socialization depends upon the needs and aims of the group. It is observed that one of the essential concerns of a social order is to sustain itself. It is to bring about social stability. The whole community of members and institutions are to be involved in it. From this view, education is an activity of the whole community and encourages peoples' participation in daily life of the society and themselves.

Promotion of health and hygiene, language, attitudes and values regarding family and kinship, a framework for understanding and managing interpersonal relations etc., remained within the family. Similarly several agencies offer education to its members. The peer groups, schools, religious bodies, state youth clubs, the mass media, and so on, are also the sources of education. So it is essential to recognize that education is not just schooling and as life oriented. Schools are only organised and specialized formal agencies of education. Social stability is maintained through education from all the agencies. Hence, education is to be interpreted in a very broader and comprehensive sense when it is intended as an instrument to promote a social order and quality of life.

Education has to realize the new social order envisioned for India. Education has demonstrated, with evidence through several research studies, that it has the potential to do so. Studies have shown that there is a high and positive relationship between education and productivity-agricultural as well as industrial. Higher levels of female education are associated with better child and mother care, better nutrition, higher levels of acceptance of health and family welfare services. Education can act as a powerful catalyst for change, development and promotion of new social order. Socialisation is an interesting process between the individual and his environment, through which the individual is shaped.

Education and its Importance: Education is a boon for the half clad, ill-fed and starving population suffering from poverty, disease, ill health, illiteracy, customs, beliefs and ignorance. The quality of the citizens depends upon the quality of their education. Democratic institutions cannot be built, nurtured and sustained with a large number of illiterate populations. In a democratic society, education allows the individual to view the things in a broader perspective, to identify the causes for deprivation, to find out several solutions and to select an appropriate solution to solve the problem. Education is a means for accelerating the pace and magnitude of economic development. It unlocks the doors to modernization. It is an investment and the value of its benefits to society cannot be assessed easily. Education helps the nation to control rapid population growth and also increase the agricultural and industrial production also helps, to reduce infant mortality rate it helps to achieve National Integration and also provide a wide range of opportunities for improving the quality of life of the people. Education is an indispensable aspect of the strategy for human resource development and for creating of a learned society. Many of the third world countries and the developing countries are now recognizing that socio-economic planning alone is not enough and also the human resource development is a key enabling factor in development.

Illiteracy is one of the formidable tasks facing the world. Nearly one third of the world population are illiterate and about seventy per cent of the world's illiterates are in Asia and 100 million school age children of the world have no place to learn. Today, unfortunately India is confronted with a massive number of 450 million illiterates in all age groups. Of this, about 110 million are in the age group of 15-35. In an illiterate environment, the efforts of the government to introduce welfare measures will not really result in meeting the expectation of the planners. The details of literacy rate in India after independence is presented in the table 1.1.

Table 1.1: Literacy Rate in India from 1901-2011 (Percentage)

Year	Total	Men	Women	
1901	5.35	9.83	0.60	(5 years & above)
1911	5.92	10.56	1.05	(5 years & above)
1921	7.16	12.21	1.18	(5 years & above)
1931	9.50	15.59	2.93	(5 years & above)
1941	16.10	24.90	7.30	(5 years & above)
1951	16.67	24.95	7.93	(5 years & above)
1961	24.02	34.44	12.95	(5 years & above)
1971	29.45	39.45	18.69	(5 years & above)
1981	36.23	46.89	24.52	(5 years & above)
1991	52.11	63.86	39.42	(7 years & above)
2001	65.38	75.85	54.16	(7 years & above)
2011	74.04	82.14	65.46	(5 years & above)

Source: Census of India

A glance at the table reveals that the growth of literacy rate has been slow up to 1951 and it has been rising at a faster level later on. Due to effective implementation of several literacy drives after independence and by introducing better strategies the results are satisfying. However, there is a lot to be done in this direction. The literacy rate as per 2011 census is 74.04 per cent. The growth of literacy among men is better in relation to that of women. Due to lack of adequate educational facilities, migration, family traditions, beliefs, early marriages, poverty and cultural constraints, the literacy rate among women is low.

There is a need apart from literacy; people will be subjected to transformation in change of life styles in all levels towards positive side. This helps to lead quality of life and direct bearing on family and indirect on society.

The development is for man, of man, all of man, whole of man and is concerned with what happens to the last man.

Development cannot, therefore, be adequately measured only in terms of GNP growth, but by how far the basic needs of the people for food, shelter, clothing, drinking water, health and education are being met; not in terms of per capita consumption of steel and power, but in terms of employment generation; not in terms of industrialization or agricultural green revolution, but by how far the unequal distribution of incomes and property in society-which is the basic cause of poverty and its consequences of malnutrition, ill-health and illiteracy-are reduced. Thus the concept of development concerns with meeting the basic needs of the people, removal of poverty, unemployment and exploitation and more equitable distribution of wealth.

Similarly, the concept of formal system of education must be replaced by a restructured educational system in which the people will have a key place. The centrality of education, particularly of adult education is to integrate adult education into the overall national educational system, which, in turn, must be integrated with the national development plans.

The problem of adult education is of equal concern to sociology and to education and as such the emphasis is for the upliftment of the deprived masses for better living and also for the desired social and economic progress in the society.

Emile Durkheim, a sociologist, clearly indicated the need for a 'sociological' approach to the study of education. Durkheim considered education 'to be something essentially social in character, in its origins and its functions, and that as a result the theory of education relates more clearly to sociology than to any other social science'. He emphasized that education is not a static phenomenon but a dynamic and even changing process. Every society with its own changing socio-cultural needs will require an appropriate education to meet these needs. Since needs change continuously education must also change. The society, thus, is the prime factor in determining the educational patterns, so that its socio-cultural and economic needs may be satisfied and it continues to grow. The society, community, people and target group must involve in the activity.

The Government of India introduce the non-formal system of education to accelerate literacy rate and to cover the illiterates and make them literate to support formal education.

Development of Adult Education in India: The formal education system always centres on the need of young, who are supposed to establish future direction. The non-formal education helps people to develop themselves in socio, political, cultural and economic aspects and change to level better life to the family. The education he learns in advanced age (non-formal) make him self-sufficient and utilize them in his daily activity like child education, health, vocation and skill development in his occupation, social and political empowerment and so on. The adult, who has maturity and experience in thinking and practicing, with education and knowledge can actively participate in social activity. The acquired knowledge through adult and continuing education provides sustainable development.

The need for adult education evolved and unfolded itself with the realization of the fact that it is the key to the future progress of mankind India (Roy, 1967) With all its manifestations of socio-economic and technical backwardness, has no other way but to take a serious view of the need of adult education and to implement it as a priority programme. With its realization, Government of India besides strengthening formal education system has launched a number of schemes to eradicate illiteracy in India. (Vasudevarao, B.S., 1988)

Post-Independence Development: Formal efforts started emerging in the field of adult education with the promotion of popular ministries in the provinces. The popular governments accorded public recognition to adult education and identified it as a definite responsibility of government.

(Bordia, 1973). Subsequently the Central Advisory Board of Education appointed an Adult Education Committee in 1938 under the chairmanship of Dr. Mahamad. The committee strongly recommended for serious effort in adult education and declared "No government can make any appreciable headway with its schemes for promotion of socio-economic welfare of its people unless the people are prepared to meet the government halfway and offer it responsive co-operation. This responsive co-operation is only possible when people posses some amount of education". (Nurullah and Naik, 1951).

After the emergence of India as an Independent country, the concept of adult education underwent significant changes. It was not only variety of socio-economic and political developments within India but also the overseas influence played no less significant part. Under various bilateral and multi-lateral agreements, India received both technical and financial support from a number of countries. It was the changing policies of the Government of India that served to have influenced the transformation of the concept of adult education from basic literacy into Civil Literacy by 1950's and further to functional literacy by 1960's. With the introduction of the National Adult Education Programmes in 1978, the focus of adult education shifted to conscientization and development. The launching of the National Literacy Mission in 1988, and the subsequent emergence of Total Literacy campaigns in different parts of India led to the emergence of the concept of development literacy, which included the components of self-reliance in basic literacy and numeracy, social awareness, acquisition of relevant skills and imbibing the values of national integration, conservation of the environment and gender equity. It is possible to discuss a pattern and certain cyclical trends in the history of Indian adult education movement. Broadly, there are four cycles which represents the four major approaches and concept of adult education in India. While the traditional approach to literacy adopted the view that learning to read and write had an innate goodness itself, the religious approach emphasized the reading of the study of the holy scriptures in order to propagate "the faith". It goes beyond the acquisition of knowledge and the emphasis is on the application of learning to daily living. The work-oriented approach dominated during the phase of functional literacy. Based on Paulo Freire Philosophy of conscientization, the social change approach made its debut during the phase of National Adult Education Programme and it continues even today (Shah. S.Y., 1999).

Table 1.2: Changing Concept of Adult Education in India

Approaches	Cycles	Key Concepts	Main Programme
Traditional or religion	First Cycle (1882-1947)	Basic Literacy	Night Schools
Life orientation (1949-1966)	Second Cycle	Civic Literacy	Social education (1952) Workers Education (1957)
Work Oriented	Third Cycle (1967-1977)	Functional Literacy	Farmers Functional Literacy programme (1966), RFLP (1966), Non-formal Education (1974)
Social Change	Forth Cycle (1978-todate)	Development Literacy	National Adult Education Programme (1978), Mass Programme for Functional Literacy (1985), Total Literacy Campaigns (1990) Post-Literacy Programme (1992), Continuing Education Programme (1996) & Saakshar Bharat (2009)

Source: Encyclopaedias of India Adult Education, 1999

In each of the four cycles, different adult educational programmes were developed and implemented in different parts of India under various nomenclatures viz. Social Education, Farmers Functional Literacy Programme, Workers Education (Shramik VIdyapeeth), National Adult Education Programme, Programme of Functional Literacy and Total Literacy Campaign and so on. Though a number of official and non-official agencies were associated with planning and implementation of these programmes, the source of funding was mainly from the Government of India, which formulated the policy and designed the programme package. Notwithstanding the changes in nomenclature, operational modalities, expansion of programmes over the years and shifts in the approach, the main trust of adult education continues to be on basic literacy (Shah, S.Y.,1999).

Some Significant Programmes of Adult Education: The imperative need and importance of adult education was recognised by the leaders of the freedom movement in India. The Central Advisory Board of Education (CABE) officially emphasised the need for adult literacy. Shri Maulana Abdul Kalam Azad, the then Education Minister, called the new programme of adult literacy as 'Social Education'. It included literacy, acquisition of skills and crafts, hygiene and training in citizenship. Social education became a part of the Community Development Programme when it was launched in 1952.

Gram Shikshan Mohim: The Satara experiment in adult education was named the Gram Shikshan Mohim (1959). Village and Taluk meetings were organised to propagate adult education in Marathi, their mother tongue. Emphasis was on imparting the ability to read and write to the neo-literate. The three-to-four-months programme on Gandhian lines ended with a village celebration on conferring of honours to the neo-literates.

Farmers' Functional Literacy Programme (FFLP): The FFLP, started in 1967-68 was jointly organised by the Ministries of Agriculture, Education and Information and Broadcasting and were involved in linking up of literacy to national developmental programmes. When the Government of India planned for the 'Green Revolution' with new technologies and methods in farming high-yielding varieties of seeds, new fertilisers, pesticides and such others were introduced. The farmers who were to use them required training and some sort of an initiation. More than a literacy programme, it was a method of training for agricultural development. The training programmes were to help farmers to adopt themselves to new techno-vocational requirements of development. The functional literacy component was to help the farmers:

(a) to read and write simple letters;
(b) complete simple application forms for loans;
(c) maintain simple farm accounts;
(d) read and identify labels on fertilizer bags and pesticide bags; and
(e) follow programmes on the radio.

Non-Formal Education (NFE): Non-formal education received a fillip since 1974 following the recommendations of the Central Advisory Board of Education (CABE). It suggested initiating non-formal education with multiple entry and part-time education programmes. Non-formal education programmes were expected to cover all age groups from 6 years onwards including drop-outs. As part of this effort Nehru Yuvak Kendras have been started to cover the non-student youth and provide training in different skills together with promotion of cultural activities, sports, social services, self-employment and recreational activities.

Worker's Education Programme: On the recommendations of a Committee of Experts on Workers Education appointed by the Government of India in 1957, the Central Board for Workers Education (CBWE) was also established. Regional Workers' Education Centres were also started in different urban centres in India. The Ministry of Education felt that urban workers should be provided opportunities for adult literacy including vocational training, functional literacy and acquisition of skills. To that end Shramik Vidyapeeths were established, at present it is named as s Jana Shikshana Samsthans.

Adult Education for Women: The Government of India has launched a number of adult literacy programmes which also cater to the literacy of adult women. The scheme is being implemented by the Integrated Child Development Services

(ICDS) project. It focuses its attention on adult women in the age group of 15 to 45 years. It helps women:

(a) acquire skills of literacy though functional literacy classes;
(b) imparts information on modern methods of health and hygiene and the importance of nutritious food and balanced diet; and
(c) provides need-based training in home management and child care.

National Adult Education Programme (NAEP): The National Adult Education Programme is a reflection of the Government's resolve "to wage a clearly conceived, well planned and relentless struggle against illiteracy to enable the masses to play an active role in social and cultural change" (Pillai, 1980). The policy statement says in this regard that the NAEP was to be: "a means to bring about a fundamental change in the process of socio-economic development, from a situation in which the poor remain passive spectators at the fringe of the development activity to being enabled to be at its centre, and as active participants" (NAEP, An Outline, 1978). In bringing about this change, the NAEP consists of three basic components of action, viz., Literacy, Functionality and Social Awareness.

Mass Programme for Functional Literacy (MPFL): In May 1986, the Ministry of Education, Government of India with the co-operation of University Grants Commission (UGC) launched Mass Programme for Functional Literacy (MPFL). The slogan of 'each one teach one' was modified to 'each one teach five'. The objective of MPFL was to involve University Adult Education Departments, Students and NSS Volunteers in eradication of illiteracy.

National Policy on Education (NPE): The National Policy on Education (1986) reviewed all earlier efforts in the area of adult education and identified the relation between poverty and illiteracy and the need for adult education for development. NPE suggested three major steps in this context for development of adult education. These steps were:

1. Mass literacy campaigns;
2. Large scale involvement of students, teachers and unemployed youth;
3. creating centres for Continuing Education (CE) in rural areas for promoting post-literacy education and women literacy.

It also suggests providing sustainable education with mission approach.

National Literacy Mission (NLM): As part of national effort to usher in latest developments in science and technology, the late Prime Minister Shri Rajiv Gandhi initiated five Technology Missions, to bring rapid developments and create a new ethos, and the National Literacy Mission was one of them. The aim of the mission was to educate 80 million illiterates in the age group of 15-35 years with a target of 30 million by 1990 and another 50 million by 1995 (revised later) by creating mass movements and through voluntary effort. Broad objectives of the National Literacy Mission (NLM 1988) were to enable the adult illiterates to:

- Achieve self-reliance in literacy and numeracy
- Become aware of the causes of their deprivation and moving towards amelioration of their condition through organisation and participation in the process of development;
- Acquire skills to improve the economic status and general well-being; and
- Imbibe the values of national integration, conservation of the environment, women's equality, and observance of small family norm.

On 5th September 2009 a new programme was launched by the Government of India and named as Saakshar Bharat. The basic unit at village level is called Loka Siksha Kendra (LSK) with only 10 illiterates to be educated and main emphasis is given to female illiterates. The kendra will act as a window for information, not only for imparting literacy but also to provide the target group all kind of help to develop their socio-economic and vocational aspects. It is known as a human development centre.

The NLM planned three pronged effort to eradicate illiteracy as:

1. Total Literacy Campaign
2. Post Literacy Programme
3. Continuing Education Programme.

Total Literacy Campaigns (TLC): The idea of TLC is to make a whole district fully literate within a stipulated period of time of six months by following the campaign approach. It is an area specific, time bound, action oriented (result), cost effective literacy promotion programme based fully on voluntarism and people's participation. It is a new concept in literacy promotion in as much as the earlier programmes for eradication of illiteracy run on the centre based approach which had several inherent weaknesses and could not achieve the desired results. TLC's emphasis is not on mere literacy. These literacy programmes have a number of objectives apart from spreading literacy such as national integration, women's employment, universal immunisation, deforestation, alleviation of poverty, universal compulsory primary education and others. Total Literacy Campaign stresses more on awareness of human liberation from oppression and bonded ness. It emphasises functional literacy. Districts taking up literacy campaigns differ from one another in their approach and implementation strategies, depending on the priorities on the various aspects of the programme.

After experimenting with successive and alternative models of adult literacy and education programme, the NLM has now adopted "Mass Campaign Approach for Total Literacy" as its principal strategy for eradication of illiteracy. Total Literacy Campaigns (TLCs), to provide basic literacy skills to the illiterate population in the age group 9-35 years, have been launched in most parts of the country. NLM has set for itself the objective of making 100 million persons functionally literate by 1997, which is the terminal year of the 8th Five Year Plan. As per latest available reports, over 40 million persons have so far been made literate.

Post-Literacy Programme: With the successful implementation of TLCs in several districts all over the country, a situation is fast emerging whereby millions of illiterates are acquiring basic literacy skills and joining the class of neo-literates each year. Without a meaningful post-literacy programme, many of these persons may relapse into the world of illiteracy. The objective of NLM is therefore, to develop systematic post-literacy programmes as a part of continuing education. With this end in view, Post-Literacy Campaigns (PLCs) are launched in the districts which complete the initial phase of imparting basic literacy skills through TLCs. PLC comprises of a two year post-literacy programme which includes about 50 hours of guided-learning as a bridge towards taking the learners a self-reliant level of learning. The subsequent phase of PLC comprises of self-directed learning through library service, newspapers for neo-literates, Charcha mandals and other activities such as vocational training and skill development. The PLC addresses itself mainly to the goal of consolidation and application of the literacy skills to the actual living and working conditions of the neo-literates.

TLCs have resulted in a positive change in attitude, a new confidence among the learners to upgrade their skills and adopt it for individual development, and eventually for social action. The enthusiasm and confidence generated among the learners in the districts which have successfully completed both the TLC as well as the PLC phases, clearly points towards the need to sustain the education process and to provide learning opportunities on a continuing basis. The rudimentary skills (3R's) acquired by the neo-literates need to be further reinforced and widened so as to enable them to fully play the crucial role for their own personal, social and economic upliftment and for the development of the country. In the face of persistent social and economic problems, application and utilization of literacy skills acquired by the neo-literates often remains a difficult proposition. The literacy process have, therefore, to be continued as to result in release of creative energies of the people, which must be sustained to enable the people to realize their potential, to help themselves and achieve self-reliance. Hence, the crucial importance is of creating satisfactory arrangements for continuing education of all learners.

The investigator undertake, to study the impact of continuing education programme on the beneficiaries, hence the concept, objectives, functioning of continuing education programme was explained in details.

Continuing Education Programme: Systematic learning opportunities in a continuing education centre to enable the neo literates to get maximum gain. CEP is not only to consolidate the basic literacy skills of reading, writing, numeric and problem solving but it also foster in individuals confidence and assurance to acquire adequate basic repertoire of skills in order to assimilate further knowledge and to incorporate new skills in their personality without personal disequilibrium and disintegration either through formal system of schooling or through open school system. (Anusuya Devi, K., 2009)

Continuing Education Programme is also an indispensable aspect of the strategy of human resource development and of the goal of creation of a learning society and third phase of NLM strategy. Formal education as an instrument of human resource development is not really effective in remedying the structural inequalities in the society. Continuing education, which provides a second chance to those who missed formal education and is responsive learners' needs, directly addresses itself to structural inequalities. Only continuing education can bring about full development of human resources.

Continuing education includes, post-literacy for neo-literates and school dropouts for retention of literacy skills, continuation of learning beyond elementary literacy and application of this learning for improving their living conditions. But continuing education goes beyond post-literacy. Continuing education includes all of the learning opportunities all people want or need outside of basic literacy education and primary education. In continuing education, human resource development becomes the focus of attention and provides access to welfare schemes. Thus, continuing education is also an essential extension of literacy to promote human resource development.

Activities and Objective of Continuing Education Programme

1. Provision of facilities for retention of literacy skills and continuing education to enable the learners to continue their learning beyond basic literacy.
2. Creating scope for application of functional literacy for improvement of living conditions and quality of life.
3. Dissemination of information on development programmes and widening and improving participation of traditionally deprived sections of the society.
4. Creation of awareness about national concerns such as national integration, conservation and improvement of the environment, women's equality, observance of small family norms, etc., and sharing of common problems of the community.
5. Improvement of economic conditions and general wellbeing as well as improvement of productivity of organizing short duration training programmes, orientation courses for providing vocational skills and by taking up linkage activities for establishing direct linkage between continuing education and development activities.
6. Provision of facilities for library and reading rooms for creating an environment conducive for literacy efforts and a learning society.
7. Organisation of cultural and recreational activities with effective community participation.

Clientele of Continuing Education Centre

The functions and objectives of the Continuing Education Centre as stated in the document reveal that it would be able to serve the following categories of persons:

(a) Neo-literates who complete the functional literacy/post-literacy courses under TLC/PLC or other programmes;
(b) School dropouts;
(c) Pass-outs of primary schools;
(d) Pass-outs of non-formal education programme; and
(e) All other members of the community interested in availing opportunities for life-long learning.

Setting up of Continuing Education Centres

Since continuing education is, by definition, provision of opportunities for life-long learning, setting up local community based Continuing Education Centres becomes indispensable for effective implementation of any continuing education programme. The following guidelines are, therefore, provided for establishment and organisation of Continuing Education Centres by NLM:

1. Establishment of Continuing Education Centres should be planned with an area-specific and community based approach. In view of the fact that the beneficiaries of continuing education programmes would include not only a very large number of adult neo-literates emerging from TLCs/PLCs but also sizeable number of pass-outs from formal and non-formal streams, the earlier policy of having one CEC (Jana Sikshna Nilyam) serving a cluster of villages having a population of 5,000 may no longer be suited to meet the continuing education needs of the targeted population.
2. Generally one Continuing Education Centre may be established for each village to serve around 500 neo-literates in a population of about 1,500 to 2,000. However, in thickly populated areas, the population covered may be more than 2,000. In sparsely populated areas such as hilly tracks, tribal and desert areas, the population covered could be less than 1,500.
3. A Continuing Education Centre may be housed in a school building, panchayat office or any other public building. A Continuing Education Centre may be

established on priority basis in a village where people come forward to support it by providing a suitable accommodation and other local resources. However, the interest of weaker sections of the society shall be especially kept in view.

4. 8 to 10 Continuing Education Centres would form a cluster, with one of them being designated as a 'Nodal Continuing Education Centre'.
5. The In-charge (Prerak) of the Nodal Continuing Education Centre would be a full-time paid worker and those of other Continuing Education Centres would have to be volunteers working on part-time basis.
6. The Nodal Continuing Education Centre besides undertaking the functions of Continuing Education Centres would facilitate networking with other Continuing Education Centres in the cluster for:
   (a) Providing avenues and facilities for Continuing Education programmes through structured and unstructured modes;
   (b) Conduct for all information, programmes of Continuing Education, vocational training, etc.;
   (c) Supply of books on regular basis;
   (d) Regular monitoring and evaluation;
   (e) Coordination with other development departments for convergence of their services at the Continuing Education Centres;
   (f) Establishing, liaison with Village Education Committees, gram panchayats, mahila mandals, voluntary organisations, etc., for active involvement of the community in the Continuing Education programmes; and
   (g) Nodal point for resource mobilisation and decentralised supply of material, equipment's, books, etc.
7. Supervision of all Continuing Education Centres in a Block would be the responsibility of the Block

Co-ordinator, who would liaison with in-charge (Prerak) of the Nodal Continuing Education Centre.

8. The Zilla Saksharatha Samithi (ZSS) will have overall responsibility for ensuring efficient functioning of the Continuing Education Centres in the district. It should establish networking arrangements to foster linkages with development programmes of other departments, secure involvement of NGOs and ensure that peoples' participatory structures at all levels are established and effectively involved in management of Continuing Education Centres and implementation of the Continuing Education programmes.

Functions of Continuing Education Centres

The principle objective of establishment of Continuing Education Centres is to serve as a window or a focal service point where diverse kinds of Continuing Education programmes and activities are taken up to provide opportunities for life-long learning to all sections of the population. The functions of Continuing Education include:

An Evening Class

For up gradation of literacy and numeracy skills evening classes are organized for 3-4 hours once a week. The learners have the option to come for an hour or so at the time of their convenience on that day.

A Library and Reading Room

Books are purchased from the non-recurring and recurring provisions; copies of old journals are maintained and useful booklets relating to development programmes will be published by concerned agencies. Wall papers and newspapers appropriate for adult learners, informative and entertaining journals, developmental literature, etc., are also made available.

A Charcha Mandal (Discussion Group)

For discussing on common problems, this forum is utilized for quality of life improvement and individual interest programme.

Training Programmes

Simple and short duration training programmes relating to such subjects as health and family welfare, new developments in agriculture and animal husbandry, conservation of energy, improved chulha, etc., are organized. Continuing Education Centres may also help the local youth to benefit from various vocational training programmes. Income generation programmes, which help participants to acquire or upgrade vocational skills and enable them to conduct income generating activities, are made available in structured packages.

Sports and Adventurous Activities

The stress is on indigenous sports, walking excursions, cycling trips in groups, etc. If savings are available, visit by bus to development projects are also arranged.

Recreational and Cultural Activities

Activities, particularly traditional and folk forms of art, rural theatre, puppetry, etc., are encouraged.

An Information Window

For securing information on various developmental programmes, information and material suitable for neo-literates are procured from the concerned development agencies.

A Communication Centre

Community radio, audio cassettes player-cum-recorder is provided (in the Nodal Continuing Education Centre only).

The Continuing Education Centre is supposed to act as a catalyst among Neo-literates, Community and Government Developmental Departments. Nodal Preraks must organize meetings face-to-face between welfare scheme people and learners of CEC. Moreover, the Prerak is supposed to act as guide, philosopher, counsellor and assisting agent for learners to receive benefits from the welfare schemes of the government without the intemperance of middlemen. The CEP has to develop the learners to be self-sufficient & self-confident and prepare them as a citizen of present day.

Continuing Education Programme is a unique programme specially designed for Indian context.

Adult Education through Five-Year Plans

Immediately after independence the Central Government faced the problem of partition on one hand and illiteracy, poverty and others on the other. It realized the importance of education in general and education of illiteracy masses in particular. In 1948, the Central Advisory Board of Education (CABE) appointed a sub-committee with M.L. Saxena as Chairman to give a report on Adult Education. The Committee report laid emphasis both on literacy and general education as part of adult education.

The adult education programmes designed and implemented plan wise were discussed comprehensively.

First Five Year Plan (April 1951 to March 1956)

Large number of Social Education Training camps were organised for training village level workers and educating illiterates. The social education programmes was shared by the Ministry of Community Development and Ministry of Education at central level along with state governments.

Second Five Year Plan (April 1956 to March 1961)

Started National Fundamental Education Centre, Institute of Library Science, Institute for Workers Education, National Book Trust, Production of Literature for Social Education Workers, and neo-literates, and assisting voluntary organisations besides social education.

Third Five Year Plan (April 1961 to March 1966)

Despite a well-conceived and planned programme, social education could not integrate literacy with functional training and developmental activities in practice. A movement known as Grama Sikshna Mohim was organised in Satara District of Maharashtra in 1959 (Patil, 1973). This was a mass literacy movement, comparable with current TLCs, and gained significance in 1963 as it spread to all the districts in the State. The Mysore State Adult Education Council, Bombay City Social Education Committee, Bengal Social Services League,

Indian Council of Churches, the Rama Krishna Mission and Literacy House, Lucknow were started during this period and made headway in adult education.

Three Annual Plans (April 1966 to March 1969)

Due to the war with China the Government of India could not finalise the fourth five-year plan. There were three annual plans for subsequent three years of third five-year plan, i.e., April 1966 to March 1969. During this period the notable feature in the field of adult education was the initiation of Farmers Functional Literacy Project in 1969 to provide a link between education and agricultural development with the three components of farmers' training, functional (FFLP) literacy and farm broadcasting.

Fourth Five Year Plan (April 1969 to March 1974)

The Farmer's Functional Literacy Project (FFLP) started in three districts initially was extended to 7 districts in 1968-70 and to another thirty-five districts in 1970-71 (Bordia, 1975). In May, 1970 the National Board of Adult Education (NBAE) came into existence which was a significant development in this plan. The aim of the Board was to co-ordinate adult education between the centre and the states and among various ministries of the Government of India. The Directorate of Adult Education was also started during this period.

Fifth Five Year Plan (April 1974 to March 1978)

In this period FFLP had covered 150 districts throughout the country. The project made an impact on adoption of agricultural practices by illiterate farmers. Non-formal Education programme for the age group of 15-25 years was also launched during 1975-76 with an objective to provide useful and purposeful education to young people.

Two Annual Plan Periods (April 1978 to March 1980)

The government, observing the low percentage of literacy level in the country, launched a massive programme known as National Adult Education Programme (NAEP) on 2nd October 1978, coinciding with the birth anniversary of

Mahatma Gandhi. The programme aimed at covering 100 million adults in the age group 15-35 years by 1983-84.

Sixth Five Year Plan (April 1980 to March 1985)

The Ministry of Education and Social Welfare set up a high level committee in October, 1979 with Dr. D.S. Kothari as Chairman to Review NAEP in all its aspects and suggest improvements. The Report of the Committee (April 1980) highlighted the fact that the literacy rate had grown at less than one per cent while the population had been growing at more than two per cent a year. Therefore the objective of universal literacy had been promoted through the twin provisions of universal education for children and massive programme of adult education.

Seventh Five Year Plan (April 1985 to March 1990)

A drastic change in the situation of adult education programme took place during the fag end of 7th plan. The programmes like Rural Functional Literacy Programme (RFLP) and State Adult Education Programme (SAEP) were started.

A major development in this plan was declaration of National Policy on Education (1986) and the new strategy on Adult Education. The launching of the National Literacy Mission Authority (NLMA) on 5th May, 1988 by the late Prime Minister, Sheri Rajiv Gandhi was another main event in this plan.

Eighth Five Year Plan (April 1992 to March 1997)

The main strategy during the eighth plan period was adoption of area approach in all adult education programmes. The Total Literacy Campaign (TLCs) was implemented by the NLM in 20 States and 4 Union Territories. Out of NLM's target of 345 districts by the end of 8th plan, 336 districts were covered fully or partially (Literacy Mission, May, 1995).

The objective kept by NLM was to achieve total literacy in 75 per cent districts in the country during the Eighth Plan Period through TLCs. TLCs were followed by Post Literacy Campaign (PLC) with duration of at least 2 years and followed by Continuing Education Programme.

Ninth Five Year Plan (1997-2002)

Eradication of illiteracy was the top priority in this plan and making 10 crores adults literate in the 9th and 10th plan periods. In addition, 38 districts have been covered under rural functional literacy projects. Hence, the total coverage comes to 485 districts. Further, gradually all districts were brought under continuing education programme. In this plan it was further proposed to strengthen state resource centres and Jana Sikshana Samsthanams.

Tenth Five Year Plan (2002-2007)

Illiteracy is largely a problem of social groups among whom literacy rates are low and who also suffer from other handicaps which make it difficult for them to participate in the adult education programmes and developmental activities. It is, therefore, most important to ensure greater participation of these groups in future adult education programmes. This requires a focused attention to their needs and problems and to the adoption of specific measures to suit their requirements. The focus in the Tenth Plan would shift to residual illiteracy and catering to difficult segments of the population.

Eleventh Five Year Plan (2007-2012)

Following are the targets and special focus areas during this plan period:

- Achieve 80 per cent literacy rate,
- Reduce gender gap in literacy to 10 per cent,
- Reduce regional, social, and gender disparities,
- Extend coverage of NLM programmes to 15+ age group Special Focus Areas
- A special focus on SCs, STs, minorities, and rural women.
- Focus also on low literacy States, tribal areas, other disadvantaged groups and adolescents.

Twelfth Five Year Plan (2012-2017)

The country has achieved a literacy rate of 74 per cent as per the Census 2011, an increase by 9.2 per cent over Census 2001. The gender gap in literacy has reduced from

21.6 per cent in2001 to 16.7 per cent in 2011. Adult Education is a major catalyst to inclusive growth. In the 12th Plan the effort will be to provide functional literacy, with focus on women, SC, ST, Minorities and other disadvantaged groups and weaker sections. The thrust will also be on providing basic education to ensure seamless transition to learning equivalent to classes V, VIII and X. Relevant skill development programmes will also be undertaken with support of institutions in the public, NGO and private sector, and in keeping with the National Vocational Education Qualifications Framework. Continuing Education programmes will provide opportunity for adults to pursue education through short duration courses in life skills.

Development of the People

The concept and nature of development and relation between education and development was discussed in the following lines. Moreover, the study area chosen was Rural in nature. Literacy is tool for development; people who are literates are more advantage position than illiterates as per general observation and findings of earlier research studies. The government is taking the measures to empower the people for self-sustain and self relation, and always advertise create requirement to people participation and approach is people intend. Hence, the welfare programmes offered by Government in the study area and concept of Rural Development were also presented.

In Indian context, development, definitional and conceptually, denotes progress - social, economic, educational, cultural, scientific and technological-brought about by planned/programmed efforts to inaugurate an era of orderly and peaceful transformation of a society in a constitutionally desired direction. The unfortunate fact, however, is that despite considerable progress, there are marked disparities in income and in poor people's access to resources, economic opportunities and social services and all because of illiteracy. The economic development is a priority given now as an instrument of social trans-function, but nobody thinks that it alone can bring about social transformation and a desired vision of development. The social tensions that we are faced with are largely the result of our single-minded pursuit to economic growth model of development, putting the broader mandate of social transformation- with social justice, equity, equality of opportunity and poor people's empowerment and participation in developmental efforts as its salient characteristics into the background.

Development has become a key word in the contemporary dialogue on human conditions. Development is now a widely accepted goal and is enunciated in policy declarations of national governments as well as the international community. It is because of an extension of this concept that societies have been distinguished as developed, underdeveloped or developing. The development of developing societies is now the universally endorsed objective of international action. Despite the fact that certain goals of development have emerged as well defined, it has not been possible to form a clear or coherent image of the process of development. This has resulted into contradicting developmental approaches and strategies. (Srivastava, Mukul, 1998)

People-Centred Development

People-centred development is defined by the UNDP as "development of the people, by the people and for the people". What so ever the precise definition given, the implications are always that people should be involved in their own development. In effect, according to COX, David (1998), people-cantered development can be said to rest on five foundation pillars viz.:

1. **Awareness Rising:** People need to be aware of the realities of their situation and their environment as necessary condition for their full participation in their development.
2. **Social Mobilisation:** People need to form into groups and local organisations as a necessary condition for

drawing on all the available local resources and for insisting on their right to participate in their own development.

3. **Participation:** Development will reflect the realities and needs of people only when the development process is a fully participatory one.
4. **Self-reliance:** If the people are to have maximum control over their own development, it is important that development rest, as much as possible, on the resources available within the local community; to maximize self-reliance is to maximize the people-centred nature of development.
5. **Sustainability:** If development has to continue to provide for people's need it must be sustainable.

Success or failure of any programme will depend on peoples participation on developmental activities and empower themselves to self sustenance. Education provides sustainable empowerment to people. In an illiteracy environment, there is a -meagre scope for development. Hence, human development is the main stress for giving quality of life to people; the prerequisite for this are literacy, people participation, availing welfare programmes, and the role of information and communication.

Concept of Rural Development

Mahatma Gandhi, Father of the Nation and the visionary architect of India's Rural Development Programmes, in his own words said - "Just as the whole universe is contained in the Self, so is India contained in the villages". The villages epitomize the soul of India. With more than 70 per cent of the Indian population living in rural areas, rural India reflects the very essence of Indian culture and tradition. No wonder then that a holistic development of India as a Nation rests on a sustained and holistic development of rural India.

The term 'Rural' does not imply a mere non-urban character in the spatial sense. It is a social and cultural concept. Rural society has its own social ethos and therefore requires full comprehension of its ingredients, while extending the process of development of this vast sector. Rural development is a positive concept of reconstructing the rural society to fully develop its potentialities and capabilities to be self reliant in basic needs. The word 'rural' thus stands for a socio cultural entity and is not merely a territorial or vocational concept. The basic character of out rural society is even now predominantly agricultural, agricultural labours, child labour and Artisans and with 70 per cent illiteracy.

In fact, the term "rural development" is a subset of the broader term "development." Development is a subjective and value-based term; thus, there cannot be a consensus as to its meaning. At best, development in the context of society could be conceptualized as a set of desirable societal objectives that a country seeks to achieve. Rural development connotes overall development of rural areas with a view to improve the quality of life of rural people. It is a comprehensive and multidimensional concept and encompasses the development of agriculture and allied activities, village and cottage industries and crafts, socio-economic infrastructure, community services and facilities, and, above all, the human resources in rural areas.

The most important landmark in the history of Indian Rural Development efforts was the setting up of an organisation called Community Projects Administration in March, 1952. The main thrust of the organisation was to administer community development programmes at grass root level. The organisation and its programmes underwent many transformations.

With reference to Rural Development programmes, the initial emphasis was on community rather than the rural areas as such. This led to emergence of Community Development programmes and Community Block concept in the beginning. Later on, the emphasis of rural development programmes was shifted to integrated approach, popularly known as Integrated Rural Development Programme (IRDP) wherein an integrated approach with a rural family as a base was taken up to translate the policy issues into programmes. Income generation programmes too gained prominence during this phase.

Since, 1990 social and human development has emerged as key element of rural development. Hence, along with income generation, capacity development, social security and safety of vulnerable groups are also emphasized. On institutional part, area specific problems and potentials required decentralized framework with a participatory mode. Institutional strengthening, and empowerment and participation of the rural people continue to remain formidable challenges towards achieving equitable and sustained rural development into the overall national development policies.

In the recent past, creating conducive environment in rural areas was the main focus of rural development programmes. This led to the programmes like SHG promotion, Self Employment programmes and Area development programmes (Watershed, DDP etc). Currently, in addition to creating appropriate social and physical environment in rural areas, rural development programmes are dominated by employment assurance programmes ultimately leading to National Rural Employment Guarantee Programme (NREGA).

State Rural Development Department

Every state or province also has a department called the State Rural Development Department (SRD). SRD has a mandate similar to that of the Ministry of Rural Development (MoRD), but confined to its own province. A state may launch its own RD programmes or jointly fund the programmes launched by MoRD, Government of India. Like MoRD the roles of SRDs are restricted to the formulation of policies & programmes relating to rural development, providing funds for the programmes, and monitoring & evaluation of the programmes.

District Rural Development Agency (DRDA)

This agency is the principal organ at the district level that is vested with the responsibility of overseeing the implementation of various anti-poverty programmes. The

DRDAs are expected to effectively coordinate with the line departments, the PRIs, the banks and other financial institutions, the NGOs, technical institutions etc. with a view to gathering the support and resources required for poverty reduction effort in the district. More recently, the DRDA have been brought under the official purview of District or Zilla Panchayats (ZP).

The Rural Development programmes implemented by the Andhra Pradesh Government through District agency in the study area at the time of investigation are:

1. Jalayagam
2. Indiramma Houses
3. Rs. 2/- Rice
4. Widow, old age, challenged persons' pensions.
5. Free current for Agriculture
6. Indira Kranth Pathakam
7. MGNREGP
8. Debt waiver for farmers
9. Social Welfare Programmes
10. Pasu Kranti
11. Debt waiver for socially deprived
12. Rajiv Arogya Sree
13. Services of 104/108
14. Family welfare (planning) programme

Living Conditions of Rural People

The nature of stakeholders, bureaucratic style were explained because the planners from the programme according to their living conditions.

The people from rural areas feel that they are powerless. They are also ignorant of law and welfare measures provided by the Government. Though the Government is publishing through media, it has not yet spread uniformly to all places. Rural people do not have forum to assist them in securing redressel for their grievances. Illiteracy is also one of the major hindrances.

Rural people, by virtue of migration or otherwise, come across variety of people with different kinds of mental traits and dispositions, both favourable and unfavourable and either known to them or strange to them. The gap that exists between the rural folk and the bureaucrats (government officials), the participation and sharing of the responsibilities between these groups of people keeps them estranged. It hardly brings them together. The rural folk are always subjected to an inferiority complex imposed by the dress and drill of the bureaucrats. Status consciousness prevails over "work ethic" during the implementation of these programmes. This results in a huge communication gap.

The large gap existing between masses and bureaucrats, Sri N. Vittal, Chairman People's Empowerment Committee said that common man has no direct approach to meet the higher authorities. Because of this fact the middleman plays an important role which leads to corruption. Sri Raghunath Rao, Secretary, Backward Class Welfare, Andhra Pradesh Government feels the same and added that today's circumstances are such that common man has no direct approach to meet IAS personnel. If any one wants to visit the secretariat, the common man has to wait long hours in hot environment which makes him half-die. All the policy issues were decided, according to the will and pleasure of political parties, not keeping in mind the interests of the common man, according to Sri J. Ram Babu, Special Secretary R & B and Sri. B. Sathyanarayana, Additional Municipal Commissioner, Hyderabad Corporation pointed out that the existing practice adopted at present is that before organising Grama Sabhas, the beneficiaries were selected. He felt that the concept of empowerment to the people is a myth. He suggested that, like USA and Saudi Arabia, 70 per cent of funds are needed to be transferred to local bodies by both the central and state Government and minimize their interference. Sri N. Vittal further expressed the functioning of authorities is the main problem faced by people today. They also feel the need to curb the activities of middleman. (Enadu-Daily paper)

The way the rural man is given audience and the way an urban capitalist is received by the bureaucratic or a Bank Officer speaks volumes of some of the reasons for the failure of many programmes. The bureaucrats, irrespective of their position within the hierarchy, are act as representative of power and prestige of the entire administrative structure. It is not the case that development administration did not seek to enlist mass participation. In spite of their efforts, still there is a lack of effective channelisation and adequate participation among administration and the rural population. One of the basic cause for this kind of scenario is lack of education on the part of the villagers, and also the bureaucrats being self-centred. These are some of the socio-economic and cultural factors which act as constraints for rural development. (Vasudeva Rao, 2004)

Development -Vs-Education

Education, health and social well-being are crucial to human productivity, while social safety nets are vital support mechanisms to cope with crises. The role of rural governance in providing these services remains important, particularly to rural communities that are both physically and economically isolated. Lack of informal and formal education restricts the capacity of rural people to take advantage of alternative job opportunities. The incidence of chronic ill-health due to poor accessibility and affordability to health services and its effect on reducing rural labour productivity has been grossly under estimated.

Secondly, education facilitates social and occupational mobility among the members of a society. Educational achievements, to a large extent, determine the nature and type of job opportunities that become available to rural people. Functional literacy programmes and rural entrepreneur-ship programmes bear out the significance of the utility of specific target oriented education.

Three approaches adopted by Government for improving the quality of life are:

1. Building capabilities of the people and improving quality of life.
2. Focusing on high potential sectors.
3. Transforming governance.

The state is committed to the devolution of power through the implementation of 73rd, 74th Constitutional Amendment Act. Participatory governance, transparency, improved services, Janma Bhoomi initiative, promoting self-help groups such as Water User's Association, Village Education Committees, Vana Samrakshana Samithis (V.S.S), DWCRA, CMEY lead to equitable social development and rapid economic growth. The people should be educated, healthy and skilled, is the ultimate aim of the Government by the year 2020.

Development is about creating an environment in which people can develop their full potential and lead productive, creative lives in accordance with their needs and interests (Human Development Report-2001 of UNDP). According to Rist (1979), the word 'development' can mean a state of affairs or a process; for instance some countries are developed whereas some others are developing. According to Marshall Wolfe, quoted by Higgins (1992), 'development consists of systematically inter-related growth and change process in human societies, delimited by the boundaries of national state, and highly independent on a world scale. He explained it further by saying that, 'development' expresses an aspiration towards better society. However, quite a different view of development is taken by Wolfgang Sachs (1992) who says that, 'development' has become shapeless amoebae-like word. It cannot express anything because the outlines are blurred. On the whole, development is perceived as an improvement in the overall spheres of life. It has come to mean a planned, stimulated movement of all sectors of social system in the direction of the overall desired goals set by a society.

In the words of Robert Chambers (1995), "Rural development is a strategy to enable a specific group of people, poor rural women and men, to gain for themselves and their children more of what they want and need. It involves helping the poorest among those who seek a livelihood in the rural areas to demand and control more of the benefits of rural development. The group includes small-scale farmers, tenants, and the landless."

Adult education plays a vital role in rural economic development. Adult Education has the potential for improving the quality of life for individuals living in rural areas by expanding their access to income and employment opportunities. Adult education is a continuing process where adults, who perform multiple social roles, participate in organized learning activities to improve their human resource skills or their human capital assets. Economists view participation in adult education as an investment in the capital assets of the individual. These investments may be viewed as existing levels of education (stock) or what is under development (flow). Benefits from investment in adult education accrue to both the individual and community. Rural economic development is linked to the existence or improvement of physical, material, capital, and human.

Education and ICT influences rural development in three ways. Firstly, it increases the awareness of the rural people. Through education, these people know about themselves, others and the outside world in general. The anti-arrack movement by the women folk of Andhra Pradesh state is a notable illustration of the impact of adult education programmes.

Education provides an insight to the rural folk about the intricacies and complexities or bureaucratic administration. It prepares them to accept and cooperate with the bureaucrats.

Impact of Education on Rural Development

The findings of external evaluation of literacy campaign revealed that women folk after attending the literacy classes are in a position to meet the authorities without fear and also in a position to explain and demand their social needs. Other benefits they achieved are:

1. Awareness about welfare programmes.
2. Participation in village development activities.
3. Demanding official to fulfil their promises in Janma bhoomi.
4. To demand appropriate wages for the work done from their employers.

Involvement of People

The continuing education programme will creates an environment for people's participation as groups in village activities. Hence, the need of involvement of people and its relevance was explained.

Every movement when emerges from people becomes successful. Though the movements are lead by some people the soul of the movement remains with the people at large. Removal of illiteracy is also one of the social movements. This movement aims at the liberation of Indian masses from slavery of illiteracy. The weapons which are used in this battle should be based on consciousness because motivated people are the backbone of this movement. It, therefore, becomes necessary to see that how this involvement can be expanded. Here one should think about the literate as well as illiterate people. The target is to make literate those who are illiterate. Hence it is the responsibility of the literate Indians to participate actively in this programme, to make others literate. The literate Indians can be involved in this programme in various ways.

Continuing Education Programme in Visakhapatnam District

Visakhapatnam District in Andhra Pradesh is one of the successful districts which have implemented the total literacy campaign during 1990-91 and out of 6.60 lakhs of illiterates as many as 3.69 lakhs were made literate. In order to retain, strengthen and further the basic literacy skills acquired by the neo-literates, the district administration has started post-literacy centres known as Jana Chaitanya Kendras (JCKs). As many as 10,000 JCKs were started and post-literacy books were provided to the centres. The JCKs were managed by the monitors who happened to be successful volunteers. With a view to cover the dropouts of total literacy campaign and the newly attained age group members (who have crossed 15 years and remained illiterate) the Zilla Saksharatha Samithi has implemented mopping up operation programmes i.e., literacy in hundred day programme from 1996 onwards. In the place of JCKs, continuing education centres were started during 1997-98 and Preraks were appointed to carryout the activities of continuing education centres. As many as 570 continuing education centres started functioning and the Preraks were trained by the district administration with regard to their roles and functions which include organisation of post-literacy programmes, equivalency programmes, income generating programmes, quality of life improvement programmes, and other functions of continuing education centre. Different committees were constituted to support the Zilla Saksharatha Samithi at the district level.

Table 1.3: Committees and its roles and responsibilities

Sl. No.	Committees	Roles and Responsibilities
1	2	3
1.	General Administration Committee	Planning, organisation, implementation, direction, evaluation etc.
2.	Academic Committee	Teaching/learning materials, volunteer guides, post-literacy and continuing education reading material, training material, preparation and distribution of materials, organisation of training programmes etc.
3.	Environment Building Committee	To create a favourable environment by organising kalajathas, processions, pada yatras, wall writing, posters, meetings etc.

(Contd...)

1	2	3
4.	Finance Committee	Proper utilisation of funds allotted, planning and direction, audit, maintenance of related records and registers.
5.	Planning and Evaluation Committee	Preparation of model forms required for planning, printing and distribution, obtaining the completed forms from lower levels, compilation and forwarding them to state level agencies.

At the Mandal level, Mandal Saaksharatha Samithi implements the continuing education programme with the support of Mandal Literacy Organiser, Mandal Development Officer, Mandal Revenue Officer, Officers of the other development departments, peoples representatives, youth associations, Mahila mandals, political parties and so on. At Mandal level, the activities of opinion building, creation of educational atmosphere, training, co-ordination, establishment of centres, material procurement and distribution, evaluation, submission of reports are carried out by the Mandal Literacy Organiser with the assistance of Mandal Resource Persons.

At the nodal level, continuing education centre nodal Prerak is the key person. He/she is responsible for the functioning of 8 continuing education centres around the nodal continuing education centre. The individual discharges this responsibility with the assistance of the Preraks and as per the instructions of Mandal Literacy Organiser. The duties and responsibilities of a nodal Prerak include the activities of survey, identifying the beneficiaries, securing accommodation for the centres, establishment of centres, procurement and distribution of materials, attending Mandal level meetings, arranging monthly meetings of Preraks, collection of reports, providing programme information to higher level officials and ensuring the services of Preraks to the beneficiaries.

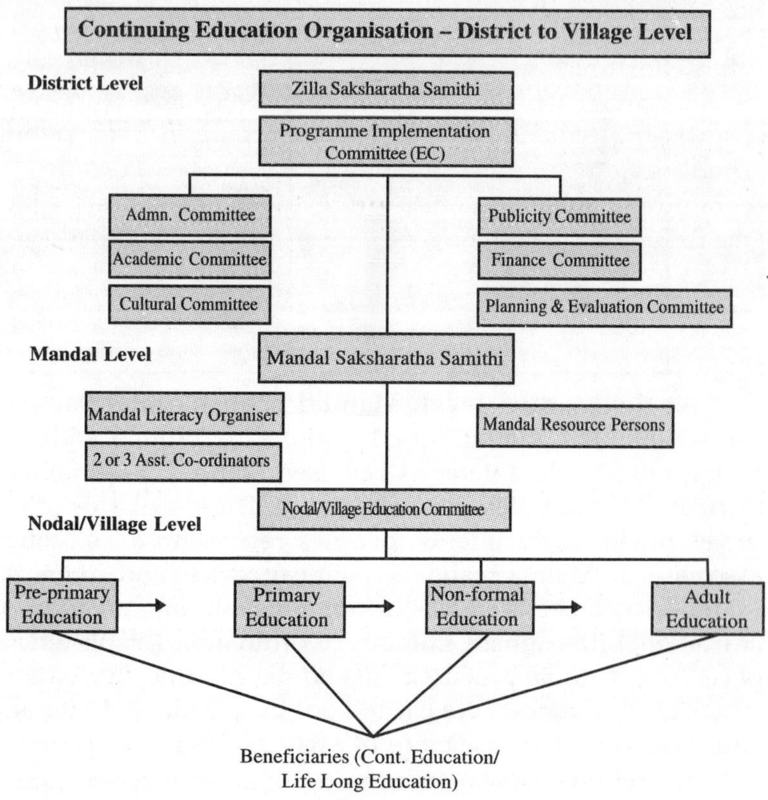

Flow Chart

The village education committee has to be formed with the joint efforts of the Prerak, nodal Prerak, Mandal Literacy Organiser. The Prerak implements the continuing education programme at village level by conducting surveys, identifying beneficiaries, providing services to beneficiaries depending upon their needs with co-ordination of other departments. Apart from village education committee, the sub-committees of pre-primary education, primary education, non-formal education help the Prerak in discharging the functions. The members of the committees are drawn from the village members. There are 250 neo-literates, 125 school dropouts and 125 others in each centre. For organising the continuing education centres, Central and State Governments release grants for first five years. After five years, the centres have to be managed by the village community. The success of continuing education centres depends upon the personal involvement and commitment of the Preraks and the community support at the local level. With this background the present study entitled *"Rural Development Through Literacy Campaigns"* was taken up.

Objectives of the Study

The study was taken up with the following objectives:

1. To study the socio economic and demographic profile of the sample respondents i.e. Preraks, Neo-literates and Community members in rural Mandals of Visakhapatnam District.
2. To find out the opinion of the Preraks and neo-literates on the organisation of continuing education centre with special reference to variables in socio-economic and demographic.
3. To investigate the details on explaining about development/welfare programmes by Preraks and neo-literates at the centre.
4. To compare the status of the neo-literates and community members on Literacy, Functionality and Awareness components.
5. To study the degree of difference on development/ welfare programmes among neo-literates and community.
6. To find out the differential impact on Continuing Education Programme with reference to variations in the socio-economic and demographic variables of neo-literates.

The concept of education, need of education for the development of individual, community and country was explained in this chapter. Though after independence, formal education is implementing effectively still 35 per cent of people are illiterates (2001). Strengthening the formal system of education, the government introduced non-formal education with a view to reduce the illiterate population, expecting to reach the developmental programmes directly to the grass-root stakeholders. The need, concept of adult education, the programmes implemented by government after post-independence and plan wise efforts were discussed.

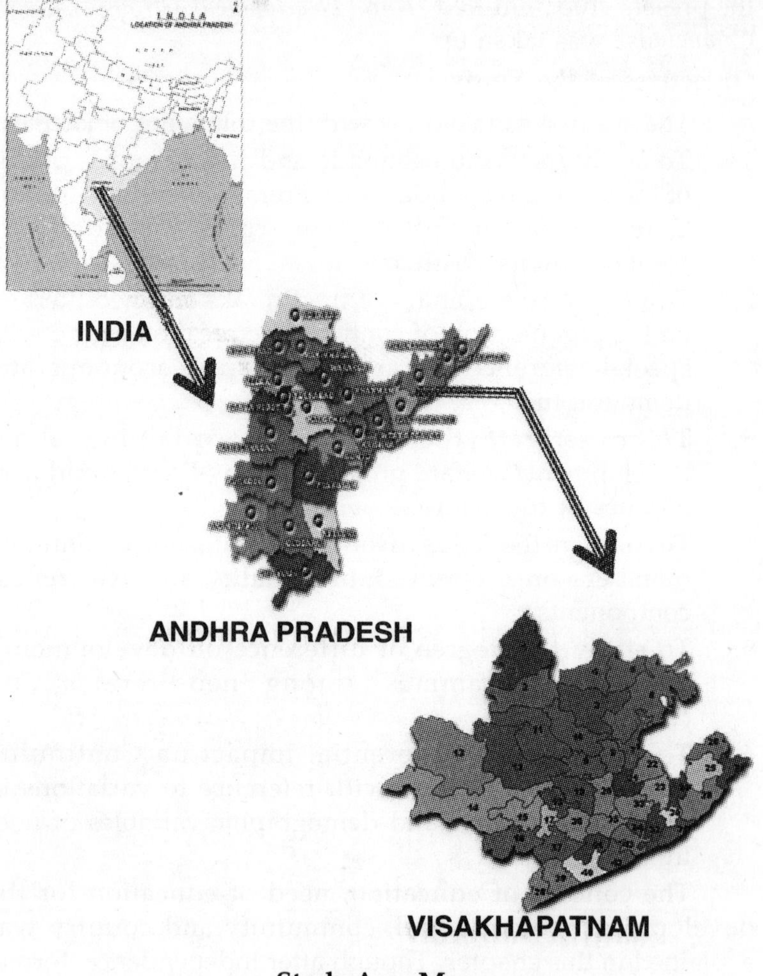

Study Area Map

In detail, the objectives of continuing education programme and functions are explained because the study related to masses the achievement and usefulness to the people. Further, the concept of development, approach, programmes, objectivises of rural development need of the people participation and characteristics of rural stakeholders were presented. Comprehensively is explained about the study area i.e. continuing education programme in Visakhapatnam district and map of the study area also enclosed.

The review of related studies is presented in the following chapter.

> *"I do not want my house to be walled in on all sides and my widows to be stuffed. I want the cultures of all lands to be blown about my house as freely as possibly but I refuse to be blown off my feet by any"*
>
> —Mahatma Gandhi

Perspectives of Adult Education

Man is only creature that could be benefited by the past experiences of his earlier generations and he need not have to begin anew in each and every field of expanding knowledge. He can make use of the already accumulated knowledge in widening his thoughts in the changing needs for centuries this has been going on and on. This is move so when research is concerned which enables a researcher to be nearer to the truth as far as possible. By doing so, the investigator feels that his problem does not exist in a vacuum and also that a considerable work had already been turned out by his predecessors, who have a direct relation with his proposed investigation. And by so depending largely on these findings made by his forerunners, his investigation would lead him to further success. Such review of related literature helps the researcher to move closer to the area of knowledge which he wants to enter into, it also helps him to be in touch with various types of research that had been employed in the field previously and it further enables him to select the best type of research that he has to undertake. It also provides the basis for formulating the valuable hypothesis for his project and to adopt an innovative approach to fulfil his ambition.

Kirlinger (1973) gives to main reasons for discussing literature related to the research problem. First, it is to clarify the theoretical rationale of the problem and secondly, to locate the present research in the existing body of research on the subject and to point out what it contributes to the subject.

The major objective of this review of the literature is to determine the significant facts, which are essentially related to the problem under investigation. Any worthwhile research in any field of knowledge requires an adequate familiarity with the work, which had been already taken place in that particular area. A summary of the previous research projects in this area provides sufficient evidence with which the investigator is already familiar with and to determine what is already known and what is still to be investigated further. Since effective research is based upon previous knowledge, this study plays a significant role in eliminating the duplication of what had already been done in this area and to arrive at the correct fixation of targets and objectives in laying out appropriate hypothesis is drawing out meaningful conclusions and in making commendable suggestions.

According to W.R. Borg (1965), "The literature is any field forms to foundation upon which all future work will be built". Failure to build a firm foundation of knowledge provided by the review of related literature leads to a shallow and naive report of the project and often it could lead to duplication of work which would have been already done better by some one else previously. Thus, a review of related literature is essential for making the study more effective, purposeful and meaningful for the investigator before he actively dives deep into the study.

The investigator, therefore, made an attempt in reviewing the available related literature in the area. The studies are incorporated regarding the programmes implemented by government of India after independence from Social Education to National Adult Education Programme and also programmes under National Literacy Mission i.e. Total Literacy Campaigns, Post Literacy and Continuing Education Programmes and presenting ongoing Continuing Education Programme in a chronological order in this chapter.

Previous Studies Relating to Study

An overview of the studies has covered dealt with socio-economic aspects of functionaries, opinions of Preraks, impact of literacy campaigns. The studies on neo-literates perceptions about various activities carried out at continuing education centres, problems of neo-literates, impact of the literacy campaigns from neo-literates perspective, performances of neo-literacy skills are few if any. Keeping these aspects in view, the present study has been formulated.

Subramaniam and Mani (1964) undertook a study on adult opinions towards literacy and findings were:

1. 75 per cent of the men and 4 5 per cent of the women interviewed were found to have interest in further education;
2. men showed keen interest in vocational education and agriculture whereas women in crafts and home improvement;
3. They showed interest in getting their children educated irrespective of sex.

The impact of social education on the life of the people in Uttar Pradesh was studies by Chaturvedi (1969) in the districts of Gorakhpur, Jhansi, Lucknow and Mathura. The investigator finds that the social education programme had definite impact on the life of the people in rural areas despite many limitations of the programme. However, there was not enough enthusiasm in either the people or the workers in the field about the programme and the attainment of its goal.

Berke (1970) studied the achievement of adult Negroes and its relation to the educational background of the family. He found that educational background of family members influenced the performance of learners. Simmons (1972) observed that the age of the participants had no influence on their reading achievement.

Dixit Asha (1975) in his study on educational need patterns of adults in the urban, rural and tribal communities of Rajasthan found that more than half of the respondents in urban population expressed that vocational training was very much helpful to them for their jobs. One fourth of the rural population indicated that they had literacy classes in the village which they could attend only at night. The majority of them had favourable attitudes towards adult education and vocation training.

Pillai (1976) through his study on participants of Farmers Functional Literacy Programme indicted that younger age group learners fared better in literacy tests as compared to those of older age group.

Venkataiah (1977) attempted to assess the impact of the Farmers Functional Literacy programme on the participants in Andhra Pradesh. A significant impact of the programme in respect of attitude towards modern agricultural practices and adult literacy was found on all age groups, caste groups and socio-economic status of the participants.

Sivadasan Pillai (1979) in a paper presented to the 32nd Annual Conference of the Indian Adult Education Association argued that de-linking adult education programmes with development programmes is not conducive for the adult education movement. The interest of the poor and illiterate masses, according to him, is concentrated on 'vocational improvement' and 'financial security' rather than gaining 'literacy'. Hence, he suggests establishment of coordination committees at the State, District, Block and Panchayat levels to implement the Rural Development Programmes and Adult Education Programmes jointly.

The detailed evaluation reports on the functioning of NAEP in the State of Rajasthan and Maharashtra gives us an in-depth position of NAEP in practice. Appraising the NAEP in Rajasthan in 1979, the public systems group found most of the learners coming from the forward castes, farming professions and predominantly illiterate, i.e., without any previous educational background. The learners were informed and motivated mostly by the Instructors, followed by neighbours, friends and family members. The learners had the objectives of enabling themselves to read and write, at the time of joining the adult education centres. Information on Agriculture, Animal Husbandry, Health and Hygiene, Banking and Panchayats found to be the desired areas of learning among the learners in general while women learners expressed more desire in the areas of swing, knitting, child care and home management.

Singh and Singh (1979) conducted a study into differential opinions of farmers towards improved agricultural practices. The findings of the study revealed that the farmers had quite a favourable opinion towards chemical fertilizers, improved form of implements and green manure. The statistical results showed that opinion tendered to be positively associated with the size of land holding and education. Thus, the more land and education the farmers had, the more favourable were their attitudes – evidence obtained also suggested that the respondents group based on the holdings size and education different significantly in respect of their opinion towards all the practices included in the study.

Social Education and Development Society (SEDS) is a voluntary organisation involved in rural development since 1980. It was started by a group of young social workers led by Mr.Rajan Joshua. Development of the rural poor has been the primary objective of SEDS. Its target population comprises of mostly the poor drawn from scheduled castes and tribes and backward committees. Emphasis on the development of women and children is given by SEDS. The major programme of the SEDS includes community organisation, education and awareness building, health, sanitation and nutrition, vocational training and employment generations and ecological restoration.

Muthuswamy (1980) measured the attitudes of the adult education organizers towards National Adult Education Programme. It was found that a good majority of the organizers were possessing positive opinion on academic and administrative aspects of the programme.

The second appraisal of NAEP in Rajasthan (Pestonjee et al. 1980), The report observed that learners had an average age of 21 years came up with many findings on NAEP in practice. They were mostly from the higher dominant castes with farming occupations. Reveals that the learners in Rajasthan were mostly motivated by their instructors and joined adult education centres with the objectives of acquiring the skills of reading, writing and accounting. Along with literacy skills, learners were acquainted with information and knowledge relating to areas of Agriculture and Animal Husbandry, Health, Hygiene, Banking and Panchayati Raj. Women learners expressed the desire to learn more about sewing knitting, home management and child care. Many learners expressed that they also undertook Bhajans and Kirtans as recreational activity in the adult education centres.

Madana Mohana Reddy (1980) conducted a study on opinion of adult learners towards National Adult Education Programme. Adult learners expressed positive opinion with respect to objectives of the programme, arrangements for popularizing the programmes, materials provided to the centres, instructional arrangements and post-literacy and continuing education aspects. Gender, age and occupation have significantly influenced the opinion of adult learners towards National Adult Education Programme.

Pillai K. Sivadasan (1980) has conducted a study of the functioning of Non-formal education in the United Kingdom with a view to suggesting practical step to be undertaken in India and particularly in Kerala. He has reported that there should be state level agencies for coordinating non-formal education programmes carried out by the Universities, Colleges, Schools and voluntary agencies.

After one year implementation of NAEP, Sharma (1981) made a review of the programme and expressed that 'all is not well with the programme'. He found the initial thrust being replaced by lack of enthusiasm on the part of the people as well as mass media. He draws out attention about the vagueness of the two components of adult education, ie., functionality and awareness. To raise the level of public participation, he suggests, "NAEP should be intimately and inextricably linked with the various ongoing developmental programmes aimed at improving the economic life or the professional skills of the poorer and deprived sections of the society". In addition to the failure on the part of the programme to raise public interest, Sharma lists the following as the other factors: lack of awareness with regard to the utility and need of NAEP among the Government functionaries, lack of enough literature on functionality and social awareness and Delays in releasing the funds to the implementing agencies.

In a study of NAEP in six villages of Bhar Block, Pune, District, Maharashtra, Muthayya and Hemalatha (1981) examined the interrelationship between programmes of Adult Education and Rural Development, motivation failures behind learners and functionaries. Some of their findings in brief are Involvement of the development functionaries or agencies in adult education activities was negligible, The adult education functionaries were not exposed to development activities; and Failure on the part of the programme to involve village leaders, village panchayat and other local organisations.

The enquiry made by Hebsur and others (1981) about NAEP in Maharashtra also obtained similar findings in addition to a few others. The findings of Hebsur and others are listed below:

- **Literacy:** The performance of the learners in literacy was fond to be good in reading and writing. The learners with the background of higher caste, higher occupation, modern exposure, regular attendance, previous schools experience, performed better than their counterparts.
- **Functionality:** NAEP is found raising the levels of functionality among the learners. The learners who were relatively old, regular in attending the centres, lower castes and classes gained more functional knowledge.
- **Social Awareness:** A positive and significant impact was created by NAEP. It has not only raised the awareness component among the learner but also enabled them to revert meaningfully to situations involving the

application of knowledge regarding social awareness'. The impact was relatively more among the learners from higher castes, those exposed to modernisation and among the learners who were regular to the adult education classes.

Umayaparvathi (1982) made a multi-faceted study seeking to find out if achievement motivation and intelligence have anything to do with literacy achievement. The study found significant difference in literacy attainments between those who have high and low achievement motivation, between high and low intelligence groups and between backward and schedulẹ castes. Significant differences were also found between literate and illiterate families in literacy attainment, achievement motivation and in mean intelligence scores.

Vasudeva Rao (1983) reported male younger age as positive factor behind the performance of learners. The performance of the learners depended on the socio-economic and attendance background of the learners, on the demographic, educational and professional background of the instructors and on the nature of the implementing agencies. In spite of financial and structural constrains, the commitment on the part of the voluntary agency enabled it to successfully implement the NAEP.

Chouhan and Rai (1984) conducted a study on perception of tribal and non-tribal farmers towards adult literacy and improved agricultural practices in the villages of Udaipur District of Rajasthan. The findings of the study revealed that the correlation between the opinion towards adult literacy and opinion towards improved agricultural practices was high, significant and positive in each of the six categories of farmers – tribals, small farmers and marginal farmers.

According to Savitha Markanda (1985), In the Indian context, continuing education assumes importance in two ways; first, for a literacy programme to be enduring, useful, and lasting. It is essential that literacy teaching is followed up and ultimately merged with the process of learning which can be made possible through continuing education; secondly, there is a need to organize continuing education programmes for school drop outs, educated employed, skilled youth, professionals and women.

David (1988) found that the educational level of people significantly influences their opinion towards different socio-economic and demographic aspects like employment, small family norms, environment, girl-child education and development programmes. It was found that educated people obtained better mean opinion scores on the above aspects when compared to semi-literates and illiterates representing the rural and urban areas.

Mistry (1988) surveyed the contributions of the Parsi community to education and allied fields. The major findings of the study revealed that through education, the Parsi community improved its social and economic standards. During the colonial rule, many Parsis migrated to the cities, especially to Bombay city, and society at large was benefited by the benevolence of Parsis. Many schools, hospitals and technical institutes developed because of the philanthropic nature of Parsis. Education enabled the Parsis to unite and revive the spirit of oneness and to seek out new areas for settlement in order to improve the lot of the community.

Vasudeva Rao (1988) found that male sex, younger age, un-married social status, joint family background, rural nativity, higher income and regular attendance helped the adult learners to gain more skills in literacy, and to raise their functionality and awareness. The caste and occupation of the learners had a little impact, compared to the other socio-economic variables. It can be stated that the performance of the learners depends to a great extent on the background of the instructor. While the instructor's sex, age and education had a definite bearing on the performance of the learners, the training background had only marginal impact. In general, male instructors in younger age group and with higher qualifications proved to be successful in imparting adult education.

Aram (1989) others the Quadrangular approach to community participation in local development planning through the institution of Village Planning Committees; the work under taken by the Gandhigram Rural Institute in the Author Block in Dindigul area has led to the formulation of the approach to people's participation in planning and management of local development efforts. In the process of this work, the villages were able to achieve nationally cherished goals such as population stabilization, eradication of illiteracy health for all, full employment and eradication of poverty.

Bhasin (1992) expressed a strong feminist view and advocates that an empowering education should cognize women's contribution and knowledge by helping women to fight out their own fears and feelings of inadequacy and inferiority. Education should liberate women from the burden of ready made answers which are given by the dominant cultural and political structures. Education should bring out the best in every individual.

Kumaraswamy (1992) found that sex, age and caste had no bearing on adult learners in reading, writing and innumeracy skills.

Nair, Omanna and Rehim (1992) evaluated the activities of the Jana Sikshana Nilayams organised by the Nehru Yuva Kendras in Kerala. It was found that an equal number of men and women participated in the programmes as Prerak. The strengths of the J.S.Ns. were found to be the reading room, teaching aids and the areas to be strengthened was the buildings of their own for J.S.N. the inadequate training for Prerak, lack of funds leading to the drop-out rate increasing. Newspapers were provided regularly in the J.S.Ns.

Adilakshmi (1993) conducted an investigation into the working conditions of Jana Shikshana Nilayams. It was found that most of the Preraks possessed positive opinion towards the programme. Majority of the Preraks organised post-literacy activities, but due to organisational and administrative difficulties and lack of capabilities they could not organize charcha mandal, simple and short duration courses, library activities, recreational and cultural activities effectively. One of the findings of the study is that there is no difference in the functioning of the centre in relation to the age and experience of the Preraks.

Sardhar Patel Institute of Economic and Social research (1993) evaluated the Kheda District Literacy Campaign. The study revealed that 86.2 per cent of the learners are successful. As far as awareness is concerned 97.7 per cent learners are aware of personal cleanliness, 45.6 per cent aware of immunization programme, 58.11 per cent are family welfare programme, 56.55 per cent are aware of sanitation in and around the houses. In addition, 87.16 per cent are aware of development programmes. 78 per cent are aware of social aspects like dowry system, social evils, minimum age for education, removal of untouchables and family planning etc.

Shah S.Y. (1993) in his study on the 'Mass Literacy campaign in Bihar' concluded that all successful adult education movements are part of the large social movements. The extent of success however depends on the degree of commitment of the leadership. By conceiving a literacy campaign as a part of a broader socio-political movement, the leadership may succeed in making it effective depending upon their initiative and involvement. Then the mobilization of the human and material resources will be comparatively easier.

Department of Adult and Continuing Education, Andhra University (1994) conducted external evaluation of Total Literacy Campaign in Srikakulam district. The study found that the campaign resulted in creating more social awareness than substantially enhancing literacy skills of the learners. The study observed that Srikakulam district, being the most backward in Andhra Pradesh state, has more physical problems like inaccessible tribal area, forest area etc., and this has resulted in relatively less performance in enhancing the literacy skills of learners. However, the study applauded the enhanced social awareness in regard to health and hygiene, environment improvement, savings etc., as a result of Total Literacy Campaign.

Reddy Adinarayana and Reddeppa (1995) in their study on 'Determinants of Prerak Effectiveness" found that the success of the post-literacy programme is largely based on the performance of the field functionaries namely Prerak. Prerak is the actual "Doer" of literacy, post literacy and continuing Education at the community level.

Shirley Walters (1995) explained the preliminary suggestions for an Adult Education research in South Africa, highlighting the impact of changes within South Africa itself and their effect in the dramatically altering the 'regional geo-politic'.

Parthasarathy (1996) studies the 'Unorganized Sector and Structural Adjustment Programme in India'. The study reported that alienated from their land and means of livelihood, the rural poor migrated to urban centres. Food subsidy through the Public Distribution System (PDS) became inaccessible to them because of migration and inability to provide proofs of residence which further impoverished them financially.

Radha Krishna Murthy (1996) in his study observed learners expressed their opinions with equal ease on all problems-social, individual and developmental. Their opinions are more towards the positive side. To illustrate this point – on the issue of 'widow remarriage' 44 per cent of the total sample agreed and 52 per cent disagreed with it. It is an indication that a considerable number agreed with this positive trend (53%) in Voluntary agencies and 34 per cent Government agencies). This point was supported by their positive opinion on other issues like 'eradication of dowry system', etc., Regarding the familiarity of social organisations, the majority (76%) of the total sample were aware of Panchayat Raj Institutions (local bodies of governance) followed by awareness about Youth Associations (68%) and women organisations (46%). Learners' participation in social organisations was very poor. Only 14 per cent of the total learners mentioned that they had participated in the activities of youth organisations. Learners' achievement on various topics under functionality component was very low, particularly in respect of skills. The topic on 'agriculture methods' with highest mean score of 2.06 followed by 'child rearing' with 1.92 and 'responsibilities at home' with 1.86 indicated that learners achievement was reasonable about knowledge aspects. The mean scores on these three topics in the case of Vas were higher than the total mean scores.

Jagannadha Sarma et.al. (1998) in their evaluation study on continuing education noticed that there was good response of Preraks towards continuing education. Some neo-literates and villagers were sponsoring for newspapers and magazines. This indicated that peoples participation and attitude were very good towards the programme.

Pandey (1998) conducted a study on 'Social mobility among the women in the transitional city of Raipur in Madhya Pradesh'. Major findings of the study include:

1. The present changes in our society have proved the social position of women and that their rights have grown.
2. Education is an important factor for social mobility among women.

Vasudeva Rao (1999) "Evaluation of Total Literacy Campaign in Nellore District, Andhra Pradesh", the findings of the study are as follows: the literacy rate of Nellore district stands at 57.08 per cent as per NLM norms. Compared to the literacy rate provided in the 1991 census, this represents an increase of 10 per cent. The learner's sex, religion, marital status and income significantly influenced their performance on the literacy performance tests as well their literacy rate.

Mastan (2000) conducted study on the performance and opinion on the performance of Preraks organising continuing education centres. It was found that gender, age, caste, education, marital status, income and experience significantly influenced the opinion of Preraks. Better mean opinion scores were obtained by Preraks representing women, 25-30 years age group, forward caste, intermediate qualified, married, higher income group and those possessing higher experience as Preraks. It was also found that opinion significantly influenced the performance of Preraks. High mean performance scores were obtained by the group having high opinion scores.

Viswanadha Gupta and Janardhana Reddy (2000) studies the functioning of continuing education centres in Chittoor District of Andhra Pradesh in terms of the profile of the Preraks, location of the centres, supply of materials, attendance of learners, co-operation form CE Committee and problem of the Preraks. The findings of the study shows that majority of the Preraks are male, middle aged, graduates, BCs and with two years experience. Furthermore half of the working Preraks are not trained but happy with the honorarium they received.

Reddeppa (2001) conducted a study on Jana Chaitanya Kendras in Chittoor District with special reference to monitor effectiveness. It was found that the performance of monitors relating to different functions was influenced by their opinion towards adult education. Out of several functions, monitors with high opinion performed better with regard to literacy and post-literacy classes, charcha mandal activities, short term training programmes, sports and adventurous activities, cultural and entertainment programmes effectively. Monitors with low opinion performed the role of maintaining the library and reading room effectively.

Egbule, Patrick E. and Njoku, Edna-Mathews C. (2001) studied the Mass Media support for Adult Education in Agriculture, in Southern Nigeria. The study concludes that it had been noted that effective dissemination of agricultural information to farmers is desirable for sustainable agricultural development. It further states that given farmers' preference for television over other mass media channels, there was a need to establish community/rural television stations, which should feature special agricultural programmes targeted at rural farmers.

Akanisi Kedrayate (2002) explains about huge changes the society is facing in Fiji especially in the socio-economic, cultural and political arena. The role of non-formal education for nation building in helping people to deal with the challenges in compensating for deficiencies in the formal education system in the field of inter cultural education, in lifelong learning, in combating poverty, and so on are explained

Jagannada Rao, D. (2002) identified the problems faced by neo-literates to attend continuing education centres in Tirupati rural mandal of Chittoor District. The major problems faced by the neo-literates in attending the CECs were lack of infrastructural facilities, Preraks inefficiency in teaching, personal, family, social, economic and health problems, lack of time, heavy work, insufficient reading materials for the neo-literates.

Schweigert, Thomas F (2002) The effect of selected predictor variables upon adult learning style with in functional chaplaincy training, The Intent of this study was to examine the relationship between adult learning style and the professional background personality type, education level and demographics of adult students with in functional chaplaincy. This new type of chaplaincy has emerged in response to recent societal changes and involves specialized qualification training incorporating critical incident response and effective counselling strategies unlike traditional chaplain preparation, functional chaplaincy training programmes are brief intensive and focus upon effective, hands on ministry in critical or crisis situations. Given the projected increase need for functional chaplains, it is imperative that these training programmes are optionally effective. In the qualitative component of quasi-experimental design, survey data was collected from two hundred and twelve functional chaplains to examine potential relationships. Then, qualitative data via personal interviews was gathered from twenty-five functional chaplains of varying involvement levels to gain additional data related to training programme effectiveness. Although partially predictive, results indicated a definite predictive relationship between personality type and a defined, categorized adult learning style. Conversely, professional background, education level and demographics were not found to be valid predictors. Recipients were also overall satisfied with the training programme perceived into to be very effective, and only offered minor upgrades for potential improvement some differences were noted with functional chaplains as a sample population and results highlighted the relevance of following androgogical guidelines for adult learners, which, beyond potentially using personality type to predict adult learning style may offer additional suggestions for improving training programmes effectiveness.

Surapa Raju, S. (2002), in his article on "Akshara Sankranthi Programme an Evaluation" It was observed that all most all the volunteers teach the learners at their respective houses. Usually they have to spend more money for additional use of their electricity/oil, etc., which is a burden to them. Attendance was more importance for the learners and give encouragement to the volunteers to teach effectively. Regular attendance implies the learner's interest, which is the most important factor for the success of the programme. But poor attendance was observed from the attendance registers in some of the centers. Many reasons for poor attendance are:

1. lack of interest among the learners to learn;
2. tiresome workers after coming from the fields could not spend their time at night to learn;
3. household problems/economic problems;
4. health problems;
5. seasonal migration/social festivals;
6. failure of power supply at night time.

It was observed that wherever the Habitation Officer resides in the village, the learners used to come regularly by his consistent observations at night times.

Vasantha Kumari and Sudha Rani (2002) conducted a study on the constraints of continuing education programme.

It was noted that 25 per cent of the Preraks were qualified up to tenth class, and 40 per cent were graduates. Only 35.00 per cent of the Preraks were satisfied with their job. Majority of the Preraks were men. 53.00 per cent of the Preraks organised different educational programmes regularly.

Baby Sarojini (2003) observed in her study that the influence of education on self help groups as. It is evident from the data presented the Illiterate members of the SHGs has lesser knowledge on all important aspects in comparison with members having certain level of education. The level of education did not have much impact on aspects like interest rate as well as attached bank. On issues like promoters of SHGs, receipt of grant and on the illiterate members has shown lesser knowledge, the impact of education has also been observed, in the process of "Financial Decisions Making". It is interesting to observe that lower the level of education lesser the role of self i.e., women SHG members, in financial decision making.

Bharathi (2003) conducted a study on Influence of training, materials, community support and opinion on the performance of Preraks organising continuing education centres. The influence of opinion on performance of prerak was also found to be significant. Preraks who obtained low opinion scores secured a mean performance score of 82.40, Preraks who obtained medium opinion scores secured a mean performance score of 86.54 and Preraks who obtained high opinion scores secured a mean performance score of 89.65. It indicates that any amount of effort to increase the efficiency of training, materials, community support and opinion of Preraks towards the programme would definitely enhance the performance of Preraks.

Bhola (2003) in his article on 'Adult and Life Long Education for Sustainable Development in India: Greater Achievements, Greater Expectations', says that adult education has been part of the development discourse from its very inception. Comprehensive systems of education were established to meet all the manpower needs of societies in transition, though hardly ever with much success. More recently, 'basic education' for children, youth and adults has come to be central to the efforts dedicated to sustainable development. It has come to be well understood that 'Education for All' is a necessary concomitant of participative democratic policies for participation in the economy, for adoption and use of technology in the processes of modernisation and for renewing and enjoying cultures. In India, the scheduled castes, scheduled tribes, other backward classes and specially girls and women require special attention.

Reddeppa Reddy (2003) made a study on Continuing Education Committees, who are supposed to associate with the Continuing Education Center activity and found, the continuing Education committee has good rapport with NGO's and non-officials rather than the developmental departments and officials. The Continuing Education Committees are not getting co-operation from the officials. The committer members are not discharging their responsibilities effectively.

Srinivasa Rao G (2004) conducted a study on opinions of Preraks and neo-literates on organisation of continuing education activities. The findings of the study revealed that Preraks and neo-literates differed significantly with regard to their opinion on the following activities carried out by the Preraks like Organisation of evening classes, Organisation of charcha mandal activities, Organisation of cultural activities, Information window, Other functions (community support, public relations, etc.) Preraks and neo-literates did not differ significantly with regard to their opinion on the following aspects viz. Organisation of library and reading room activities; Organisation of short duration training programmes; Organisation of games and sports activities; Organisation of total activities. As per the trend of the means, the Preraks have obtained:

(a) a better opinion scores on:

 1. organisation of evening classes;

2. charcha mandal activities;
3. short duration training programmes;
4. games and sports activities;
5. other functions (community support, public relations, etc.); and
6. total activities.

(b) a lower opinion score on:

1. organisation of library and reading room activities;
2. information window.

Vasudeva Rao B S and Viswanadha Gupta P (2004) studied on the problems and strategies on continuing education programme, the findings of the study are as follows: Problems as indicated by the respondents, lack of separate building facility and electricity in many centres; collection of membership fee from neo-literates and corpus fund from the public; delay in supply of weekly newspaper meant for neo-literates; lack of provision for buying new games materials in the place of worn out materials; lack of understanding and awareness among the public about the importance of CEC.

Bhat, R.L. and Sharma, Namita (2005) in their article "External benefits of women's education: Some evidence from developing countries", Education indirectly decreases fertility, it changes the perceptions of the costs and benefits of having children, it influences age at marriage, reduces the infant mortality rate, and also changes the attitude to contraception which ultimately leads to reduction infertility rate. Education is also found to have a positive impact on the health status of person concerned and other members of the family. Education of women results in improvement in the nutrition level, better sanitation, cleanliness of home and neighbourhood and knowledge and use of available health care facilities.

Kulasekhar (2005) studied the influence of personal variables on the opinion of neo-literates participating in the continuing education centres. It was found that community support, self-motivation to learn, availability of leisure time and occupation have significantly influenced the participation of learners attending the continuing education centres.

Niranjan Reddy (2005) made an evaluative study of continuing education centres. The findings of the study are Majority of the continuing education centres covered in the study are located in government schools followed by temple, Prerak's house, rented building and small house, Zilla Saksharatha Samiti, Chittoor has provided a wide range of post-literacy and continuing education materials to the centres. The material about democracy, education, agriculture, children and their rights, health care and communicable diseases, women and health issues, AIDS, animal husbandry, social evils, national integration, forests and environment, women's emancipation, folk arts, development programmes, consumer protection, human values and local issues. The response pattern of Preraks revealed that more than half of the sample is satisfied with the material.

Robert Devdoss (2005) conducted a study on the evaluation of continuing education programme in Chittoor District. The following are the findings related to the activities of Preraks. Out of the different activities carried out by the Preraks in the centres, majority of the learners are satisfied with a few areas namely, Organisation of evening classes; Creating favourable environment to achieve the objectives of 'Education For All'; Providing books and magazines to learners to read at home; Helping the neo-literates to read and understand the reading materials; Maintaining different registers in the centre; Maintaining the equipment of the centre; Identifying the learning needs of neo-literates; and Organisation of programmes to promote mental peace, happiness and values among beneficiaries.

Sikligar, P.C (2005) in his study titled "Social mobilisation for sustainable agriculture development: A study with reference to "MS Swami Nathan Research Foundation" studied the importance of mobilization of community in ensuring sustainable development in rural areas. Study observes that both the units have conducive atmosphere in favour of promoting agricultural production. The bio-pesticide unit helped the women in their economic empowerment. The women member have reported an improvement in their income level up to Rs. 2,000/- per month individually. This increase in income helps these women to educate their children and fulfil their other domestic needs.

Vasudeva Rao, Viswanadha Gupta and Srinivasa Rao (2005) "Akshara Bharathi Programme: Volunteers' Perceptions" they found that the problems of the volunteers are lack of honorarium and incentives, non availability of proper building to organize class, delay in supply of primers/ books in some centres, inconvenient location of the centres to learners, lack of awareness and understanding about the importance of education and objective of Akshara Bharathi programme among the masses

Viswanadha Gupta, Adinarayana Reddy and Vasudeva Rao (2006) undertaken a Study of the Functioning of Continuing Education Centres as Perceived by Continuing Education Committee Members and the findings of the study are as follows, all the sample committee members have expressed that they have received very poor cooperation from the higher officers for their representations. Sixty per cent of the committee members have revealed that their CECs have organized income-generating programmes followed by cultural programmes and health related programmes. One third of CECs have organized individual programmes.

Rodriguez, Liza M (2007) Adult learning for social action in a Latino Community: Integrating and sustaining skills development, community organizing and advocacy in a grassroots organisation. Latinos are the fastest growing population group in the U.S. The growth of this population has taken place at a time of economic restructuring and funding cuts for adult education. The urban 'hourglass' economy with most jobs concentrated of the top and bottom of the earning scale coupled with limited access to adult education programmes, provides Latino immigrants with little opportunity for social mobility. In this context adult educators have proposed integrated learning models that combine work place with social action skills in order to give learners a meaningful voice in local decision making. The dissertation examines an adult learning model in a north-eastern, urban Latino community that aims to integrate work place and social action skills. The study's theoretical frame work illiterates the possibility of learning for social among historically marginalized groups. It ethnographic methodology, relying on participant observations, interviews and life histories, captures how specific organisational practices help shape a sense of shared community, goals and social action plans. In its examination of specific practices that enable an organisation to assist immigrants with the transition from newcomers to active residents, the study provides vital information to local policy makers on decisions that can best support the integration of a growing Latino immigrant population.

Adinarayana Reddy, P. et.al (2007) suggested in their article Rural Development through Continuing Education Programme suggested the following indicators of Rural Development which need an integrated approach through Continuing Education Programme viz. Developing social consciousness, Collective decision – making and collective action, Dedicated village leadership, Use of science & Technology, Development of Agriculture and allied section, Provision of subsidiary occupation and income and Development of cottage and village industries.

Padma Kumari (2007), in her study pointed out that due to lack of proper sanitation facilities the rural people are facing various health problems. They even don't have adequate medical facilities to overcome these health disorders. This is one of the problem being faced by the rural population. Preparing illicit liqueur is means in the villages and selling the same in rural areas as appoint the family and youth and many associations victims are women. The Rural Development Sector Policy of the World Bank (1975) observed that "Rural Development is a strategy designed to improve the economic and social life of a specific group of people – the rural poor. It involves extending the benefits of development to the poorest among those who seek a livelihood in the rural areas. The group includes small scale farmers, tenants and the landless".

The world Bank Publication again defines the Rural Development as "Improving the living standards of the masses of the low-income population residing in rural areas making the process of rural development self-sustaining".

Chaudhury, Sahadat H (2008) Choices and voices of Adult illiterate: Exploring their literacy needs in rural Bangladesh, Literacy researchers have some times been puzzled by the modest results of literacy programmes in developing countries. One of the key areas identified as a possible cause for limited success of literacy programmes is the inadequate understudying of the literacy needs and perspectives of beneficiaries. Unlike many studies that draw mostly on provides' accounts. In addition to using beneficiaries providers, some of the key findings were rural adults tended to identify themselves as educated or uneducated instead of as literate or illiterate; there was hardly any difference in perspective between neo-literates and illiterates, adults engaged irregular rural occupations like selling labour or farming are less likely to feel motivated to pursuer literacy., older made adults preferred to spend their time on religious pursuits instead of on literacy; and older women attached higher priority to skills training as than did younger women. Based on the findings, the researcher argued in favour of developing some common ground to help reduce the perspective gap. Such middle grand could foster increased understanding and cooperation among all actors and contribute to the development of more useful literacy programmes for rural adults.

Mamata Das (2008) in his study "Capacity building for rural development" organised by SNDT University, the impact of the training programmes, Shedashi-Wavoshi Watershed in Khalapur Talukas of Raigad district, Maharashtra has been considered as a sample. RC, with the support of NABARD, has implemented the watershed activities in the village. The community members have undergone various skill development programmes on watershed management. The study reveals the impact of the capacity building programmes adopting a process as well as outcome oriented study. It acknowledges that capacity building of the local people is fundamental for sustainable rural development. An appropriate people oriented approach of human resource development has the ability to transform the rural scenario in India. It stresses that theoretical inputs accompanied with experiential learning play an important role in developing attitude, knowledge and skill of a trainee, shaping up the vision and providing him confidence to carry the task of development forward.

Sabine Strassburg (2008) Adult Education and Poverty Alleviation – What can be learnt from Practice? Four case studies from South Africa, the results of case studies and identifies good practice and effectiveness indicators. Information from all the case studies is triangulated. The effectiveness indicators indentified cover location (accessibility for the poor), approach, training offered targeting of the poor, strategies and poverty issues addressed financial sustainability of the organisation, institutional and human capacity, concept appropriateness, monitoring and evaluation, outcome and impact.

Thus the review has provided a background for the present study. Only limited studies are presented because limitations of the thesis. On the basis of the empirical evidences of the earlier studies, the present study aims differential impact of the Continuing Education programme in Visakhapatnam district.

The methodology of the study is presented in the following chapter.

> *"If I learn carpentry from an illiterate carpenter only I know, how to do work, but if I learn from a literate carpenter, my thoughts will be stimulated"*
>
> – Mahatma Gandhi

CHAPTER 3 Methodology

The purpose of this chapter is to present a detailed process of statement of the problem, method adopted, nature of the study, objectives formulated, area of the study, sample taken for the study, research tools selected and statistical techniques used and limitations of the study.

Statement of the Problem

India consists of 638,596 villages and nearly 16.6 per cent of people are illiterates; among them the illiteracy rate of males are (17.9%) and females (53.3%). The village people in India are mainly engaged in agriculture and allied occupations. We can find four kinds of people in villages as agriculturists, agricultural labour, child labour and artisans. All these sections are backward in terms of the social-economic development, irrespective of their caste and creed. In their daily occupation they are dependent upon natural resources, environment, climate and economic aspects. The Andhra Pradesh Government and Central Government introduced many welfare programmes for the benefit of rural people. Due to ignorance, illiteracy and interference of middlemen, the rural development programmes are not reaching the target groups up to expectation of the planners. Realizing this fact the Government of India introduced many educational programmes under non-formal sector. Continuing Education Programme is one of the strategies under National Literacy Mission to provide Literacy and creating awareness for income generating activities to the neo-literates at the centre level. Andhra Pradesh is known as a pioneering state for effective implementation of both continuing education programmes and rural development programmes. Government is particular to link continuing education programmes and welfare schemes for conveying the benefits to the target group properly. The functionaries of CEP arrange face - to - face interaction between neo-literates and developmental officials regularly. With this background the present study entitled *"Rural Development through Literacy Campaigns* was taken up.

Scope of the Study

This study is an attempt to measure the impact of the continuing education programme on the set goals in Visakhapatnam district, measuring the impact of the programme on the neo-literates, Literacy, Functionality, Awareness, Benefits received from developmental programmes and also eliciting the opinion of the Preraks towards organisation of the centre, to elucidate information from community members (non-enrolled) and also to identify the difference. This study analyses the impact in relation to the socio-economic background of neo-literates, community members.

Type of the Study

The discussion over the methodological aspects of the study, to begin with, focuses upon the research design applicable for the study. Describing research design as a tool of guidance in seeking required information, in processing the data and in combining the data with a purposeful procedure, Sliltiz (1959) classified the research designs into three types, namely, exploratory, descriptive and explanatory. Exploratory studies are aimed at gaining new insights into a phenomenon and are generally formulate in nature. The major emphasis of these studies is on discovery of ideas that help in the development of hypothesis at a later stage. In the descriptive design, the research design proceeds, with or without hypothesis to portray the accurate characteristics of a given phenomenon. In the explanatory research, normally the researcher tests a hypothesis in relation to different variables in an already investigated field. So the present study falls under exploratory research.

Aim of the Study

The present investigation aims to asses the socio-economic status of beneficiaries and non-beneficiary, opinion, awareness of neo-literates and community members and advantage gained by the neo-literate by attending the continuing education centre and status of community members (Members not attending centre), the problems faced to utilize the development/welfare programmes by the neo-literate and non neo-literates and opinion of the Preraks in running the centre activities. In addition to improve the programme, better implementation and providing access to Rural Development and welfare programme, suggestions to improve the programme context to seek remedies for draw backs, deficiencies and problems encountered by the Preraks and neo-literates were also enlisted for them. Also elucidate the opinion of the Preraks and neo-literates on the functioning of the centre activities, moreover the knowledge on literacy and benefit acquired by the neo-literates were gathered. The opinion of the community members were also gathered about their knowledge on literacy, welfare programmes and benefits from continuing education programme.

Need and Significant of the Study

University literacy is recognized to be an important factor in contributing to social and economic development. The linkages between literacy on one hand and other aspects of social and economic development are quire strong. Literacy facilitates better and more effective communication of new technology in agriculture; and, extension agencies could work better in a climate of literate environment. Illiterate peasants rarely succeed in transforming co-operative and Panchayat institutions to their benefit. In an illiterate environment such institutions are either controlled by bureaucrats or by exploitative landlords and usurers. The linkages between adoption of family planning and literacy are known to be even stronger. Adoption rates are higher among literate females as compared to illiterate people. Such strong linkages between literacy and other aspects of social development result in high benefits to investments in literacy, apart from the fact that universal literacy should be valued as an end in itself. Yet, this is an area in which achievements have lagged behind expectations. Literacy progresses only slowly, and the number of illiterates have been rising. Even today the rate of illiteracy of rural folk is very high. There needs to be a two-pronged attack, enrolment rates in the primary schools need to be improved. But as J.P. Naik points out, this is not adequate. Given the levels of poverty, many children do drop out from schools and add to the number of illiterates. They do not benefit from the formal school system. There is a need for programmes outside the formal school system to meet the requirements of these groups. The task of spreading literacy among the disadvantaged sections of the community cannot be left alone to bureaucratic agencies. There is also a need for innovative approaches. Illiterates will have to be motivated to learn. Techniques of imparting instructions will have to be appropriate. Subject matter of instruction should be relevant to environment of work and life of the learner. Modern systems of Communication such as audio visual aids will have to be employed.

Recognizing the need for the education of the masses in the country, the Government has introduced many number of adult education programmes like Social Education Programme (1949), Farmers Functional Literacy Programme (1966-67), Non-Formal Education for Women (1975), National Adult Education Programme (1978), Point No. 16 of the New 20 Point Programme (1982), Mass Programme for Functional Literacy (1986), National Literacy Mission (1988). The objectives of these programmes basically are:

1. to extend educational opportunities to illiterates in terms of reading, writing and numeracy;
2. to create awareness among the beneficiaries of the programmes about social concerns, social problems, development initiatives and about various facilities and opportunities available to the masses;
3. to provide scope for the neo-literates to strengthen and further the basic literacy skills acquired by them through the post-literacy and continuing education centres; and
4. to pave the way for enhancing the quality of life of the beneficiaries of the continuing education centres in social, economic and cultural aspects through different types of programmes.

Mode of Data Collection

The schedule meant for the Preraks covered their socio-economic, professional and educational background, extent of experience in Continuing Education Programmes, activities including opinion and attitude of the prerak on seven objectives of CEP and their efforts in explaining to neo-literate about developmental programmes for their benefit. Data are collected over a period of seven months. Initially the basic statistics about the centres, location, Neo-literates and their overall characteristics are listed out from the records available with the agency in the district. After selecting the sample centres, the respective Preraks of the centres are contacted in person. Subsequently, a pre-test is conducted to test the validity of the schedule by canvassing it. During the phase of data collection, the researchers gained unstinted cooperation from the Neo-literates, Community Members and Preraks. Neo-literates showed very keen interest while responding to the questions in the schedule. There was slight difficulty in tracing the nodal Preraks for canvassing the schedule since they were involved in frequent and mostly unscheduled field visits.

Variables of the Study

Age, sex, caste, nativity, family background, individual income, family income, occupation, and other individual characteristics of the Neo-literates, Community Members, and Preraks are analyzed. The same variables are considered for measuring the variations on the impact of the programme.

Objectives of the Study

The following are the objectives of the study:

1. To study the socio economic and demographic profile of the sample respondents i.e. Preraks, Neo-literates and Community members in rural Mandals of Visakhapatnam District.
2. To find out the opinion of the Preraks and neo-literates on the organisation of continuing education centre with special reference to variables in socio-economic and demographic.
3. To investigate the details on explaining about development/welfare programmes by Preraks and neo-literates at the centre.
4. To compare the status of the neo-literates and community members on Literacy, Functionality and Awareness components.
5. To study the degree of difference on development/welfare programmes among neo-literates and community.
6. To find out the differential impact on Continuing Education Programme with reference to variations in the socio-economic and demographic variables of neo-literates.

Development of the Tools

Research tools are the sole factors in determining the sound data and in drawing accurate conclusions about the problem on hand. The conclusions ultimately help in providing suitable remedial measures to the problem concerned. The selection and use of tools can be done in two ways. The first one is to construct a tool independently by the researcher for his study. The second way of selection and use of tools is right selection of tools from already standardized ones available in the field of study. For the purpose of the study the investigator prepared two scales and one scheduled and standardized the scales as per the procedure. Two scales are attitude/opinion towards organisation of continuing education centre activity and benefits literacy inventory, and the schedule for awareness aspects and development/welfare programmes' knowledge and benefits.

Attitude/Opinion Scale

As it has been described earlier, it is proposed to study the opinion of Preraks and neo-literates on different aspects of organisation of continuing education activities and its impact on the human resource development i.e. health, education, rural development etc. Therefore, two questionnaires meant for the groups are to be developed. To collect the data pertinent personal and programme related variables of Preraks and neo-literates personal data was used. The procedures adopted in the development of the tools are described in the following pages:

Development of Attitude/Opinion Scale on Organisation of Continuing Education Activities

The present study required a measure to assess the attitude of Preraks and neo-literates towards organisation of continuing education activities. In the absence of standardized tool the investigator developed a measure of attitude/opinion towards organisation of continuing education activities. The scale was developed on the lines of Likert type of attitude scale construction. The Likert technique was preferred as it is believed to be easier and simpler in respect of construction, perceived to be relatively more reliable, valid, better understood and easier to fill in and claimed to provide more information about subjects' attitude since responses would be given to each of the many items.

Preparation of Preliminary Form

Statements that are supposed to indicate favourable or unfavourable attitude towards various activities of continuing education centre like organisation of evening classes, library and reading room, charcha mandal, simple and short duration programmes, cultural and recreational activities, games and sports activities, supportive facilities were pooled together from the available literature. To supplement the list 5 Mandal Literacy Organisers, 5 supervisors, 5 Nodal Preraks, 20 Preraks and 50 neo-literates were contacted (chosen randomly from the study area). They were asked to list either favourable or unfavourable statements that are supposed to indicate the attitude towards organisation of continuing education activities. The statements thus obtained were subjected to scrutiny and the relevant statements were picked up. At the next stage, all the statements together were reviewed and rewritten to avoid ambiguity and overlapping. Item pool thus developed consisted of 106 statements, about 56 positive and 50 negative items. The list was submitted to 3 university level teachers and 2 project officers working in adult and continuing education with a request to suggest omissions and modifications wherever necessary. The experts suggested the following aspects.

1. Since the study involves comparison of attitudes of both Preraks and neo-literates, there is no need to develop two scales for Preraks and neo-literates separately on the organisation of continuing education activities.
2. As far as possible clarity with regard to language and presentation should be maintained.
3. Further explanation has to be given when the subjects fail to understand the statements.
4. Items relating to each unit should be presented at one place.

The suggestions of the experts were duly considered and only one scale was developed to study the attitude of Preraks and neo-literates towards organisation of continuing education activities. In all 92 statements remained in the form were thus finalized. A five point rating scale was suggested by the panel of experts for this purpose wherein the respondents can check the statements on the descriptive cues, namely, strongly agree, agree, undecided, disagree and strongly disagree. Attitude scale thus developed was translated into regional language and administered to 30 Preraks and 30 neo-literates to check the language errors and to know whether the statements were easily understandable or not and the errors and doubts raised were duly carried out.

Pilot Study

The attitude/opinion scale thus prepared with 92 items was subjected to pilot study on a random sample of 30 Preraks and 30 neo-literates. Care was taken to see that the subjects represented different gender, age, education, experience, marital status and income groups. The tool was administered individually to neo-literates and to Preraks or in small groups (5-10 members) and their ratings were obtained and analysed.

Selection of Items for the Final Form

In order to determine the discriminative power and usefulness of the statements of the measure, the 't' values were calculated. Statements that had calculated equal or greater than 1.96 were selected for the final form. Based on this procedure out of 92 statements 12 statements were discarded and 80 statements remained in the final form. The final form consists of 80 students spread over 8 areas i.e., organisation of evening classes, library and reading room, charcha mandal (simple and short duration training programmes), cultural and recreational activities, games and sports activities, information window, development programmes and supportive facilities. There are 10 items in each area and altogether there are 40 positive and 40 negative statements.

Reliability

For the purpose of establishing reliability for the measure on attitude, test retest method was followed. This was done to know the consistency of the measure and the measure was administered to 30 Preraks and 30 neo-literates with a gap of 2 weeks. The correlation co-efficient between the ratings was 0.762 for Preraks and 0.695 for neo-literates which is highly reliable.

Validity

For the purpose of the measure of attitude, content validity, item validity and intrinsic validity were established.

Content Validity

The attitude scale was developed based on field observations, policy documents, discussions with Preraks, nodal Preraks, Mandal literacy organizers, review of literature, university level experts, neo-literates and community members. Hence it can be presumed that the measure was possessing content validity.

Item Validity

Item validity depends upon the number of discriminations of the desired sort that the item is capable of making. It emphasises the extent to which the item predicts segregation of the examinees with high versus low criteria scores. The discriminatory power of each of these items can be established and tested for significant difference between the criterion groups before including them in the final form.

Intrinsic Validity

Intrinsic validity is stated in terms of how well the obtained scores measure the tests true score components. This validity is given by the square root of the proportion of the true variance i.e., the square root of its reliability. The intrinsic validity of the measures of attitude is therefore for Preraks and for neo-literates.

Schedule

The schedule intended for the neo-literates and community members covering their level of literacy gained, functional particulars, availability of the neo-literate materials, level of awareness on social, health, cultural and rural developmental aspects and questions relating to benefits and utilization of the developmental programmes. Schedule included who informed about the developmental programmes.

The community schedule includes socio economic background, literacy, functionality, awareness of welfare, health problems faced and to what extent they are benefited from welfare programmes. The community members were also enquired about the suggestions for better implementation of the programmes for neo-literates.

Benefits of Literacy Inventory

One of the aims of the study is to identify the benefits of the literacy in continuing education Neo-literates. Keeping this in view, the available literature is reviewed and found that not much effort has been made in developing a suitable and comprehensive scale for measuring the benefits of literacy. Hence, an attempt is being made by the investigator to develop benefits of literacy inventory on scientific lines not only to identify the benefits of the literacy but also to see the intensity of the benefits acquired by the Neo-literates.

In developing the benefits inventory method mentioned above, the following steps are taken.

Preparation of Preliminary Form

Benefits of literacy can be identified and studied by adopting various methods and sources. They can be identified by using various methods such as interview, observation, checklist, questionnaire, ratings and other suitable parameters. The sources of identification of the benefits of the literacy can be personal interview with the Neo-literates, observation of actual proceedings of the continuing education programme, enquiry with the field administrators and others etc.

Each of the above methods and sources has its own merits and demerits. However, for the purpose of the present study, the rating scale method is considered appropriate not only for identifying the benefits but also to study their intensity. With regard to the sources, Neo-literates themselves are appropriate sources for identification of the benefits. Hence, the rating scale method for identifying the benefits and their intensity is being used. Further, this method helps in categorized the benefits based on their intensity expressed by the Neo-literates.

Development of the Tool

A list of benefits of literacy is gathered from different sources like personal interview with the Neo-literates, village committees, participants of the programme, Preraks consultation with experts in the field and the review of related literature. The items pooled are re-written again for removing the ambiguous items, items without clarity, repetition and inaccuracies. These items are arranged under different sub-headings. The list thus prepared was presented to a panel of 10 experts and suggestions of the experts were carried out. At this stage, there were 65 items in the inventory.

Rating Procedure

As the aim of the study is not only to identify the benefits but also to measure the intensity of the benefits; appropriate method is a numerical rating scale consisting of five descriptive cues for rating the items by the sample with ease and accuracy. Hence, a five point numerical rating scale consisting of five descriptive cues viz., Very Good, Good, Moderate, Poor and Very Poor with the scores 5, 4, 3, 2 and 1 respectively was constructed. Respondents were supposed to agree with any one of the alternative cues to indicate the intensity of benefits that they were exposed in getting the literacy.

Pilot Study

A sample of 75 Neo-literates representing all social segments of the society was selected at random from different continuing education centres in Visakhapatnam district of Andhra Pradesh. They were explained about the mode of marking the scale so that data gathered is accurate as far as possible.

Selection of Items

Based on obtained benefit scores, the benefits of the literacy inventory responses sheets were arranged in descending order. The top and bottom response sheets were chosen to find out the discriminative power and usefulness of the items. The 't-test' values for each items of the two categories of response sheets were calculated and all the items with 't' values of 1.96 and above were retained for the final form and rest of the items with less than 't' value of 1.96 were discarded, as suggested by Edward (1969). Based on the above procedure 29 items were discarded and the final number of inventory consisted of 36 benefits.

Reliability of the Tool

For the purpose of the present study, Test, Re-test reliability of the scale was adopted. This was done by obtaining the ratings for the scale twice with an interval of one month between the first and the second administration of the scale to the sample. The obtained correlation coefficient between the two ratings was 0.919 which was significant. Therefore, the benefit of literacy inventory used in the study is highly reliable.

Validity of the Tool

Any instrument developed for measuring a particular aspect will be considered appropriate only when its validity is proved. Construct validity refers to the extent to which a test reflects constructs presumed to underline the test performance and also the extent to which it is based on theories regarding these constructs. The benefits of literacy inventory developed on the lines described above process satisfactory validity with reference to the content, items and intrinsic validity. The description of details of the validity of the inventory is as follows.

Content Validity

Content validity indicates how adequate is the content of the test sampling, the domain about which inferences are to be drawn. Further, when taken collectively, the items should constitute a representative sample of the variable that is measured. The present benefit of literacy inventories were developed keeping the above in view i.e., while selecting the items the functionaries of the programme, researchers and review of literature were consulted. Thus, it can reasonably be assumed that the instrument possesses satisfactory content validity.

Item Validity

Item validity stresses the extent to which the item predicts segregation of examiners into those with high versus and those with low criterion scores. The discriminative power of each of the item of the present scale was established by calculating their 't' values as described under the heading 'Section of Items'. Thus, the items chosen for both sections of the scale were found to be effectively valid.

Intrinsic Validity

Intrinsic validity is the degree to which a test measures what it purports to measure. This can also be stated as how well obtained scores measure the tests true score component. Intrinsic validity refers to the square root of its reliability. Thus, the intrinsic validity of the benefit of literacy inventory was the square root of its reliability Ö0.92 = 0.96 which can be assumed that the scores have highly satisfying intrinsic validity. Reliability value of the scale is nothing but intrinsic validity.

Brief Description of the Benefit of Literacy Inventory

The final form of the Neo-literates benefit of literacy inventory developed in the lines described above consisted of 53 items. Each item can be rated on any of the five responses category namely Very Good, Good, Moderate, Poor and Very Poor which carried numerical values 5, 4, 3, 2 and 1 respectively. The score on the inventory ranges between 53 and 265 points.

Locale and Sample of the Study

Visakhapatnam district in Andhra Pradesh was selected for the purpose of study. The Visakhapatnam district consists of 42 Mandals. A total of 570 continuing education centres and 570 sub continuing education centres are functioning in the district under the supervision of Zilla Saaksharatha Samithi. For the purpose of this study 3 Mandals were selected at random, the data was collected in three rural Mandals to elicit unbiased responses from the sample. From the selected Mandals, nearly fifty per cent of the centres were selected for the study. All the Preraks from the selected centres were interviewed. Five Neo-literates from each of the selected centres and three community members' responses from the selected centre area were also recorded.

The sample frame of the study is as follows:

District	- 1
Mandals	- 3
Preraks	- 78
Neo-literates	- 219
Community Representatives	- 176

Analysis of the Data

The data/information gathered in the present research fall under two categories viz.:

1. quantitative; and
2. qualitative data.

Therefore, for the quantitative data, the MS-Excel and Statistical Package for Social Sciences (SPSS) was utilized for finding Mean, Standard Deviation, t-test, Analysis of Variance and correlation. The 'F' or 't' test was applied to find out the differences, if any, between the mean scores obtained by any two groups. Whereas, the ANOVA techniques were utilised to find out the difference amongst three or more groups.

Scheme of Presentation

The study is presented in five chapters and presented as follows:

- *Chapter – I:* An Introduction is on different aspects of adult and continuing education programmes, different adult education programmes, status of continuing education programme in Andhra Pradesh and in India. Concept of development and different development/ welfare programmes are presented in this chapter, profile of the study area, profile of continuing education programmes in Visakhapatnam and progress in development of continuing education programme in respect of study area as well as Andhra Pradesh also presented.

- *Chapter – II:* A brief review of research studies in relation to adult and continuing education programmes as well as development/welfare programmes and their impact was presented in this chapter to capture the contemporary thinking and findings. The studies conducted in India and abroad are presented in this chapter.
- *Chapter – III:* This chapter is devoted to study division the scope, need, objectives of the study, methodological aspects, Chapterisation and the limitations of the study are discussed in this chapter. This section is devoted to preparation of the scales and schedules and their reliability & validity of the scales was explained. The study area, mode of data collection, and analysis of the data are presented.
- *Chapter – IV:* This chapter mainly concentrates to describe and analyse the profile of preraks, neo-literates and community members. The areas focussed were sex, age, marital status, caste, nativity, education, occupation and individual and family income.
- *Chapter V:* This chapter discusses and analyses the perspectives of Preraks and neo-literates towards eight themes viz., Organisation of Evening Classes, Library and Reading Room, Charcha Mandal, Cultural and Recreational Activities, Short Term Training Programmes, Games and Sports Activities, Information Window Programmes and Supportive Facilities.
- *Chapter VI:* This chapter is dedicated for comparison of neo-literates and community members in relation with Literacy, functionality and social awareness aspects viz., Institutional membership, social taboos, social beliefs. Analysis was made on these aspects.
- *Chapter VII:* This chapter explains and analyses the impact of continuing education programme on neo-literates.
- *Chapter – VIII:* In this chapter outlook of continuing education programme in the form of a brief summary of the introduction and review of literature and

methodology is presented in the beginning. This chapter also includes a list of major findings in different aspects of the study and concludes with a discussion on the major findings. The discussion focuses upon the positive and negative implication of the findings and thus enables us to evolve suitable suggestions for effective implications of the Continuing Education Programme in future.

Limitations of the Study

1. The study was limited to Continuing Education Centres of 3 rural mandals of Visakhapatnam district, 78 Preraks, 219 Neo-literates and Community Representatives176.
2. Control method was used to obtain the difference between neo-literates and community members towards knowledge and benefits of the rural development programmes.
3. The sample was very specific and related to continuing education programmes, neo-literates and their activities.
4. As appropriate standardized tools were not available, the researchers constructed the attitude/opinion scales and schedule/questionnaire was canvassed in the field after standardized process of the tools.

The results obtained from the analysis are presented in the following chapters.

> *Adult education neither begins nor ends with literacy. Literacy can not be forced upon the toiling masses desperately engaged in just living somehow. A lonely and tired people will have no genuine interest in literacy. Literacy, most some as the response to the inner urge of the people themselves, who have eaten some food during the day and have marginal energy. The best way to bring literacy to such people is to make the programme life centered..."*
>
> –Mahatma Gandhi

Profile of Preraks, Neo-literates and Community Members

The success or failure of any programme depends upon the personnel associated with the programme the continuing education Programme is conceived for the benefit of the people and also for the educated people of the community and to create income generation by providing required facilities and environment. The continuing education programme envisaged that the benefit of the programme should go to the target i.e. unemployed, youth, neo-literates, educated and the community as a whole. In order to facilitate the functioning of the programme, functionaries are appointed by the implementation agency and monitoring the work of Preraks who is supposed to be organizing centre activity i.e. key field functionary.

The socio-economic background in general and the educational and professional background in particular of the sample respondents i.e. Preraks, neo-literates and community members are analyzed in this chapter, basing upon the assumption that these factors do play a significant role in determining the impact of the programme in doing so. Our study covers a total number of 78 Preraks, 219 neo-literates are engaged in continuing education programme and 176 community members from the study area of Visakhapatnam district.

Profile of the Preraks

The Prerak who is in-charge of the continuing education centre selected for the study. The socio-economic background of the Preraks is presented in the following analysis.

Sex, Age and Marital Status of the Preraks

Out of total 78 Preraks selected, only 17 (21.8%) are females while 61 (78.2%) are males. The Female Preraks are found to be less comparatively to Male, though more number of females is enrolled in the centres.

Table 4.1: Sex, Age and Marital Status of the Preraks

Variable	Group	Number	Percentage
Sex	Male	61	78.2
	Female	17	21.8
Age	Below 20	20	25.6
	21 - 35	27	34.6
	Above 36	31	39.7
Marital Status	Unmarried	17	21.8
	Married	55	70.5
	Widow/widower	6	7.7

The age of the Preraks ranged from below 20 years to above 36 years of age, 31 (39.7%) of Preraks were above 36 years while the 20 (25.6%) are below 20 years and remaining 27 (34.6%) are between 21-35 years of the age group. Out of the total 78 Preraks, 55 (70.5%) are married, 17 (21.8%) unmarried and remaining only 6 (7.7%) are either widow or widower.

Preraks under study belonged to different social classes. More than one fifth (21.5%) are from upper castes and 16 (20.5%) are from schedule castes. 45 (57.7%) are from the backward classes, who are following rural traditional skills and are also economically weak. Our data shows that 48 (51.3%) Preraks are native of rural areas, and 30 (38.5%) are from urban nativity.

Caste and Nativity of the Preraks

Table 4.2: Caste and Nativity of the Preraks

Variable	Group	Number	Percentage
Caste	O.C.	17	21.8
	B.C.	45	57.7
	S.C.	16	20.5
Nativity	Rural	48	61.5
	Urban	30	38.5
	Tribal	0	0.0

Education, Occupation and Income of the Preraks

Table 4.3: Education, Occupation, Individual and Family Incomes of the Preraks

Variable	Group	Number	Percentage
Education	10th	19	24.4
	Intermediate	36	46.2
	Graduation	19	24.4
	Post graduation	4	5.1
Occupation	Agriculture	29	37.2
	Business	14	17.9
	Employed	7	9.0
	Artisans	23	29.5
	Others	5	6.4
Individual income	Below Rs. 1000/- PM	29	37.2
	Rs. 1000/- to Rs. 2000 PM	34	43.6
	Above Rs. 2000/- PM	15	19.2
Family income	Below Rs. 1000/- PM	9	11.5
	Rs. 1000/- to Rs. 2000 PM	31	39.7
	Above Rs. 2000/- PM	38	48.7

The education background of the Preraks shows that nearly half (46.2%) are educated till intermediate and 19 (24.4%) are graduates and only 4 (5.1%) of the Preraks are post graduates. The remaining 19 (24.4%) studied up to 10th class. From this study, it can be stated that considerable number of Preraks is having collegiate or university education. Higher qualification of the Preraks really helps in transforming the benefits to the neo-literates and also helps in improving the effectiveness of the organisation and the centre.

The occupational background of the Preraks is taken in to study and have found that the Preraks are engaged in different occupation from very a long time, in addition to the existing position of Prerak in continuing education programme. Majority of the Preraks 29 (37.2%) are occupied with agricultures and 23 (29.5%) are from artisan. Only 7 (9.0%) are employed. The business people also 14 (17.9%) are also involved in CEC activity and remaining 5 (6.4%) Preraks are doing other works.

The income levels of the Preraks other than the honorarium from continuing education programme shows that it is in tune with their occupational background. Only 15 (19.2%) of the Preraks are having monthly income of Rs. 2000/- and above. Preraks 34 (43.6%) are have income ranging between Rs. 1000/- to Rs. 2000/- per month and the remaining 29 (37.2%) Preraks are with monthly income is Rs. 1000/- and below per month.

With regard to the family income, the income groups are categorised them into three groups as Rs. 1000/- and below PM, Rs. 1000/- to Rs. 2000/- and above Rs. 2000/- per month. It has been found that majority 38 (48.7%) of the sample Preraks family income is Rs. 2000/- per month and above, 31 (39.7%) of the Preraks are earning between Rs. 1000/- to 2000/- income per month and the remaining 9 (11.5%) of the Preraks family income is below Rs. 1000/- per month. This shows that almost all the Preraks belongs to below to middle class family.

Experience of the Preraks

Table 4.4: Experience of the Prerak

Sl. No.	Experience	Number	Percentage
1.	Below 2 years	40	51.3
2.	2 - 4	25	32.1
3.	4 and above	13	16.7
	Total	78	100.0

The working experience of Preraks in the Continuing Education Centres are classified into three different groups based on their experience as less than two years, 2 to 4 years and 4 and more years. The findings show that majority 40 (51.3%) of them are having less than 2 years of experience 25 (28.2%) of the Preraks having experience of 2 - 4 years and the remaining 13 (16.7%) of the sample Preraks are having more than 4 years experience in the Continuing Education Centre. The field observation and discussion with the field functionaries revealed that due to heavy work load on the Prerak a few of them have discontinued from the position of Preraks with different personal reasons. Hence it is suggested that the implementing agencies should take steps to provide pre and in service training to Preraks and also it is requisite motivate the Preraks to train them with required skills and to handle continue in the programme.

Family Background of the Preraks

The working sample Preraks are classified into five groups based on their family background as agriculture, business, employed, artisans and others. The performance of the Preraks depends on their availability and sparing of their time and support available from the family in discharging their functions.

The information available from the table 4.5 indicates that 32 (41.0%) Preraks are belong to agriculture family background followed by 23 (29.5%) of the Preraks are artisans, 13 (16.7%) are doing business followed by 6 (7.7%) engaged in other works and only 4 (5.1%) of them are employed.

Table 4.5: Family Background of the Preraks

Sl. No.	Family Background	Number	Percentage
1.	Agriculture	32	41.0
2.	Business	13	16.7
3.	Employed	4	5.1
4.	Artisans	23	29.5
5.	Others	6	7.7
	Total	78	100.0

Profile of the Neo-literates

The socio-economic and demographic background of sampled neo-literates is presented.

Sex, Age and Marital Status of the Neo-literates

It is noted from earlier studies that illiteracy is more prevalent among women compared to men. However, the distribution of the learners shows that in spite of high illiteracy among women, equal number of women comes forward to make use of the continuing education programme. Among the sample respondents 111 (50.7%) are males and 108 (49.3%) are females. It is pertinent to note that women are in a disadvantages position in the society as in most the society is restricting the women to the four walls of the house (Bhatia SC 1982) and it thus putting a restriction on them to make use of the existing facilities. Hence, there is a need to create social awareness in the society towards more involvement of women in the developmental activities.

Continuing Education Programme aims at promoting over all sustainable development among target group in the age group of 15 - 35 years. From the data it is observed that 39 (17.8%) of neo-literates are above 35 years, while 30% are below 20 years and remaining 114 (52.1%) respondents are between 21 - 35 years. However, the study shows that most of the neo-literates 82.1 per cent belonged to the target group.

Table 4.6: Sex, Age and Marital Status of the Neo-Literates

Variable	Group	Number	Percentage
Sex	Male	111	50.7
	Female	108	49.3
Age	Below 20	66	30.1
	21 - 35	114	52.1
	Above 36	39	17.8
Marital Status	Unmarried	47	21.5
	Married	154	70.3
	Widow/widower	18	8.2

The marital status of the neo-literates in general shows that the 154 (70.3%) are married and 47 (21.5%) are unmarried. Very few neo-literates (8.2%) belonged to the widow or widower category.

Caste, Nativity and Family Background of Neo-literates

Table 4.7: Caste, Nativity and Family Background of the Neo-Literates

Variable	Group	Number	Percentage
Caste	O.C.	53	24.2
	B.C.	119	54.3
	S.C.	47	21.5
Nativity	Rural	136	62.1
	Urban	83	37.9
	Tribal	0	0.0
Family background	Agriculture	99	45.2
	Business	25	11.4
	Employed	20	9.1
	Artisans	48	21.9
	Others	27	12.3

The caste wise distribution of the sample learners shows that majority 119 (54.3%) of the neo-literates are from Backward Castes followed by the Forward Castes 53 (24.2%) and Scheduled Castes 47 (21.5%). The trend clearly demonstrates that majority of the learners are from backward castes, which is the dominant category in the district. The learners of Continuing Education Centre are classified into three groups depending upon their nativity as Rural, Urban and Tribal. The divisions of the sample presented in the table 4.7 shows that majority, 136 (62.1%) of them are from rural background and remaining 83 (37.9%) of them are from urban background. The absence of the tribal nativity learners due to the study area belongs to rural background. The family background wise distribution of the sample informs that 99 (45.2%) of the sample are coming from the agricultural family background followed by artisans 48 (21.9%), others 27 (12.3%), business 25 (11.4%) and employed 20 (9.1%). The trend clearly shows that majority of the sample represented agriculture and artisans groups. It is a fact that the centres are organized in rural and semi-rural areas and people depends upon agriculture and allied activities.

With regard to the level education, the sample is classified into three groups i.e. illiterate, literate and primary. The division shows that majority 114 (52.1%) of the sample selected are found to be literates and 69 (31.5%) of them are illiterates. The remaining 36 (16.4%) of them are having primary education and some are found to be dropouts from formal schooling. The occupation wise distribution of the sample shows that majority 103 (47.0%) of the sample are from the agricultural and allied occupations followed by artisans 69 (31.5%), business 37 (16.9%) and employed 10 (4.6%). The occupation background indicates that there is a need for more welfare programmes to be conducted at the centres.

Education, Occupation and Income of the Neo-literates

Table 4.8: Education, Occupation, Individual and Family Income of the Neo-Literates

Variable	Group	Number	Percentage
Education	Illiterate	69	31.5
	Literate	114	52.1
	Primary Education	36	16.4
Occupation	Agriculture	103	47.0
	Business	37	16.9
	Employed	10	4.6
	Artisans	69	31.5
Individual income	Below Rs. 1000/- PM	63	28.8
	Rs. 1000/- to Rs. 2000 PM	116	53.0
	Above Rs. 2000/- PM	40	18.3
Family income	Below Rs. 1000/- PM	38	17.4
	Rs. 1000/- to Rs. 2000 PM	86	39.3
	Above Rs. 2000/- PM	95	43.4

Above table 4.8 reveals that the individual income earning status of the sample learners inform that, majority 116 (53.0%) of the sample members are earning Rs. 1000 to Rs. 2000/- PM, 63 (28.8%) of the members are earning below Rs. 1000/- PM and only 40 (18.3%) of the members are earning above Rs. 2000/- PM. Family income has been categorized into three groups according to which, majority 95 (43.4%) of the sample members are from above Rs. 2000/- PM of family income, and followed by 86 (39.3%) sample learners are between Rs. 1000/- to 2000/- PM income group. Only 38 (17.4%) of the sample respondents reported that their family earned income is below Rs. 1000/- per month.

Profile of the Community Members

The Continuing Education Centres are established in the villages not only for the benefit of the learners, but also to cater the needs of all sections of the population. The aim of continuing education programme is to help the community. In other words it will be catering to the needs of wider community. Hence, the entire community has access to utilizing the programmes of the Continuing Education Centres and the continuing education programme is supposed to be transparent in terms of its functions and activities. In view of this, community members are also selected as sample to identify their awareness on literacy and social and developmental aspects and as a control group i.e. not attending the continuing education centres In this process the social-economic and demographic background information of the community was collected, analysed and presented in table given below.

Sex, Age and Marital Status of the Community Members

Table 4.9: Sex, Age and Marital Status of the Community Members

Variable	Group	Number	Percentage
Sex	Male	92	52.3
	Female	84	47.7
Age	Below 20	58	33.0
	21-35	85	48.3
	36 and above	33	18.8
Marital Status	Unmarried	37	21.0
	Married	127	72.2
	Widow/widower	12	6.8

The sex wise representation of the community members of the sample shows that 84 (47.7%) of them are females and 92 (52.3%) are males. The trend of the representation of the community members clearly demonstrates that the woman has come forwarded to respond to the enquiry. Further it is an indication and it shows that irrespective of gender, they showed enthuse and interest in the activities of Continuing Education Centres. The age wise distribution of the sample in the table 4.9 indicates that 85 (48.3%) of the community members are between 21 - 35 years age followed by below 20 years (33.0%), and 33 (18.8%) of respondents are above 36 years. According to their marital status presented in the table 4.9, majority 127 (72.2%) of the sample are married and 37 (21.0%) of them are unmarried. Very few of the respondents 12 (6.8%) are either widow or widower.

Caste, Nativity and Family background of the Community

Table 4.10: Caste, Nativity and Family Background of the Community Members

Variable	Group	Number	Percentage
Caste	O.C.	40	22.7
	B.C.	97	55.1
	S.C.	39	22.2
Nativity	Rural	108	61.4
	Urban	68	38.6
	Tribal	0	0.0
Family background	Agriculture	79	44.9
	Business	20	11.4
	Employed	16	9.1
	Artisans	40	22.7
	Others	21	11.9

The caste wise distribution of the community members presented in the table 4.10 reveals that majority 97 (55.1%) of the respondents are belongs to Backward Castes, followed by 40 (22.7%) from others castes and 39 (22.2%) are scheduled castes. The trend clearly demonstrates that majority of the community members are from Backward Castes and they have shown inclination towards the developmental aspects.

The community members are classified into three groups with regard to their native place viz., rural, urban and tribal areas. The divisions of the sample presented in the table 4.10 shows that majority 108 (61.4%) of them are with rural area background and remaining 68 (38.6%) arc urban background and in the study there are no tribal respondent because of the taken sample is rural and semi-urban geographical area.

The community members are classified into five groups based on their family background as agriculture, business, employed, artisans and others. The information available from the table 4.10, demonstrates that 79 (44.9%) of the community members belong to agriculture background, artisans 40 (22.7%), 21 (11.9%) belongs to other works business 20 (11.4%) and employed 16 (9.1%).

Education, Occupation and Income levels of the Community

The distribution of the community members according to their level of education identified that majority 92 (52.3%) of them are literates. On the other hand 55 (31.3%) of them are illiterates and remaining 29 (16.5%) are up to primary level. The classification of the community members according to their occupational background, presented in the table 4.11, disclosed that majority 83 (47.2%) of the respondents are doing agriculture and allied works, 57 (32.4%) community members are artisans, 28 (15.9%) business occupation and 8 (4.5%) of them are employees. The table 4.11 reveals that the individual income earning of the sample community members reveals that the majority 95 (54.0%) of the sample community members are earning Rs. 1000 to Rs. 2000/- PM, 49 (27.8%) of the members are earning below Rs. 1000/- PM, only 32 (18.2%) of the members are earning above Rs. 2000/- PM.

While coming to the family income earning, the sample community members, majority 79 (44.9%) of the sample members are earning above Rs. 2000/- PM, 69 (39.2%) of the members are earning Rs. 1000/- to Rs. 2000, only 28 (15.9%) of the members are earning below Rs. 1000/- PM.

Table 4.11: Education, Occupation Individual & Family Income of the Community Members

Variable	Group	Number	Percentage
Education	Illiterate	55	31.3
	Literate	92	52.3
	Primary	29	16.5
Occupation	Agriculture	83	47.2
	Business	28	15.9
	Employed	8	4.5
	Artisans	57	32.4
Individual income	Below Rs. 1000/- PM	49	27.8
	Rs. 1000/- to Rs. 2000 PM	95	54.0
	Above Rs. 2000/- PM	32	18.2
Family income	Below Rs. 1000/- PM	28	15.9
	Rs. 1000/- to Rs. 2000 PM	69	39.2
	Above Rs. 2000/- PM	79	44.9

Prerak is the key person in implementation of the continuing education programme at centre level. The overall socio-economic and demographic profile of the Preraks presented mixed picture, in brief, it can be stated that the sample Preraks from male sex, above 36 years of age, married, belongs to backward castes, with rural nativity, agricultural and artisans occupation studied up to intermediate level, individual income between Rs. 1000/- to Rs. 2000/-, belongs to family income of Rs. 1000/- to 2000/- per month, below 2 years of working experience as Prerak and comes from agricultural family backgrounds.

The socio-economic background of neo-literates shows that most of the sample respondents belong to equal gender distribution, between 21-35 years of age, married, backward class community, rural areas, agriculture and artisans family background, literates, with agriculture occupations, individual income of Rs. 2000/- per month and family income is above Rs. 2000/- per month.

The profile of the community members, who are control group to study the impact of continuing education programme on neo-literates, identified that majority belongs to male sex, 21-35 years of age group, married, backward classes community, rural nativity, belong to agriculture and artisans families, with agriculture occupations individual income of below Rs. 1000/- per month and family income is above Rs. 2000/- per month.

The following chapter dealing with the comparison between Preraks and neo-literates towards the functioning of the continuing education programme and developmental aspects. And also comparison between the neo-literates and community towards awareness of development/welfare programmes and its benefits utilized.

Perspectives of Preraks and Neo-literates Towards Continuing Education

Continuing education centres are established at village level and the Preraks are kept in-charge to organise the activities. The functions of Preraks as stipulated by National Literacy Mission (1988) include organisation of evening classes for improving literacy levels, provision of library and reading room facilities, organizing Charcha Mandal activities for discussing on common problems, organising short term training programmes relating to vocation and development aspects, organising games and sports activities, recreational and cultural activities. The centres has to be kept as an information window for securing information from developmental agencies and as a communication centre where community radio, audio cassettes player-cum-recorder will be provided. Neo-literates are the main beneficiaries of the continuing education programme. The Prerak has to act as motivator, mobilisation of neo-literates, recorder, planner and co-ordinator to organise the various activities effectively and efficiently with the help of Zilla Saksharatha Samithi. It is necessary to ensure the opinion of Preraks and neo-literates towards the various activities that are organised in the continuing education centres to understand the situation.

Analysis of Themes

The analysis has 80 items into eight themes, which were labelled according to suggestions of the experts. The details of the themes and the analysis in the study are presented in the following pages.

Preraks and learners (Neo-literates) opinions towards the following aspects were gathered and divided into eight themes as follows, Organisation of Evening Classes, Library and Reading Room, Charcha Mandal, Cultural and Recreational Activities, Short Term Training Programmes, Games and Sports Activities, Information Window Programmes, Supportive Facilities. Analysis was made on the eight themes. The mean value scores of the total responses were calculated.

For up gradations of literary and numeracy skills the Continuing Education centre to be organised for three to four hours once a week. The learner would have the option to come for an hour or so at the time of their convenience on the given day. Keeping in view this aspect, ten items have been included under this dimension and are provided in the Table 5.1; four items i.e., Assessment of performance of neo-literates in literacy skills leads to their dissatisfaction (2.9103>2.2146), the timings for organisation of evening classes should be decided based on the leisure time of beneficiaries (2.9103>2.2146), it is difficult for a Prerak to organise evening classes for neo-literates and semi-literates simultaneously (2.5641>1.9589) and it is not the responsibility of a Prerak to identify the volunteers for literacy programme(3.1026>2.5525) are high level difference. Four items i.e., Maintenance of attendance register is necessary for organizing evening classes (2.7949>2.4201), the assistance of Prerak is necessary for neo-literates to appear for 5th or 7th class examinations (2.3846 > 1.9361), there is no need to organise separate classes for women learners (3.1154 > 2.7626) and Literacy games will be useful to strengthen the literacy skills of neo-literates are medium level (2.9872 > 2.4932) these two items are low level difference between Preraks and neo-literates.

Theme – 1: Organisation of Evening Classes

Table 5.1: Items relating to Organisation of Evening Classes

Sl. No.	Statement	Preraks	Neo-literates
1.	Organisation of evening classes is theresponsibility of Prerak.	1.9615	1.7397
2.	Nco literates do not evince interest to participate in the evening classes.	2.2308	1.8128
3.	Assessment of performance of neo-literates in literacy skills leads to their dissatisfaction.	2.9103	2.2146
4.	Maintenance of attendance register is necessary for organising evening classes.	2.7949	2.4201
5.	The timings for organisation of evening classes should be decided based on the leisure time of beneficiaries.	2.5641	1.9589
6.	It is difficult for a Prerak to organise evening classes for neo-literates and semi-literates simultaneously.	2.5641	1.9589
7.	It is not the responsibility of a Prerak to identify the volunteers for literacy programme.	3.1026	2.5525
8.	The assistance of Prerak is necessary for neo-literates to appear for 5th or 7th class examinations.	2.3846	1.9361
9.	There is no need to organise separate classes for women learners.	3.1154	2.7626
10.	Literacy games will be useful to strengthen the literacy skills of neo-literates.	2.9872	2.4932

There is difference of opinion between Preraks and neo-literates in all items; Preraks obtained better mean scores than the neo-literates. The more difference is observed in the case of assessment leads to dissatisfaction (0.677), timing of the centre (0.6052), dual teaching (0.6052) responsible for assistance (0.504). the analysis shows that the neo-literates are mostly depends upon Preraks about the centre.

Theme – 2: Library and Reading Room

Table 5.2: Items relating to Library and Reading Room

Sl. No.	Statement	Preraks	Neo-literates
1.	There is no need for a separate reading room in continuing education centres.	3.1923	2.6301
2.	Neo-literate evince more interest to read at home than in the library.	2.8077	2.4429
3.	It is only due to lack of good books and magazines that the neo-literates are not attending to the centres.	2.5256	1.9680
4.	Neo-literates need regular reading habit.	2.4615	1.7534
5.	Proper co-ordination is necessary between Preraks and local librarians.	3.5128	2.8858
6.	Books meant for neo-literates need not be provided for general public.	2.6538	2.1598
7.	Eye sight is a problem to neo-literates above 45 years to read newspapers and books.	2.0385	1.9772
8.	Keeping the books in a systematic manner will help the neo-literates to pick up them easily.	2.9231	2.5662
9.	Neo-literates do not return the books if they are given for reading at home.	3.2179	2.6986
10.	The continuing education centre library should be opened even in the absence of the Prerak	2.4744	1.8630

Library and reading room is one of the functions of the Continuing Education Centre, books would be purchased from the non-recurring and recurring provisions, copies of old journals, wall papers and news paper appropriate for adult learner, informative and entertaining magazines , developmental literature etc., keeping in view this aspect ten items have been included in the table 5.2, in regard to the items; it is only due to lack of good books and magazines that the neo-literates are not attending to the centres (2.5256>1.968), neo-literates need regular reading habit (2.4615>1.7534), proper co-ordination is necessary between Preraks and local librarians (3.5128>2.8858) neo-literates do not return the books if they are given for reading at home (3.2179>2.6986) and the continuing education centre library should be opened even in the absence of the Preraks (2.4744>1.863) are more difference scores compared to neo-literates. With to the items like there is no need for a separate reading room in continuing education centres (3.1923>2.6301), neo-literate evince more interest to read at home than in the library (2.8077>2.4429), books meant for neo-literates need not be provided for general public (2.6538>2.1598) and keeping the books in a systematic manner will help the neo-literates to pick up them easily (2.9231>2.5662) medium difference scores. And regarding other items viz. eye sight is a problem to neo-literates above 45 years to read newspapers and books (2.0385 > 1.9772) is low level difference.

Preraks are obtained better mean scores than neo literates in the items relating to library and reading room.

Charcha Mandal or discussion group is one of the functions of the Continuing Education Programme., for discussing on common problems, this forum could be utilized for quality of life improvement and individual interest programmes. This helps to know the awareness of the people in related issues. And build up capacity to present their views requirement and problems relating to community and individual to acquire benefits. Keeping in view of this aspect ten items have been included under this theme and are depicted in the table 5.3. The opinions between Preraks and neo-literates are more difference in Charcha Mandal activities. With regard to the items viz. Charcha Mandal activities not helpful for neo-literates to improve their knowledge (2.8718>2.2420), better results can be obtained by involving adult education officials in Charcha Mandal activities (2.3077>2.2420) and decision taken at Charcha Mandal need not be informed to its members aspects (2.374>1.8858) these are the high level difference. With regard to the items viz. any problem relating to the village can be taken up for discussion in the Charcha Mandal (2.3974>1.9543), Preraks should have sufficient understanding about the method of organising Charcha Mandal activities

Theme – 3: Charcha Mandal

Table 5.3: Items Relating to Charcha Mandal

Sl. No.	Statement	Preraks	Neo-literates
1.	Any problem relating to the village can be taken up for discussion in the Charcha Mandal.	2.3974	1.9543
2.	Preraks should have sufficient understanding about the method of organising Charcha Mandal activities.	2.4615	2.0183
3.	Charcha Mandal activities are not helpful for neo-literates to improve their knowledge.	2.8718	2.2420
4.	Better results can be obtained by involving adult education officials in Charcha Mandal activities.	2.3077	1.8904
5.	Decision taken at Charcha Mandal need not be informed to its members.	2.3974	1.8858
6.	The participation of development department officials in discussions are more useful to neo-literates.	2.7051	2.3333
7.	It is better to limit the Charcha Mandal activities to women.	2.4615	2.1096
8	The leaders of self-help groups need not be invited for Charcha Mandal activities.	2.4872	2.2877
9.	Sarpanches and village secretaries have nothing to do with Charcha Mandal activities.	2.6795	2.3744
10.	Training is necessary for Preraks to organise Charcha Mandal activities effectively.	2.8205	2.4201

(2.4615>2.0183), participation of development department officials in discussions are more useful to neo-literates (2.7051>2.3333) and training is necessary for Preraks to organise Charcha Mandal activities effectively (2.8205>2.4201) these items having medium level difference. And remaining items viz. it is better to limit the Charcha Mandal activities to women (2.4615>2.1096), the leaders of self-help groups need not be invited for Charcha Mandal activities (2.4872>2.2877) and Sarpanches and village secretaries have nothing to do with Charcha Mandal activities (2.6795>2.3744) are low level difference. The Preraks and neo-literates suggested that the Charcha Mandal discussion should be organised in the presence of women, self help group leaders and people's representatives.

Theme – 4: Cultural&Recreational Activities

Table 5.4: Items relating to Cultural and Recreational Activities

Sl. No.	Statement	Preraks	Neo-literates
1.	Cultural and recreational activities are not necessary for neo-literates.	2.5000	2.3790
2.	Trained artists can give good performances.	2.3590	2.2511
3.	Cultural activities are more necessary to illiterates than neo-literates.	2.5513	2.2192
4.	There is no need to organsie cultural activities periodically in continuing education centres.	2.1667	1.7808
5.	Prior intimation about cultural activities will enable the neo-literates to observe the performances.	2.7051	2.1735
6.	Importance of literacy need not be incorporated as an element in cultural activities.	2.6795	2.3790
7.	Regular organisation of cultural activities is not expensive.	2.2821	1.9132
8.	It is better to plan the recreational activities with the beneficiaries of the centre.	3.1282	2.4155
9.	A Prerak should have knowledge about different types of cultural and recreational activities.	2.8346	2.3333
10.	Community support is not necessary for organising cultural and recreational activities in the villages.	3.0000	2.6210

The Prerak should conduct recreational and cultural activities for sustaining their interest to attend the continuing education centre. Particularly traditional and folk forms of art, rural theatre, puppetry etc., are the activities of this aspect. A total of ten items have been included the items the items viz. Prior intimation about cultural activities will enable the neo-literates to observe the performances (2.7051>2.1735), it is better to plan the recreational programmes in consultations with the beneficiaries (3.1282>2.4155), and Prerak should have knowledge about different types of cultural and recreational activities (2.8846>2.3333) the mean difference score is high. Incase of the items viz. there is no need to organise cultural activities periodically in continuing education centres (2.1667>1.7808) and Community support is not necessary for organising cultural and recreational activities in the villages (3.00>2.6210) mean difference score is medium and remaining items i.e., cultural and recreational activities are not necessary for neo-literates (2.50>2.3790), trained artists can give good performances (2.359>2.2511), cultural activities are more necessary to illiterates than neo-literates (2.5513>2.5513), importance of literacy need not be incorporated as an element in cultural activates (2.6795>2.3790) and regular organisation of cultural activities is not expensive (2.2821>1.9132) are low level mean difference scores.

Neo-literates have differed with the views of Preraks about the cultural programmes, helping neo-literates, regular planning in advance and Preraks knowledge in culture activities. Regular organizing of recreational activities and taking help of community is some extent necessary according Preraks and neo-literate. The mean score difference different is insignificant in the case of other items.

Short term programmes relating to subjects like health and family welfare, new developments agriculture and animal husbandry, conservation of energy, improved quality of life and so on. Continuing Education Centres may also help the local community and beneficiaries to benefit from various vocational training programmes. Income generation programmes, up gradation of vocational skills to enable them for better life practices.

Theme – 5: Short-Term Training Programmes

Table 5.5: Items relating to Short Term Training Programmes

Sl. No.	Statement	Preraks	Neo-literates
1.	Preraks should possess sufficient understanding about the organisation of short term training programmes.	2.5385	2.2374
2.	Short duration training programmes need not be limited to neo-literates.	2.7692	2.4429
3.	Local needs need not be considered while organising short duration training programmes.	2.0000	1.9635
4.	Short duration training programmes are more necessary for men than women.	2.0897	1.7900
5.	Arranging visits to government offices and historical places requires proper planning.	2.1026	1.7854
6.	Preraks should be trained in as many short duration programmes as possible.	2.0000	1.7306
7.	Officials of concerned development departments need not participate in the short duration programmes.	2.0128	1.8447
8.	Neo-literates need training programmes relating to income generation and vocational aspects.	2.5769	2.1370
9.	Jana Sikshana Sansthans are the right agencies for organising vocational courses in the continuing education centres.	2.2436	1.8767
10.	The availability of Mandal resource persons need not be ensured for organising vocational courses.	2.7179	2.4064

In this theme ten items have been included. The Preraks opinion is more mean score difference with neo-literates i.e., Arranging visits to government offices and historical places requires proper planning (2.1026>1.7854), neo-literates need training programmes relating to income generation and vocational aspects (2.5769>2.137) and Jana Sikshana Sansthans are the right agencies for organising vocational courses in the continuing education centres (2.2436>1.8767) are high level mean difference scores. Medium level mean difference scores observed as in items of Preraks should possess sufficient understanding about the organisation of short term training programmes (200>1.7306), short duration training programmes need not be limited to neo-literates (2.7692>2.4429) short duration training programmes are more necessary for men than women (2.0987>1.79), Preraks should be trained in as many short duration programmes as possible (2.00>1.7306), Neo-literates need training programmes relating to income generation and vocational aspects (2.5769>2.137) and availability of Mandal resource persons need not be ensured for organising vocational courses (2.7179>2.4064). In case of local needs need not be considered while organising short duration training programmes (2.00>1.9635) and officials of concerned development departments need not participate in the short duration programmes (2.0128>1.8447) has low level difference.

The Preraks are better opined that proper planning in visits, training for neo-literates in income generating activities compare to neo-literates. There is no significant difference among them in consideration of local needs presence of developmental department officials is not necessary in organizing training.

Games and sports/adventurous activities are also one of the functioning of the Continuing Education Centre to create encouragement. Preraks and learners opinion is high mean difference scores on neo-literates need not participate in the games and sports activities at village level (2.4359>1.8539) and there is no need to provide prizes to neo-literates who win in the games and sports (2.0513>1.5845). Medium mean difference scores are found on the items of "neo-literates evince more interest to see games and sports activities than to participate (2.4872>2.0548), the games and sports materials supplied to continuing education centres need not be of good quality (2.4487>2.1963), neo-literates need orientation about meditation and simple physical exercises (2.00>1.7397), district level athletes should be invited to continuing education centres to motivate neo-literates to participate in games and sports (2.1667>1.8721), games and sports should be separately organised for women neo-literates (2.5128>2.1963)". And remaining items viz. Preraks should be trained in games and sports activities (1.6282<1.6347), activities like football, cricket are not necessary for neo-literates (1.7692<1.7945), and Preraks need not have the knowledge of rules and regulations of games and sports activities (2.3590>2.2237) is low level mean difference scores are obtained.

Theme – 6: Games and Sports Activities

Table 5.6: Items relating to Games and Sports

Sl. No.	Statement	Preraks	Neo-literates
1.	Neo-literates need not participate in the games and sports activities at village level.	2.4359	1.8539
2.	There is no need to provide prizes to neo-literates who win in the games and sports.	2.0513	1.5845
3.	Preraks should be trained in games and sports activities.	1.6282	1.6347
4.	Activities like football, cricket are not necessary for neo-literates.	1.7692	1.7945
5.	Neo-literates evince more interest to see games and sports activities than to participate.	2.4872	2.0548
6.	The games and sports materials supplied to continuing education centres need not be of good quality.	2.4487	2.1324
7.	Neo-literates need orientation about meditation and simple physical exercises.	2.0000	1.7397
8.	District level athletes should be invited to continuing education centres to motivate neo-literates to participate in games and sports.	2.1667	1.8721
9.	Games and sports should be separately organised for women neo-literates.	2.5128	2.1963
10.	Preraks need not have the knowledge of rules and regulations of games and sports activities.	2.3590	2.2237

There is high degree of difference of opinion expressed by Preraks and neo-literates in views of participation by neo-iterates in games and sports and prizes for winners. The difference of mean scores is low in case of Preraks should be trained in sports and games, necessity of playing foot ball, cricket and knowledge of Preraks on rules and regulation of games sports.

Theme – 7: Information Window

Table 5.7: Items Relating to Information Window Programmes

Sl. No.	Statement	Preraks	Neo-literates
1.	It is necessary to keep the basic information of the village in continuing education centres.	2.5000	2.2877
2.	Information relating to the activities of local voluntary organisations need not be furnished in continuing education.	2.3205	2.1005
3.	Development department officials need not provide details about their programmes to the Prerak.	2.3462	1.8356
4.	Proper co-ordination between adult education officials and officials of development departments is necessary.	2.8846	2.4201
5.	It is necessary to maintain radio, television, projector etc., in the continuing education centres.	2.3846	2.1279
6.	Details relating to transport and communication facilities need not be kept in the continuing education centres.	2.4103	2.2511
7.	Information relating to the literacy level of the village, panchayat, district should be furnished in the centres.	2.4487	2.0868
8.	The details of self-help group leaders need not be kept in continuing education centre.	2.5256	2.1598
9.	Continuing education centre need not serve as a centre for different development activities.	2.3846	2.0776
10.	Neo-literates do not utilise the information even though it is available in the continuing education centre.	2.7179	2.4521

The continuing education centre as per objective may act as a information providers for the people in regard to the development programmes. The difference between Preraks and neo-literates opinion is high i.e., Development department officials need not provide details about their programmes to the Prerak (2.3462>1.8356), proper co-ordination between adult education officials and officials of development departments is necessary (2.8846>2.4201), information relating to the literacy level of the village, panchayat, district should be furnished in the centres (2.4487>2.0868) and details of self-help group leaders need not be kept in continuing education centre (2.5256>2.1598). medium mean difference scores on development department officials need not provide details about their programmes to the Prerak (2.3462>1.8356), continuing education centre need not serve as a centre for different development activities (2.3846>2.0776) and neo-literates do not utilise the information even though it is available in the continuing education centre (2.7179>2.4521) and remaining items i.e. information relating to the activities of local voluntary organisations need not be furnished in continuing education (2.3205>2.1005), it is necessary to maintain radio, television, projector etc., in the continuing education centres (2.3846>2.1279) and details relating to transport and communication facilities need not be kept in the continuing education centres (2.4103>2.2511) is low level.

The difference of mean scores is high between Preraks and neo-literates in items like provide information and coordination with developmental officials and public about literacy levels and SHG leaders.

Supportive facilities are also one of the functions of the Continuing Education Centre activity. Preraks is supposed to do all the activities and key field levels functions of the centre, basing on this the investigator elicit the opinions of Preraks as well as the neo-literates. In this ten items have been included and are projected in the table 5.8. It was found that Preraks opinion is more difference mean scores with neo-literates. The opinions of Preraks high in three items, four items in medium and remaining three items are low category.

Theme – 8: Supportive Facilities

Table 5.8: Items relating to Supportive Facilities

Sl. No.	Statement	Preraks	Neo-literates
1.	There is no need for supervision of continuing education centres.	2.9487	2.6164
2.	It is a mere waste to continue the continuing education centres without the participation of neo-literates.	2.1410	2.1598
3.	It is better to limit the continuing education centres to rural areas.	2.4231	2.2100
4.	Adequate provision of finances will lead to effective organisation of the activities of the centre.	1.9744	1.5068
5.	Preraks should have self-interest. to organise various activities of the centre.	2.1667	1.9361
6.	Success stories do not help to strengthen the activities of continuing education centre.	2.4487	2.1872
7.	There is no need for the Prerak to take the support of assistant Prerak and nodal Prerak in performing his/her duties.	2.3590	2.0868
8.	Participation of neo-literate in the activities of continuing education centre will not improve their living conditions.	2.6923	2.2968
9.	Preraks appointed on part time basis cannot do justice to their job.	2.3333	1.9680
10.	Press has to give publicity to the activities of continuing education centre	2.3077	2.1096

The details given as follows: High mean difference in the items of adequate provision of finances will lead to effective organisation of the activities of the centre (1.9744>1.5068), participation of neo-literate in the activities of continuing education centre will not improve their living conditions (2.6923>2.2968) and Preraks appointed on part time basis cannot do justice to their job (2.3333>1.968). The medium level mean difference scores on the items of there is no need for supervision of continuing education centres (2.9487>2.6164), Preraks should have self-interest to organise various activities of the centre (2.1667>1.9361), success stories do not help to strengthen the activities of continuing education centre (2.4487>2.1872), there is no need for the Prerak to take the support of assistant Prerak and nodal Prerak in performing his/her duties (2.3590>2.0868). And remaining items are having low level mean difference scores on, it is a mere waste to continue the continuing education centres without the participation of neo-literates (2.1410>2.1598) and Press has to give publicity to the activities of continuing education centre (2.3077>2.1096)

The Preraks feels that for effective run the centre more financial provision is necessary and participation in continuing education centre will not change life conditions of neo-literates. Further, he/she want full time appointment as Prerak. But neo-literates regarded with the Preraks. There is no significant difference about the role of press and media to develop under functioning.

The preceding analysis based on comparison about the opinion of Preraks and neo-literates on eight themes by calculating the individual mean scores. This helps to identify the degree of difference about the opinions listed in the themes.

Attitude/Opinion of Preraks and Neo-Literates towards Organisation of Continuing Education Centre Activities

A comparison was also made as whole themes to identify the difference between Preraks and neo-literates and to calculate the significance levels.

Continuing education centres are established at village level and the Preraks are kept in-charge to organise the activities. The functions of Preraks as stipulated by National Literacy Mission (1988) include organisation of evening classes for improving literacy levels, provision of library and reading room facilities, organizing Charcha Mandal activities for discussing on common problems, organising simple and short duration training programmes relating to vocation and development aspects, organising games and sports activities, recreational and cultural activities. The centres has to be kept as an information window for securing information from development agencies and as a communication centre where community radio, audio cassettes player-cum-recorder will be provided. Neo-literates are the main beneficiaries of the continuing education programme. The Prerak has to act as motivator, mobiliser, recorder, planner and co-ordinator to organise the various activities effectively and efficiently. It is necessary to ensure the attitude of Preraks and neo-literates towards the various activities that are organised in the continuing education centres to understand the situation.

The observation indicates the information pertaining to the opinion of Preraks and neo-literates towards the organisation of continuing education activities (A1) are as presented in table 5.9. It can be observed that the Preraks and neo-literates have secured mean opinion score of 33.79 and 21.84 towards the organisation of evening classes. The difference between the means is high and the't' value is 9.497 which is statistically significant at 0.01 level.

With respect to organisation of library and reading room activities (A2) Preraks have obtained a better mean opinion score in relation to neo-literates (34.98 > 22.94). The calculated 't' value is 8.508 which indicates that the differences between the means are statistically significant at 0.01 level.

The information about the organisation of Charcha Mandal (A3) reveals that the Preraks have obtained a mean opinion score of 32.76 and neo-literates have obtained a mean opinion score is 21.51. The 't' test was employed to find out the significance of difference between the means and the calculated 't' value of 8.925 which is statistically significant at 0.01 level.

The mean opinion score of Preraks about the organisation of short term training programmes (A4) meant for the benefit of neo-literates, mean of Preraks is 33.43 whereas that of neo-literates is 22.46. There is difference of 10.97 points in the mean opinion scores. The calculated 't' value of 8.605 denotes that the mean differences are statistically significant at 0.01 level.

Table 5.9: Mean, Standard Deviation and 'F' value for Preraks and Neo-literates on the Themes of Opinions Towards Continuing Education Programme

Sl. No.	Theme	Group	N	Mean	S D	't'-Value
1.	A1	Preraks	78	33.7949	9.2741	9.497**
		Neo-Literate	219	21.8493	9.6308	
2.	A2	Preraks	78	34.9872	9.1218	8.508**
		Neo-Literate	219	22.9452	11.2489	
3.	A3	Preraks	78	32.7692	9.6953	8.925**
		Neo-Literate	219	21.5160	9.5145	
4.	A4	Preraks	78	33.4359	9.1759	8.605**
		Neo-Literate	219	22.4658	9.8359	
5.	A5	Preraks	78	30.2308	10.0478	8.575**
		Neo-Literate	219	20.2146	8.3986	
6.	A6	Preraks	78	29.0385	10.3515	9.179**
		Neo-Literate	219	19.0868	7.3239	
7.	A7	Preraks	78	32.1026	9.3982	8.102**
		Neo-Literate	219	21.7991	9.7301	
8.	A8	Preraks	78	30.9744	9.5536	8.306**
		Neo-Literate	219	21.0776	8.8467	
	Total	Preraks	78	257.3333	70.3324	9.243**
		Neo-Literate	219	170.9543	71.0642	

** Significant at 0.01 level, * Significant at 0.05 level

Further, the Preraks (30.2308) and neo-literates (20.2146) have obtained opinion on the organisation of cultural and recreational activities (A5) and games and sports activities (A6), mean scores obtained by the Preraks and neo=literates are 29.03 and 19.08 respectively. The mean differences in both the cases are found to be statistically significant at 0.01 levels.

The information relating to the opinion of Preraks and neo-literates about information window (A7) indicates that the Preraks have obtained a mean opinion of 32.10 where the mean opinion obtained by neo-literates is 21.79. The calculated 't' value of 10.31 reveals that the mean differences are statistically significant at 0.01 level.

It can be observed from the table 5.9, that Preraks and neo-literate differed significantly in their opinion on the supportive facilities (A8) (supervision, basic facilities, community support, publicity, and so on). Preraks have obtained more favourable opinion than neo-literates (30.97 > 21.07). The calculated 't' value of 8.306 indicates that the mean differences are statistically significant at 0.01 level.

With regard to total opinions, the Preraks have secured a mean score of 257.33 with a standard deviation of 70.33 whereas the neo-literates have secured a mean opinion score of 170.95 with a standard deviation of 71.06. 't' test was employed to find out the significance of difference between the means and the 't' value of 9.243 is statistically significant at 0.01 level. Preraks have more favourable opinion towards organisation of continuing education activities, when compared to neo-literates.

Influence of Personal Variables on Attitude/Opinion of Preraks Towards Organisation of Continuing Education Centre Activities

The role of the Prerak in maintaining the Continuing Education centre is very crucial. The Prerak must be aware of all the objectives of continuing education centre. He/she must also know all his / her responsibilities completely before joining as Prerak. He must have the attachment to the village, commitment, honesty, clarity about the work, tendency to encourage and motivate people towards literacy, rapport with officials, amicable nature and intention to serve people. Then, only he can fulfil his duties as the Prerak. The role and main responsibilities of the Preraks are as follows:

- To create the necessary environment for Continuing Education programme.
- To motivate the learners to enrol and attend the centre regularly.
- To conduct games and cultural activities, Charcha Mandals and organise short-term training programmes to improve the living conditions of members.
- To act as a counsellor, guide, philosopher in the field situation.
- To maintain the register of the centre and reporting the activities to MLOs and ZSS

Besides all these duties the Prerak with his talent and dynamism can take up many social service activities to make the learner to get the benefit.

In this section of analysis, the Preraks opinion was gathered in relation to his/her socio-economic and demographic variables. This shows that the Preraks attitude/ opinion towards the centre activity depending upon his/her personal variables. According to previous studies the personal characteristic have an impact is undertaken the work. Hence, the mean, standard deviation and "t/F" values were calculated to find out their opinion/attitude belongs to various groups.

Opinion of the Preraks Towards Organisation of Continuing Education Centre Activity - Gender – wise

In the Preraks opinion towards organisation of the evening class (A1), the male Preraks scored higher mean value of 33.8033 and minimum Standard Deviation of 9.1685 than that of female category. The female Preraks mean score is 33.7647 and Standard Deviation of 9.9346. Further, the 't' test also shows that the difference between male and female has no significant different. It shows that both the male and female category respondents expressed on the same opinion towards organisation of evening class theme.

In the Preraks opinion towards library and reading room theme (A2), male Preraks mean score (35.0984) is more than the female mean scores (34.5882). Standard Deviation of male and female are 8.9883 and 9.8619 respectively and the 't' test value shows that the difference between male and female Preraks is found not significantly different from each other in this aspect.

Table 5.10: Mean, Standard Deviation and 't' value for various gender groups on the Themes of opinions of Preraks towards Continuing Education Programme

Sl. No.	Theme	Group	N	Mean	S D	't'-Value
1.	A1	Male	61	33.8033	9.1685	0.015
		Female	17	33.7647	9.9343	
2.	A2	Male	61	35.0984	8.9883	0.203
		Female	17	34.5882	9.8619	
3.	A3	Male	61	32.0984	9.6293	1.16
		Female	17	35.1765	9.8377	
4.	A4	Male	61	33.0164	8.9340	0.763
		Female	17	34.9412	10.1395	
5.	A5	Male	61	29.6557	9.7346	0.957
		Female	17	32.2941	11.1678	
6.	A6	Male	61	28.7049	10.0769	0.537
		Female	17	30.2353	11.5300	
7.	A7	Male	61	31.4590	9.4067	1.148
		Female	17	34.4118	9.2740	
8.	A8	Male	61	30.2459	9.3517	1.281
		Female	17	33.5882	10.0999	
	Total	Male	61	254.0820	68.7676	0.771
		Female	17	269.0000	76.7276	

** Significant at 0.01 level, * Significant at 0.05 level

The observation indicates the Preraks opinion towards Charcha Mandal theme (A3), the female Preraks scored maximum mean value of 35.1765 and maximum Standard Deviation of 9.8377. The male Preraks mean score is 32.0984 and Standard Deviation of 9.6293. Further, the 't' test value shows that the difference between male and female Preraks is found not significant.

As per the Preraks opinion towards cultural and recreational activity theme (A4), female Preraks mean score (34.9412) is more than the male mean scores (33.0164). Standard Deviation of male and female are 8.934 and 10.1395 respectively and the 't' test value is 0.763 which is not found statistically significant.

It was found that the Preraks opinion towards short term programmes theme (A5), female Preraks mean score (32.2941) is more than the male mean scores (29.6557). Standard Deviation of male and female are 9.9346 and 11.1678 respectively and the 't' test value shows that the difference between male and female Preraks is found not significantly different from each other in this aspect.

The Preraks opinion towards games and sports theme (A6), the female Preraks scored mean value of 30.2353 and Standard Deviation of 11.53. The male Preraks mean score is 28.7049 and Standard Deviation of 10.0769. Further, the 't' test also shows that the difference between male and female Preraks is found not significantly different from each other.

It can be observed from the Preraks opinion towards information window programmes theme (A7), the female Preraks scored mean value of 34.4118 and Standard Deviation of 9.274. The Male Preraks mean score is 31.459 and Standard Deviation of 9.4067. Further, the 't' test also shows that the difference between male and female Preraks is found not significantly different from each other.

Here, the Preraks opinion towards supportive facilities activity theme (A8), female Preraks mean score (33.5882) is more than the male mean scores (30.2459). Standard Deviation of male and female are 9.3517 and 10.0999 respectively and the 't' test value is 1.281 which is not significantly different from each other in this aspect.

An attempt was made in the present study to find out the influence of personal variable i.e. gender on the opinion of Preraks towards the organisation of continuing education activities, the details of which are as shown in table 5.10. It can be observed that Preraks representing women group have obtained a mean opinion score of 269.00 with a standard deviation of 76.72. The Preraks representing men group have secured a mean opinion score of 254.08 with a standard deviation of 68.7676. Preraks representing women group have obtained a more favourable mean attitude score in relation to their counterparts. The 't' test was employed to find out the difference between the means and the 't' value obtained (0.771) is found to be statistically not significant even at 0.05 level.

It has been found that the sex of the Preraks has no impact on their opinion towards over all opinion and the sub themes Organisation of Evening Classes (A1), Library and Reading Room (A2), Charcha Mandal (A3), Cultural and Recreational Activities (A4), Short Term Training Programmes (A5), Games and Sports Activities (A6), Information Window (A7), Supportive Facilities (A8)

Opinion of the Preraks Towards Organisation of Continuing Education Centre Activity – Age-wise

It is evident from the study the Preraks opinion towards organisation of the evening class (A1), the above 36 years of age Preraks scored higher mean value of 34.3548 and maximum Standard Deviation of 10.1046 than that of other two categories. The 21-35 years of age Preraks mean score is 32.8519 and Standard Deviation of 9.4735. Further, the 'F' test also shows that the difference between three age groups of Preraks is found not significantly different from each other.

Table 5.11: Mean, Standard Deviation and 'F' Value for Various Age Groups on the Themes of Opinions of Preraks Towards Continuing Education Programme

Sl. No.	Theme	Group	N	Mean	S D	'F'-Value
1.	A1	Below 20	20	34.2000	7.9114	0.211
		21-35	27	32.8519	9.4735	
		Above 36	31	34.3548	10.1046	
2.	A2	Below 20	20	33.1500	7.6384	0.548
		21-35	27	35.4444	9.2709	
		Above 36	31	35.7742	9.9523	
3.	A3	Below 20	20	30.5000	8.7630	1.165
		21-35	27	32.2963	10.3879	
		Above 36	31	34.6452	9.5831	
4.	A4	Below 20	20	31.8500	8.3809	0.537
		21-35	27	33.2963	9.2479	
		Above 36	31	34.5806	9.7186	
5.	A5	Below 20	20	27.3500	9.0279	1.144
		21-35	27	30.8519	9.9565	
		Above 36	31	31.5484	10.6735	
6.	A6	Below 20	20	26.5000	8.6603	0.866
		21-35	27	29.4074	10.4854	
		Above 36	31	30.3548	11.2266	
7.	A7	Below 20	20	31.7000	8.0466	0.275
		21-35	27	31.2963	9.7933	
		Above 36	31	33.0645	10.0463	
8.	A8	Below 20	20	29.1000	8.0256	0.583
		21-35	27	31.1111	9.8969	
		Above 36	31	32.0645	10.2467	
	Total	Below 20	20	244.3500	58.3386	0.593
		21-35	27	256.5556	72.6325	
		Above 36	31	266.3871	75.9683	

** Significant at 0.01 level, * Significant at 0.05 level

In the Preraks opinion towards library and reading room theme (A2), above 36 years of age Preraks mean score (35.7742) is more than the 21-35 years (35.4444) and below 20 years (33.15). Standard Deviation of below 20 years, 21-35 years and above 36 years are 7.6384, 9.2709 and 9.9523 respectively and the 'F' test also shows that the difference between these three age groups of Preraks is found not significantly different from each other in this aspect.

It is observed that the Preraks opinion towards Charcha Mandal theme (A3), the above 36 years of age Preraks scored maximum mean value of 34.6452 and Standard Deviation of 9.5831. The below 20 years of age Preraks mean score is 30.50 and Standard Deviation of 8.7630. Further, the 'F' test shows that the difference between the three age groups of Preraks is found not significant.

It can be noted from the Preraks opinion towards cultural and recreational activity theme (A4), above 36 years of age Preraks mean score (34.5806) is more than the 21-35 years (33.2963) and below 20 years mean scores (31.85). Standard Deviation of below 20 years, 21-35 years and above 36 years are 8.3809, 9.2479 and 9.7186 respectively and the 'F' test value is 0.537 which is not significant even at 0.05 level.

As per the Preraks opinion towards short duration programmes theme (A5), above 36 years of age Preraks mean score (31.5484) is more than that of 21-35 years (30.8519) and below 20 years of age mean scores (27.35). Standard Deviation of below 20 years, 21-35 years and above 36 years are 9.0279, 9.9565, and 10.6735 respectively and the 'F' test also shows that the difference among below 20 years, 21-35 years and above 36 years of Preraks is found not significantly different from each other in this aspect.

The table reveals that the Preraks opinion towards games and sports theme (A6), the above 36 years of age Preraks scored mean value of 30.3548 and Standard Deviation of 11.2266. The below 20 years of age Preraks mean score is 26.50 and Standard Deviation of 8.6603. Further, the 'F' test also shows that the difference between these three age groups of Preraks is found not significantly different from each other.

As per the Preraks opinion towards information window programmes theme (A7), the above 36 years of age Preraks scored mean value of 33.0645 and Standard Deviation of 10.0463. The 21-35 years of age Preraks mean score is 31.2963 and Standard Deviation of 9.7933. Further, the 'F' test also shows that the difference between these three groups of Preraks is found not significant.

The result of the Preraks opinion towards supportive facilities activity theme (A8), above 36 years of age Preraks mean score (32.0645) is more than the 21-35 years (31.1111) and below 20 years (29.10) and the 'F' test value is 0.583 which is not significantly different from each other in this aspect.

The information relating to the influence of age on the opinion of Preraks towards the organisation of continuing education activities reveals that the above 36 years group have secured a better mean attitude score in relation to the other age groups (below 20 and 21-35 years). The mean opinion score of above 36 years age group is 266.3871. The mean opinion score of 21-35 years age group is 255.5556 whereas the mean attitude score of below 20 years of age group is 244.35. 'F' test was employed to find out the significance of difference among the means and the calculated 'F' value is 0.593 which is not statistically significant at 0.05 level.

This finding indicates that the age has no impact on the organisation of the centre. The Preraks in the above 36 years of age better than the other two age groups in all eight themes which reveals that the age has no influence to cater the needs of centre.

Opinion of the Preraks Towards Organisation of Continuing Education Centre Activity – Marital Status-wise

Based on the findings the Preraks opinion towards organisation of the evening class (A1), the married Preraks scored higher mean value of 35.6545 and maximum Standard Deviation of 9.7187 than that of other two categories. The widow/widower Preraks mean score is 29.1667 and Standard Deviation of 5.1153 and less than unmarried and married.

Further, the 'F' test also shows that the difference between three groups of Preraks is found significantly different from each other. The significant value is 4.049 which is significant at 0.05 level.

It is clearly evident form the Preraks opinion towards library and reading room theme (A2), married Preraks mean score (36.0727) is more than the unmarried (32.7647) and widow/widower (31.3333). Standard Deviation of married, unmarried and widow/widower are 10.079, 5.6406 and 6.0553 respectively and the 'F' test also shows that the difference between these three groups of Preraks is found not significantly different from each other in this aspect.

It is found that the Preraks opinion towards Charcha Mandal theme (A3), the married Preraks scored maximum mean value of 34.2142 and maximum Standard Deviation of 10.4575. The widow/widower Preraks mean score is 28.5 and Standard Deviation of 3.8859. Further, the 'F' test also shows that the difference between the three groups of Preraks is found not significant different from each other.

It is observed that the Preraks opinion towards cultural and recreational activity theme (A4), married Preraks mean score (34.9636) is more than the unmarried (30.0000) and widow/widower mean scores (29.1667). Standard Deviation of married, unmarried and widow / widower are 10.0682, 5.9161 and 1.472 respectively and the 'F' test value is 3.153 which is significant at 0.05 levels in this aspect.

The table shows that the Preraks opinion towards short duration programmes theme (A5), married Preraks mean score (31.9818) is more than that of widow/widower (28.00) and unmarried mean scores (25.3529). Standard Deviation of married, widow/widower and unmarried are 11.1214, 4.1473 and 5.0366 respectively and the 'F' test also shows that the difference among married, unmarried and widow/widower of Preraks is found not significantly different from each other in this aspect.

Table 5.12: Mean, Standard Deviation and 'F' Value for Various Marital Status Group Respondents on the Themes of opinions of Preraks towards Continuing Education Programme

Sl. No.	Theme	Group	N	Mean	S D	'F'-Value
1.	A1	Unmarried	17	29.4118	6.8288	4.049*
		Married	55	35.6545	9.7187	
		Widow/widower	6	29.1667	5.1153	
2.	A2	Unmarried	17	32.7647	5.6406	1.389
		Married	55	36.0727	10.0790	
		Widow/widower	6	31.3333	6.0553	
3.	A3	Unmarried	17	29.5882	7.3319	2.175
		Married	55	34.2182	10.4575	
		Widow/widower	6	28.5000	3.8859	
4.	A4	Unmarried	17	30.0000	5.9161	3.153*
		Married	55	34.9636	10.0682	
		Widow/widower	6	29.1667	1.4720	
5.	A5	Unmarried	17	25.3529	5.0366	2.72
		Married	55	31.9818	11.1214	
		Widow/widower	6	28.0000	4.1473	
6.	A6	Unmarried	17	24.9412	4.0229	2.769
		Married	55	30.7818	11.6535	
		Widow/widower	6	24.6667	4.2740	
7.	A7	Unmarried	17	28.7647	3.7505	1.711
		Married	55	33.3455	10.7776	
		Widow/widower	6	30.1667	1.1690	
8.	A8	Unmarried	17	27.1765	3.6782	2.197
		Married	55	32.4000	10.8723	
		Widow/widower	6	28.6667	2.8048	
	Total	Unmarried	17	228.0000	25.0998	2.89
		Married	55	269.4182	79.6764	
		Widow/widower	6	229.6667	12.2420	

** Significant at 0.01 level, * Significant at 0.05 level

It is found that the Preraks opinion towards games and sports theme (A6), the married Preraks scored mean value of 30.7818 and Standard Deviation of 11.6535. The widow/ widower Preraks mean score is 24.6667 and Standard Deviation of 4.274. Further, the 'F' test also shows that the difference between these groups of Preraks is found not significantly different from each other. The unmarried Preraks obtained better mean scores than widow/widower.

The findings indicate that the Preraks opinion towards information window programmes theme (A7), the married Preraks scored mean value of 33.3455 and Standard Deviation of 10.7776. The unmarried Preraks mean score is 28.7647 and Standard Deviation of 3.7505. Further, the 'F' test also shows that the difference between these three groups of Preraks is found not significantly different from each other.

As per the Preraks opinion towards supportive facilities activity theme (A8), married Preraks mean score (32.40) is more than the widow/widower (28.6667) and unmarried (27.1765) and the 'F' test value is 2.197 which is not significantly different from each other in this aspect.

In the present study an attempt was made to know the influence of marital status on the opinion of Preraks towards the organisation of continuing education activities. The details as shown in the table 5.12 reveal that the Preraks belonging to the married (269.67) group have secured a better mean opinion score in relation to their counterparts i.e. unmarried (228.00) and widow/widower (229.67) group. The 't' value obtained to test the significance of difference between the means is statistically not significant.

In order to estimate the influence of the marital status on the opinion of the Preraks, the different backgrounds of Preraks marital status expressed one and the same opinion towards Library and Reading Room (A2), Charcha Mandal (A3), Short Term Training Programmes (A5), Games and Sports Activities (A6), Information Window (A7), Supportive Facilities (A8) and over all opinion, in case of Organisation of Evening Classes (A1), Cultural and Recreational Activities (A4) has significant difference at 0.05 level.

Opinion of the Preraks Towards Organisation of Continuing Education Centre Activity – Caste-wise

The observation indicates the Preraks opinion towards organisation of the evening class (A1), the O.C. Preraks scored higher mean value of 39.4118 and maximum Standard Deviation of 10.5597 than that of other two categories. The B.C Preraks mean score is 31.0444 and Standard Deviation of 7.2831. Further, the 'F' test also shows that the difference between three groups of Preraks is found highly significantly different from each other. The significant value is 6.101 which is significant at 0.01 level.

The findings indicate that the Preraks opinion towards library and reading room theme (A2), O.C Preraks mean score (39.7647) is more than the S.C. (37.0625) and B.C. (32.4444). Standard Deviation of O.C., B.C. and S.C. are 9.9532, 7.5062, and 10.3116 respectively and the 'F' test also shows that the difference between these three groups of Preraks is found highly significant different from each other in this aspect.

As per the observation in the table the Preraks opinion towards Charcha Mandal theme (A3), the O.C. Preraks scored maximum mean value of 36.4706 and maximum Standard Deviation of 12.2583. The B.C. Preraks mean score is 30.0667 and Standard Deviation of 7.8607. Further, the 'F' test also shows that the difference between the three groups if Preraks is found highly significant different from each other.

It is found that the Preraks opinion towards cultural and recreational activity theme (A4), O.C. Preraks mean score (37.1176) is more than the S.C. (36.6875) and B.C. Preraks mean scores (30.8889). Standard Deviation of O.C., B.C. and S.C. are 11.7574, 7.2589 and 9.1704 respectively and the 'F' test value is 4.478 which is significant at 0.05 level in this aspect.

The result is indicating that the Preraks opinion towards short duration programmes theme (A5), O.C. Preraks mean score (35.5882) is more than that of S.C. (32.4275) and B.C. (27.4222). Standard Deviation of O.C., B.C. and S.C. are 13.0051, 7.2252 and 11.1054 respectively and the 'F' test also shows that the difference among these three groups of Preraks is found highly significant different from each other in this aspect. The significant value is 5.039 which is significant at 0.01 level.

Table 5.13: Mean, Standard Deviation and 'F' Value for Various Caste Groups Respondents on the Themes of Opinions of Preraks Towards Continuing Education Programme

Sl. No.	Theme	Group	N	Mean	S D	'F'-Value
1.	A1	O.C.	17	39.4118	10.5597	6.101**
		B.C.	45	31.0444	7.2831	
		S.C.	16	35.5625	10.2565	
2.	A2	O.C.	17	39.7647	9.9532	4.956**
		B.C.	45	32.4444	7.5062	
		S.C.	16	37.0625	10.3116	
3.	A3	O.C.	17	36.4706	12.2583	4.509**
		B.C.	45	30.0667	7.8607	
		S.C.	16	36.4375	9.4444	
4.	A4	O.C.	17	37.1176	11.7574	4.478*
		B.C.	45	30.8889	7.2589	
		S.C.	16	36.6875	9.1704	
5.	A5	O.C.	17	35.5882	13.0051	5.039**
		B.C.	45	27.4222	7.2252	
		S.C.	16	32.4375	11.1054	
6.	A6	O.C.	17	34.0000	13.9866	4.584*
		B.C.	45	26.2000	7.1561	
		S.C.	16	31.7500	11.4572	
7.	A7	O.C.	17	38.0588	11.2276	5.716**
		B.C.	45	29.5778	6.6246	
		S.C.	16	32.8750	11.4127	
8.	A8	O.C.	17	35.8824	12.4040	5.033**
		B.C.	45	28.2667	6.9328	
		S.C.	16	33.3750	10.3915	
	Total	O.C.	17	296.2941	91.1721	5.948**
		B.C.	45	235.9111	49.0449	
		S.C.	16	276.1875	77.4220	

** Significant at 0.01 level, * Significant at 0.05 level

As per the Preraks opinion towards games and sports theme (A6), the O.C. Preraks scored mean value of 34.00 and Standard Deviation of 13.9866. The B.C. Preraks mean score is 26.20 and Standard Deviation of 7.1561. Further, the 'F' test also shows that the difference between these groups of Preraks is found significant difference at 0.05 level.

The study indicates the Preraks opinion towards information window programmes theme (A7), the O.C. Preraks scored mean value of 38.0588 and Standard Deviation of 11.2276. The B.C. Preraks mean score is 29.5778 and Standard Deviation of 6.6246. Further, the 'F' test also shows that the difference between these three groups of Preraks is found highly significant difference at 0.01 level.

In the Preraks opinion towards supportive facilities activity theme (A8), O.C Preraks mean score (35.8824) is more than the S.C. (33.3750) and B.C. (28.2667) and the 'F' test value is 5.033 which is significance at 0.01 level in this aspect.

In the present investigation, an attempt was made to find out whether the Preraks belonging to different castes differ significantly in their opinion towards organisation of continuing education activities. As the table 5.13 reveals, Preraks belonging to forward caste (296.29) have obtained a better mean opinion score than scheduled castes (276.18) and backward castes (235.911). The calculated 'F' value denotes that the mean differences are statistically significant at 0.01 level.

To estimate the influence of the caste of the Preraks on their opinion, there is high level significant difference in the themes of Organisation of Evening Classes (A1), Library and Reading Room (A2), Charcha Mandal (A3), Short Term Training Programmes (A5), Information Window (A7), Supportive Facilities (A8) and over all opinion. And remaining two themes there is a significant difference is found.

Opinion of the Preraks Towards Organisation of Continuing Education Centre Activity - Nativity-wise

In the Preraks opinion towards organisation of the evening class (A1), the rural Preraks scored higher mean value of 33.8333 and maximum Standard Deviation of 10.0326 than that of urban category. The urban Preraks mean score is 33.7333 and Standard Deviation of 8.0769. Further, the 't' test also shows that the difference between rural and urban Preraks is found not significantly different from each other. It shows that both the rural and urban category respondents expressed on the same opinion towards organisation of evening class theme.

Table 5.14: Mean, Standard Deviation and 'F' Value for Various Nativity Groups Respondents on the Themes of Opinions of Preraks Towards Continuing Education Programme

Sl. No.	Theme	Group	N	Mean	S D	't'-Value
1.	A1	Rural	48	33.8333	10.0326	0.046
		Urban	30	33.7333	8.0769	
2.	A2	Rural	48	35.2292	9.5611	0.295
		Urban	30	34.6000	8.5161	
3.	A3	Rural	48	32.8125	10.5056	0.05
		Urban	30	32.7000	8.4083	
4.	A4	Rural	48	33.3958	9.8925	0.048
		Urban	30	33.5000	8.0590	
5.	A5	Rural	48	30.1875	10.6724	0.048
		Urban	30	30.3000	9.1356	
6.	A6	Rural	48	29.4167	11.1295	0.406
		Urban	30	28.4333	9.1187	
7.	A7	Rural	48	32.8750	9.8836	0.917
		Urban	30	30.8667	8.5812	
8.	A8	Rural	48	31.6250	9.9073	0.759
		Urban	30	29.9333	9.0246	
	Total	Rural	48	259.3750	75.8968	0.322
		Urban	30	254.0667	61.4862	

** Significant at 0.01 level, * Significant at 0.05 level.

The study reveals the Preraks opinion towards library and reading room theme (A2), rural Preraks mean score (35.2292) is more than the urban Preraks mean scores (34.60). Standard Deviation of rural and urban are 9.5611 and 8.5161 respectively and the 't' test also shows that the difference between rural and urban Preraks is found not significantly different from each other in this aspect.

The study indicates the Preraks opinion towards Charcha Mandal theme (A3), the rural Preraks scored maximum mean value of 32.8125 and maximum Standard Deviation of 10.5056. The urban Preraks mean score is 32.70 and Standard Deviation of 8.4083. Further, the 't' test also shows that the difference between rural and urban Preraks is found not significant. The findings shows that the Preraks opinion towards cultural and recreational activity theme (A4), urban Preraks mean score (33.50) is more than the rural mean scores (33.3958). Standard Deviation of rural and urban are 9.8925 and 8.059 respectively and the 't' test value is 0.048 which is not significantly different from each other.

The results of the study shows that the Preraks opinion towards short duration programmes theme (A5), urban Preraks mean score (30.30) is more than the rural mean scores (30.1875). Standard Deviation of rural and urban are 10.6724 and 9.1356 respectively and the 't' test also shows that the difference between rural and urban Preraks is found not significantly. In the Preraks opinion towards games and sports theme (A6), the rural Preraks scored mean value of 29.4167 and Standard Deviation of 11.1295. The urban Preraks mean score is 28.4333 and Standard Deviation of 9.1187. Further, the 't' test also shows that the difference between rural and urban Preraks is found in significance. In the Preraks opinion towards information window programmes theme (A7), the rural Preraks scored mean value of 32.875 and Standard Deviation of 9.8836. The urban Preraks mean score is 30.8667 and Standard Deviation of 8.5812. Further, the 't' test also shows that the difference between rural and urban Preraks is found not significantly different from each other.

From the observation made the Preraks opinion towards supportive facilities activity theme (A8), rural Preraks mean score (31.625) is more than the urban mean scores (29.9333). Standard Deviation of rural and urban are 9.9073 and 9.0246 respectively and the 't' test value is 0.759 which is not significantly different from each other in this aspect.

In the present study an attempt was made to know the influence of native place on the opinion of Preraks towards the organisation of continuing education activities. The details as shown in the table 5.14 reveal that the Preraks belonging to the rural (259.375) area group have secured a better mean opinion score in relation to their counterpart i.e. urban (254.0667) group. The 't' value obtained to test the significance of difference between the means is statistically not significant. The results clearly shows that the influence of the native place i.e. rural and urban on the opinions of the Preraks. There is no significant difference in the over all opinion and eight sub themes.

In the Preraks opinion towards organisation of the evening class (A1), the intermediate qualification of Preraks scored higher mean value of 36.2222 and Standard Deviation of 10.0828 than that of other three categories. The 10th class qualification of Preraks mean score is 29.1053 and Standard Deviation of 4.5692. Further, the 'F' test also shows that the difference between four groups of Preraks is found significantly different from each other. The significant value is 2.718 which is significant at 0.05 level. In the Preraks opinion towards library and reading room theme (A2), intermediate qualification Preraks mean score (36.5833) is more than Graduate (35.4737), Post Graduate (31.50) and 10th (32.2105). Standard Deviation of 10th, intermediate, graduation and post graduation are 6.1244, 10.3437, 9.3236 and 6.6081 respectively and the 'F' test also shows that the difference between these four groups of Preraks is found significant difference at 0.05 level.

Opinion of the Preraks Towards Organisation of Continuing Education Centre Activity – Education-wise

Table 5.15: Mean, Standard Deviation and 't' Value for Various Educational Status Groups Respondents on the Themes of Opinions of Preraks Towards Continuing Education Programme

Sl. No.	Theme	Group	N	Mean	S D	'F'-Value
1	2	3	4	5	6	7
1.	A1	10th	19	29.1053	4.5692	2.718*
		Intermediate	36	36.2222	10.0828	
		Graduation	19	34.3684	10.4521	
		P.G.	4	31.5000	4.6547	
2.	A2	10th	19	32.2105	6.1244	1.175
		Intermediate	36	36.5833	10.3437	
		Graduation	19	35.4737	9.3236	
		P.G.	4	31.5000	6.6081	
3.	A3	10th	19	26.8421	4.7757	3.497*
		Intermediate	36	35.0000	10.2511	
		Graduation	19	34.4211	10.9965	
		P.G.	4	33.0000	4.9666	
4.	A4	10th	19	29.6842	2.9824	1.611
		Intermediate	36	35.2500	10.5489	
		Graduation	19	34.0000	10.0664	
		P.G.	4	32.2500	8.3016	
5.	A5	10th	19	25.7895	3.5368	1.944
		Intermediate	36	32.3056	11.6492	
		Graduation	19	31.2105	10.7836	
		P.G.	4	28.0000	6.7823	
6.	A6	10th	19	23.5263	3.4216	3.037*
		Intermediate	36	31.6389	11.7672	
		Graduation	19	30.3684	11.1316	
		P.G.	4	25.5000	4.4347	

(Contd...)

1	2	3	4	5	6	7
7.	A7	10th	19	27.9474	3.5820	2.716*
		Intermediate	36	34.6111	10.6805	
		Graduation	19	32.6316	10.0676	
		P.G.	4	26.7500	5.1235	
8.	A8	10th	19	27.6316	3.3034	1.277
		Intermediate	36	32.8056	11.0242	
		Graduation	19	31.2105	10.7888	
		P.G.	4	29.2500	6.7515	
	Total	10th	19	222.7368	17.4032	2.539
		Intermediate	36	274.4167	80.8549	
		Graduation	19	263.6842	78.1004	
		P.G.	4	237.7500	20.6942	

** Significant at 0.01 level, * Significant at 0.05 level.

It is found that the Preraks opinion towards Charcha Mandal theme (A3), the intermediate Preraks scored maximum mean value of 35.00 and Standard Deviation of 10.2511. The 10th class Preraks mean score is 26.8421 and Standard Deviation of 4.7757. Further, the 'F' test also shows that the difference between the four groups of Preraks is found significant difference at 0.05 levels from each other. As per the Preraks opinion towards cultural and recreational activity theme (A4), intermediate Preraks mean score (35.25) is more than the graduation (34.00), post graduation (32.25) and 10th Preraks mean scores (29.6842) and the 'F' test value is 1.611 which is not significant even at 0.05 level in this aspect.

The study reveals that the Preraks opinion towards short duration programmes theme (A5), intermediate Preraks mean score (32.3056) is more than that of graduation (31.2105), post graduation (28.00) and 10th class (25.7895). Standard Deviation of 10th, intermediate, graduation and post graduation are 3.5368, 11.6492, 10.7836 and 6.7823 respectively and the 'F' test also shows that the difference among these four groups of Preraks is found in significant. The finding of the study indicate the Preraks opinion towards games and sports theme

(A6), intermediate Preraks scored maximum mean value of 31.6389 and Standard Deviation of 11.7672. The 10th class Preraks minimum mean score of 23.5263 and Standard Deviation of 3.4216. Further, the 'F' test also shows that the difference between these groups of Preraks is found significant difference at 0.05 level.

It clearly indicates the Preraks opinion towards information window programmes theme (A7), the Preraks who are studied up to intermediate scored mean value of 34.6111 and Standard Deviation of 10.6805. The post graduation Preraks mean score is 26.75 and Standard Deviation of 5.1235. Further, the 'F' test also shows that the difference between these four groups of Preraks is found significant difference at 0.05 level. The observation from the Preraks opinion towards supportive facilities activity theme (A8), Preraks with qualification of intermediate mean score (32.8056) is more than the graduation (31.2105), post graduation (29.25) and 10th class (27.6316) and the 'F' test value is 1.277 which is not significant even at 0.05 level in this aspect.

In the present investigation, an attempt was made to find out whether the Preraks having different educational qualifications differ significantly in their opinion towards organisation of continuing education activities. As the table 5.15 reveals, Preraks having intermediate qualification (274.41) have obtained a better mean opinion score than graduates (263.68) and post graduates (237.75). The calculated 'F' value denotes that the mean differences are statistically not significant and education is not a significant predictor.

To estimate the influence of the educational qualification of the Preraks on their opinion, the difference categories of respondents expressed same opinion towards the themes Library and Reading Room (A2), Cultural and Recreational Activities (A4), Short Term Training Programmes (A5), Supportive Facilities (A8) and over all opinion. There is a significant difference in Organisation of Evening Classes (A1), Charcha Mandal (A3), Games and Sports Activities (A6), Information Window (A7).

Opinion of the Preraks Towards Organisation of Continuing Education Centre Activity – Occupation-wise

In the Preraks opinion towards organisation of the evening class (A1), the Preraks engaged agricultural occupation scored higher mean value of 36.5862 and Standard Deviation of 9.7926 than that of other four categories. The employed Preraks mean score is 28.2857 and Standard Deviation of 5.0568. Further, the 'F' test also shows that the difference between five groups of Preraks is found significantly different from each other. The significant value is 2.442 which is significant at 0.05 level. It is found that the Preraks opinion towards library and reading room theme (A2), agriculture occupation Preraks mean score (38.1379) is more than other groups and the 'F' test also shows that the difference between these five groups of Preraks is found significance difference at 0.05 level from each other in this aspect. The significant value is 3.854.

The findings indicate that the Preraks opinion towards Charcha Mandal theme (A3), the Preraks with agriculture occupation scored maximum mean value of 36.00 and Standard Deviation of 10.4471. The business occupational Preraks mean score is 26.8571 and Standard Deviation of 4.0546. Further, the 'F' test also shows that the difference between the five groups of Preraks is found significance value is 2.598 which is significant at 0.05 level. As per the Preraks opinion towards cultural and recreational activity theme (A4), agriculture Preraks mean score (36.8621) is more than the others (34.20), artisans (33.913), employed (29.00) and business (27.50) and the 'F' test value is 3.248 which is significant at 0.05 level in this aspect.

It can be seen from the Preraks opinion towards short duration programmes theme (A5), agriculture Preraks mean score (33.0345) is more than that of artisans (31.913), others (27.00), employed (25.7143) and business (25.0714) and the 'F' test also shows that the difference among these five groups of Preraks is found not significant.

Table 5.16: Mean, Standard Deviation and 'F' Value for Various Occupation Groups Respondents on the Themes of Opinions of Preraks Towards Continuing Education Programme

Sl.No.	Theme	Group	N	Mean	S D	'F'-Value
1	2	3	4	5	6	7
1.	A1	Agriculture	29	36.5862	9.7926	2.442*
		Business	14	29.2857	5.2393	
		Employed	7	28.2857	5.0568	
		Artisans	23	33.9565	10.8648	
		Others	5	37.2000	3.4928	
2.	A2	Agriculture	29	38.1379	9.1952	3.854**
		Business	14	28.7857	4.2820	
		Employed	7	30.2857	5.0897	
		Artisans	23	35.0870	10.6127	
		Others	5	40.2000	3.5637	
3.	A3	Agriculture	29	36.0000	10.4471	2.598*
		Business	14	26.8571	4.0546	
		Employed	7	29.1429	5.9000	
		Artisans	23	33.0000	11.3458	
		Others	5	34.6000	2.5100	
4.	A4	Agriculture	29	36.8621	8.9711	3.248*
		Business	14	27.5000	5.0345	
		Employed	7	29.0000	5.2599	
		Artisans	23	33.9130	10.8457	
		Others	5	34.2000	6.4576	
5.	A5	Agriculture	29	33.0345	11.1146	2.272
		Business	14	25.0714	4.2691	
		Employed	7	25.7143	3.9881	
		Artisans	23	31.9130	11.7895	
		Others	5	27.0000	4.0000	

(Contd...)

1	2	3	4	5	6	7
6.	A6	Agriculture	29	32.1724	11.7506	3.148*
		Business	14	23.9286	2.6736	
		Employed	7	22.0000	2.7080	
		Artisans	23	31.3043	11.7180	
		Others	5	24.6000	1.8166	
7.	A7	Agriculture	29	35.2069	9.6376	2.706*
		Business	14	28.2143	7.1487	
		Employed	7	27.4286	5.3807	
		Artisans	23	33.3478	10.4864	
		Others	5	25.8000	4.0249	
8.	A8	Agriculture	29	33.3793	10.9948	1.956
		Business	14	26.7857	3.0929	
		Employed	7	29.0000	3.5119	
		Artisans	23	32.4348	11.1715	
		Others	5	24.8000	2.1679	
	Total	Agriculture	29	281.3793	77.0438	2.837*
		Business	14	216.4286	19.7278	
		Employed	7	220.8571	14.8597	
		Artisans	23	264.9565	84.4573	
		Others	5	248.4000	5.8566	

** Significant at 0.01 level, * Significant at 0.05 level

The opinion of the Preraks towards games and sports theme (A6), agriculture Preraks scored maximum mean value of 32.1724 and Standard Deviation of 11.7506. The employed Preraks minimum means score of 22.00 and Standard Deviation of 2.7080. Further, the 'F' test also shows that the difference between these groups of Preraks is found significant difference at 0.05 level. In the Preraks opinion towards information window programmes theme (A7), the agriculture Preraks scored mean value of 35.2069 and Standard Deviation of 9.6376. The others occupations Preraks mean score is 25.80 and Standard Deviation of 4.0249. Further, the 'F' test also shows that the difference between these five groups of Preraks is found significant difference at 0.05 levels. The significant value is 2.706.It is observed from the table that the Preraks opinion towards supportive facilities activity theme (A8), agriculture Preraks mean score (33.3793) is more than the artisans (32.4348), employed (29.00), business (26.7857) and others (24.80) and the 'F' test value is 1.956 which is not significant even at 0.05 level in this aspect.

In the present study an attempt was made to find out the influence of personal variable i.e. occupation on the opinion of Preraks towards the organisation of continuing education activities, the details of which are as shown in table 5.16. It can be observed that Preraks from agriculture occupation group have obtained a mean opinion score of 281.3793 with a standard deviation of 77.0438. The Preraks from business occupation have secured a least mean opinion score of 216.4286 with a standard deviation of 19.7278. Preraks from agriculture occupation group have obtained a more favourable mean attitude score in relation to their counterparts. 'F' test was employed to find out the difference between the means and the 'F' value obtained (2.837) is found to be statistically significant even at 0.01 level.

In order to understand the differential opinions of the different occupation groups, the trend of the mean opinion scores illustrates that there is no significant difference in Short Term Training Programmes (A5), Games and Sports Activities (A6), Information Window (A7), Supportive Facilities (A8). There is high level significant difference is found in the themes of Organisation of Evening Classes (A1), Library and Reading Room (A2), Charcha Mandal (A3). And remaining the theme Cultural and Recreational Activities (A4) and over all opinion is found significant at 0.05 level.

Opinion of the Preraks Towards Organisation of Continuing Education Centre Activity — Individual income-wise

The observation indicates that the Preraks opinion towards organisation of the evening class (A1), Preraks with Rs. 1000/- to 2000/- PM of income scored higher mean value of 37.1176 and Standard Deviation of 10.2743 than that of other two categories. Preraks with above Rs. 2000/- PM of income mean score is 28.8667 and Standard Deviation of

4.7188. Further, the 'F' test also shows that the difference between three groups of Preraks is found highly significantly different from each other. The significant value is 5.096 which is significant at 0.01 level.

The Preraks opinion towards library and reading room theme (A2), Rs. 1000/- to Rs. 2000/- PM Preraks mean score (38.8235) is more than below Rs. 1000/- (33.1379), and above Rs. 2000/- mean scores is 29.8667. Standard Deviation of below Rs. 1000/-, Rs. 1000/- to Rs. 2000/- and above Rs. 2000/- are 8.0122, 9.5107 and 6.7174 respectively and the 'F' test also shows that the difference between these three groups of Preraks is found highly significance difference at 0.01 level from each other in this aspect.

It is can be seen from the Preraks opinion towards Charcha Mandal theme (A3), Rs. 1000/- to Rs. 2000/- PM income category Preraks scored maximum mean value of 35.4412 and Standard Deviation of 10.9023. The above Rs. 2000/- PM Preraks mean score is 28.6667 and Standard Deviation of 4.8206. Further, the 'F' test also shows that the difference between the three groups of Preraks is found significant difference at 0.05 level.

The observation indicates that the Preraks opinion towards cultural and recreational activity theme (A4), Rs. 1000/- to 2000/- PM Preraks mean score (35.5588) is more than above Rs. 2000/- PM (30.5333), and below Rs. 1000/- PM Preraks mean scores (32.4483) and the 'F' test value is 1.870 which is not significant even at 0.05 level in this aspect.

In the Preraks opinion towards short duration programmes theme (A5), Rs. 1000/- to Rs. 2000/- PM Preraks mean score (33.00) is more than that of below Rs. 1000/- PM (29.2069), and above Rs. 2000/- PM (25.9333). Standard Deviation of below Rs. 1000/-, Rs. 1000/- to 2000/- and above Rs. 2000/- PM are 9.5183, 11.6827 and 3.4323 respectively and the 'F' test also shows that the difference among these three groups of Preraks is found significant different from each other in this aspect. In the Preraks opinion towards games and sports theme (A6), Rs.1000/- to 2000/- PM Preraks scored maximum mean value of 32.3529 and Standard Deviation of 12.0627. The above Rs. 2000/- PM Preraks minimum mean score of 24.6667 and Standard Deviation of 3.9036. Further, the 'F' test also shows that the difference between these groups of Preraks is found significant difference at 0.05 level.

Table 5.17: Mean, Standard Deviation and 'F Value for Various Individual Income Groups Respondents on the Themes of Opinions of Preraks Towards Continuing Education Programme

Sl. No.	Theme	Group	N	Mean	S D	'F'-Value
1.	A1	Below Rs. 1000/- PM	29	32.4483	8.5255	5.096**
		Rs. 1000/- to Rs. 2000 PM	34	37.1176	10.2743	
		Above Rs. 2000/- PM	15	28.8667	4.7188	
2.	A2	Below Rs. 1000/- PM	29	33.1379	8.0122	6.877**
		Rs. 1000/- to Rs. 2000 PM	34	38.8235	9.5107	
		Above Rs. 2000/- PM	15	29.8667	6.7174	
3.	A3	Below Rs. 1000/- PM	29	31.7586	9.3833	2.932*
		Rs. 1000/- to Rs. 2000 PM	34	35.4412	10.9023	
		Above Rs. 2000/- PM	15	28.6667	4.8206	
4.	A4	Below Rs. 1000/- PM	29	32.4483	9.1791	1.870
		Rs. 1000/- to Rs. 2000 PM	34	35.5588	10.3987	
		Above Rs. 2000/- PM	15	30.5333	4.2066	
5.	A5	Below Rs. 1000/- PM	29	29.2069	9.5183	2.957*
		Rs. 1000/- to Rs. 2000 PM	34	33.0000	11.6827	
		Above Rs. 2000/- PM	15	25.9333	3.4323	
6.	A6	Below Rs. 1000/- PM	29	27.4138	9.4473	3.677*
		Rs. 1000/- to Rs. 2000 PM	34	32.3529	12.0627	
		Above Rs. 2000/- PM	15	24.6667	3.9036	
7.	A7	Below Rs. 1000/- PM	29	31.5172	8.9547	2.953*
		Rs. 1000/- to Rs. 2000 PM	34	34.5294	10.6123	
		Above Rs. 2000/- PM	15	27.7333	4.9493	
8.	A8	Below Rs. 1000/- PM	29	29.5862	9.1866	4.27*
		Rs. 1000/- to Rs. 2000 PM	34	34.1765	10.7435	
		Above Rs. 2000/- PM	15	26.4000	3.1351	
	Total	Below Rs. 1000/- PM	29	247.5172	65.0909	4.384*
		Rs. 1000/- to Rs. 2000 PM	34	281.0000	81.1250	
		Above Rs. 2000/- PM	15	222.6667	19.2972	

** Significant at 0.01 level, * Significant at 0.05 level

As per the Preraks opinion towards information window programmes theme (A7), Rs. 1000/- to 2000/- PM Preraks scored mean value of 34.5294 and Standard Deviation of 10.6123. The above Rs. 2000/- PM Preraks mean score is 27.7333 and Standard Deviation of 4.9493. Further, the 'F' test also shows that the difference between these three groups of Preraks is found significant difference at 0.05 level. In the Preraks opinion towards supportive facilities activity theme (A8), Rs. 1000/- to 2000/- PM Preraks mean score (34.1765) is more than the below Rs. 1000/- PM (29.5826), and above Rs. 2000/- PM (26.40) and the 'F' test value is 4.27 which is significant at 0.05 level in this aspect.

In the present study an attempt was made to know the influence of individual income on the opinion of Preraks towards the organisation of continuing education activities. The details as shown in the table 5.17, reveal that the Preraks belonging to the income of Rs. 1000/- to 2000/- per month group have secured a better mean opinion score in relation to their counterparts and above Rs. 2000/- per month of income group having least mean attitude scores. The 'F' value obtained to test the significance of difference between the means is statistically significant at 0.05 levels.

To calculate the influence of the individual income of the Preraks on their opinion, the trend of mean scores found that there is no significant in the theme of Cultural and Recreational Activities (A4). There is high level significant difference in the themes of Organisation of Evening Classes (A1), Library and Reading Room (A2) and remaining all sub themes and over all opinion is found significant at 0.05 levels.

Opinion of the Preraks Towards Organisation of Continuing Education Centre Activity – Family Income-wise

The study indicates that the Preraks opinion towards organisation of the evening class (A1), Preraks have family income of Rs. 1000/- to 2000/- PM scored higher mean value of 35.4839 and Standard Deviation of 9.5634 than that of other two categories. Above Rs. 2000/- PM of family income of

Preraks mean score is 32.3684 and Standard Deviation of 8.8788. Further, the 'F' test also shows that the difference between three groups of Preraks is found not significant difference from each other.

Findings of the study indicates the Preraks opinion towards library and reading room theme (A2), Rs. 1000/- to Rs. 2000/- PM of family income of Preraks mean score (36.7742) is more than above Rs. 2000/- (33.8421), and below Rs. 1000/ - (33.6667). Standard Deviation of below Rs. 1000/-, Rs. 1000/ - to Rs. 2000/- and above Rs. 2000/- are 9.8362, 8.8608 and 9.1726 respectively and the 'F' test also shows that the difference between these three groups of Preraks is found not significance difference even at 0.05 level from each other in this aspect.

In the Preraks opinion towards Charcha Mandal theme (A3), below Rs. 1000/- PM of family income of Preraks scored maximum mean value of 35.6667 and Standard Deviation of 8.8459. The above Rs. 2000/- PM of family income of Preraks mean score is 31.6842 and Standard Deviation of 9.0944. Further, the 'F' test also shows that the difference between the three groups of Preraks is found not significant difference even at 0.05 levels.

As per the Preraks opinion towards cultural and recreational activity theme (A4), below Rs. 1000/- PM of family income Preraks mean score (34.6667) is more than Rs. 1000/- to 2000/- PM (33.8387), and above Rs.2000/- PM of family income of Preraks mean scores (32.8158) and the 'F' test value is 0.193 which is insignificant. It is the Preraks opinion towards short duration programmes theme (A5), below Rs. 1000/- PM of family income of Preraks mean score (31.6667) is more than that of Rs. 1000/-to 2000/- PM (31.4194), and above Rs. 2000/ - PM (28.9211). Standard Deviation of below Rs. 1000/-, Rs. 1000/- to 2000/- and above Rs. 2000/- PM are 11.3358, 10.8221 and 9.1604 respectively and the 'F' test also shows that the difference among these three groups of Preraks is found not significant different from each other in this aspect.

Table 5.18: Mean, Standard Deviation and 'F' Value for Various Family Income Groups Respondents on the Themes of Opinions of Preraks Towards Continuing Education Programme

Sl. No.	Theme	Group	N	Mean	S D	'F'-Value
1.	A1	Below Rs. 1000/- PM	29	34.0000	9.9750	0.965
		Rs. 1000/- to Rs. 2000 PM	34	35.4839	9.5634	
		Above Rs. 2000/- PM	15	32.3684	8.8788	
2.	A2	Below Rs. 1000/- PM	29	33.6667	9.8362	0.988
		Rs. 1000/- to Rs. 2000 PM	34	36.7742	8.8608	
		Above Rs. 2000/- PM	15	33.8421	9.1726	
3.	A3	Below Rs. 1000/- PM	29	35.6667	8.8459	0.674
		Rs. 1000/- to Rs. 2000 PM	34	33.2581	10.6832	
		Above Rs. 2000/- PM	15	31.6842	9.0944	
4.	A4	Below Rs. 1000/- PM	29	34.6667	10.6654	0.193
		Rs. 1000/- to Rs. 2000 PM	34	33.8387	10.0635	
		Above Rs. 2000/- PM	15	32.8158	8.2228	
5.	A5	Below Rs. 1000/- PM	29	31.6667	11.3358	0.625
		Rs. 1000/- to Rs. 2000 PM	34	31.4194	10.8221	
		Above Rs. 2000/- PM	15	28.9211	9.1604	
6.	A6	Below Rs. 1000/- PM	29	29.8889	11.5374	0.563
		Rs. 1000/- to Rs. 2000 PM	34	30.3548	11.2858	
		Above Rs. 2000/- PM	15	27.7632	9.3619	
7.	A7	Below Rs. 1000/- PM	29	34.4444	11.0353	1.027
		Rs. 1000/- to Rs. 2000 PM	34	33.2903	9.8020	
		Above Rs. 2000/- PM	15	30.5789	8.6419	
8.	A8	Below Rs. 1000/- PM	29	32.1111	11.0730	0.884
		Rs. 1000/- to Rs. 2000 PM	34	32.4516	10.1516	
		Above Rs. 2000/- PM	15	29.5000	8.6891	
	Total	Below Rs. 1000/- PM	29	266.1111	77.9382	0.723
		Rs. 1000/- to Rs. 2000 PM	34	266.8710	75.5260	
		Above Rs. 2000/- PM	15	247.4737	64.5072	

** Significant at 0.01 level, * Significant at 0.05 level

Findings indicate that the Preraks opinion towards games and sports theme (A6), Rs. 1000/- to 2000/- PM family income of Preraks scored maximum mean value of 30.3548 and Standard Deviation of 11.2858. The above Rs. 2000/- PM family income of Preraks minimum mean score of 27.7632 and Standard Deviation of 9.3619. Further, the 'F' test also shows that the difference between these groups of Preraks is found not significant difference even at 0.05 level.

The Preraks opinion towards information window programmes theme (A7), below Rs. 1000/- PM family income of Preraks scored mean value of 34.4444 and Standard Deviation of 11.0353. The above Rs. 2000/- PM family income of Preraks mean score is 30.5789 and Standard Deviation of 8.6419. Further, the 'F' test also shows that the difference between these three groups of Preraks is found not significant difference even at 0.05 levels. In the Preraks opinion towards supportive facilities activity theme (A8), Rs. 1000/- to 2000/- PM family income of Preraks mean score (32.4516) is more than the below Rs. 1000/- PM (32.1111), and above Rs. 2000/- PM (29.50) and the 'F' test value is 0.884 which is not significant difference at 0.05 level in this aspect.

It is observed that the present study an attempt was made to know the influence of family income on the opinion of Preraks towards the organisation of continuing education activities. The details as shown in the table 5.18 reveal that the Preraks belonging to the family income of Rs. 1000/- to 2000/- per month group have secured a better mean opinion score in relation to their counterparts and above Rs. 2000/- per month of income group having least mean attitude scores are get. The 'F' value is 0.723 obtained to test the significance of difference between the means is statistically not significant.

To calculate the influence of the family income of the Preraks on their opinion, the trend of mean scores found that there is no significant in the themes of Organisation of Evening Classes (A1), Library and Reading Room (A2), Charcha Mandal (A3), Cultural and Recreational Activities (A4), Short Term Training Programmes (A5), Games and Sports Activities (A6), Information Window (A7), Supportive Facilities (A8) and over all opinion.

Opinion of the Preraks Towards Organisation of Continuing Education Centre Activity – Experience-wise

In the Preraks opinion towards organisation of the evening class (A1), the 2-4 years of experienced Preraks scored higher mean value of 37.32 and Standard Deviation of 10.0983 than that of other three categories. The below 2 years of experienced Preraks mean score is 31.300 and Standard Deviation of 7.8747. Further, the 'F' test also shows that the difference between three groups of Preraks is found significantly different from each other. The significant value is 3.532 which is significant at 0.05 level.

In the Preraks opinion towards library and reading room theme (A2), 2-4 years of experienced Preraks mean score (36.16) is more than above 4 years (36.0769), and below 2 years (33.90). Standard Deviation of below 2 years, 2-4 years and above 4 years are 8.3691, 10.4868 and 8.8455 respectively and the 'F' test also shows that the difference between these three groups of Preraks is found not significance difference even at 0.05 level from each other in this aspect.

It is clearly indicate that the Preraks opinion towards Charcha Mandal theme (A3), the 2-4 years of experienced Preraks scored maximum mean value of 35.72 and Standard Deviation of 10.5693. The below 2 years of experienced Preraks mean score is 30.725 and Standard Deviation of 8.3727. Further, the 'F' test also shows that the difference between the three groups of Preraks is found not significance difference even at 0.05 level.

In the Preraks opinion towards cultural and recreational activity theme (A4), 2-4 years of experienced Preraks mean score (35.56) is more than the above 4 years (33.3077), and below 2 years of experienced Preraks mean scores (32.15) and the 'F' test value is 1.066 which is not significant even at 0.05 level in this aspect.

In the Preraks opinion towards short term programmes theme (A5), 2-4 years of experienced Preraks mean score (33.72) is more than that of above 4 years (29.6154), and below 2 year (28.25). Standard Deviation of below 2 year, 2-4 years and above 4 years are 8.0535, 11.9705 and 10.5636 respectively and the 'F' test also shows that the difference among these three groups of Preraks is found not significant different from each other in this aspect.

Table 5.19: Mean, Standard Deviation and 'F' Value for Various Experiences Groups Respondents on the Themes of Opinions of Preraks Towards Continuing Education Programme

Sl. No.	Theme	Group	N	Mean	S D	'F'-Value
1.	A1	Below 2 years	40	31.3000	7.8747	3.532*
		2-4	25	37.3200	10.0983	
		4 and above	13	34.6923	9.9447	
2.	A2	Below 2 years	40	33.9000	8.3691	0.577
		2-4	25	36.1600	10.4868	
		4 and above	13	36.0769	8.8455	
3.	A3	Below 2 years	40	30.7250	8.3727	2.134
		2-4	25	35.7200	10.5693	
		4 and above	13	33.3846	10.9281	
4.	A4	Below 2 years	40	32.1500	7.4233	1.066
		2-4	25	35.5600	11.0343	
		4 and above	13	33.3077	10.1356	
5.	A5	Below 2 years	40	28.2500	8.0535	2.398
		2-4	25	33.7200	11.9705	
		4 and above	13	29.6154	10.5636	
6.	A6	Below 2 years	40	26.4000	8.4027	3.727*
		2-4	25	33.3600	11.9718	
		4 and above	13	28.8462	10.4550	
7.	A7	Below 2 years	40	30.0750	7.7803	2.489
		2-4	25	35.3200	10.8694	
		4 and above	13	32.1538	9.9234	
8.	A8	Below 2 years	40	29.0250	7.7641	1.883
		2-4	25	33.6000	11.7047	
		4 and above	13	31.9231	9.3672	
	Total	Below 2 years	40	241.8250	56.2881	2.458
		2-4	25	280.7600	84.7183	
		4 and above	13	260.0000	71.6705	

** Significant at 0.01 level, * Significant at 0.05 level

As per the Preraks opinion towards games and sports theme (A6), 2-4 years of experienced Preraks scored maximum mean value of 33.36 and Standard Deviation of 11.9718. The below 2 years of experienced Preraks minimum mean score of 26.40 and Standard Deviation of 8.4027. Further, the 'F' test also shows that the difference between these groups of Preraks is found significant difference at 0.05 level.

It is evident from the Preraks opinion towards information window programmes theme (A7), the 2-4 years of experienced Preraks scored mean value of 35.32 and Standard Deviation of 10.8694. The below 2 years of experienced Preraks mean score is 30.075 and Standard Deviation of 7.7803. Further, the 'F' test also shows that the difference between these three groups of Preraks is found not significant difference even at 0.05 level.

The observation indicates the Preraks opinion towards supportive facilities activity theme (A8), 2-4 years of experienced Preraks mean score (33.60) is more than the above 4 years (31.9231), and below 2 years (29.025) and the 'F' test value is 1.883 which is not significant even at 0.05 level in this aspect.

The information relating to the influence of experience on the opinion of Preraks towards the organisation of continuing education activities reveals that the 2-4 years of experience group have secured a better mean attitude score in relation to the other experience groups (below 2 years and above 4 years). The mean opinion score of 2-4 years of experience group is 280.76. The mean opinion score of below two years experience group is 241.82 whereas the mean attitude score of above 4 years of experience group is 260.00. 'F' test was employed to find out the significance of difference among the means and the calculated 'F' value is 2.458 which is not statistically significant even at 0.05 level.

Table 5.20: Opinion of the Preraks Towards Organisation of Continuing Education Centre Activity - Family background:

Mean, Standard Deviation and 'F' Value for Various Family Background Groups Respondents on the Themes of Opinions of Preraks Towards Continuing Education Programme

Sl. No.	Theme	Group	N	Mean	S D	'F'- Value
1	2	3	4	5	6	7
1.	A1	Agriculture	29	33.2500	9.7881	5.881**
		Business	14	28.9231	5.7367	
		Employed	7	27.0000	2.9439	
		Artisans	23	40.0435	8.1323	
		Others	5	27.8333	5.7067	
2.	A2	Agriculture	29	35.5000	9.1051	5.297**
		Business	14	29.4615	5.6364	
		Employed	7	26.5000	4.2032	
		Artisans	23	40.1304	8.8693	
		Others	5	30.1667	6.7946	
3.	A3	Agriculture	29	33.0625	10.4817	3.497**
		Business	14	26.9231	4.8384	
		Employed	7	30.0000	1.4142	
		Artisans	23	37.5217	10.1393	
		Others	5	27.5000	4.8888	
4.	A4	Agriculture	29	33.9063	8.9022	3.369*
		Business	14	28.3077	6.1290	
		Employed	7	30.0000	4.0825	
		Artisans	23	37.7391	10.6311	
		Others	5	27.8333	2.4014	
5.	A5	Agriculture	29	30.5625	10.2073	1.652
		Business	14	26.1538	4.5064	
		Employed	7	25.2500	4.0311	
		Artisans	23	33.6957	12.6435	
		Others	5	27.3333	4.2269	

(Contd...)

1	2	3	4	5	6	7
		Agriculture	29	29.7188	10.4147	
		Business	14	25.4615	3.5967	
6.	A6	Employed	7	22.5000	4.2032	2.237
		Artisans	23	32.8261	13.0302	
		Others	5	23.0000	2.9665	
		Agriculture	29	32.3438	9.6206	
		Business	14	28.5385	3.7775	
7.	A7	Employed	7	29.7500	6.1305	0.963
		Artisans	23	34.5652	12.2357	
		Others	5	30.6667	1.6330	
		Agriculture	29	31.5000	9.6017	
		Business	14	26.5385	4.1355	
8.	A8	Employed	7	28.2500	4.6458	1.351
		Artisans	23	33.6957	12.4149	
		Others	5	29.1667	2.2286	
		Agriculture	29	259.8438	72.6161	
		Business	14	220.3077	20.5564	
	Total	Employed	7	219.2500	18.9978	3.117*
		Artisans	23	290.2174	83.5986	
		Others	5	223.5000	19.7762	

** Significant at 0.01 level, * Significant at 0.05 level.

To calculate the influence of the experience of the Preraks on their opinion, the trend mean opinions scores found that there is no significant difference on the themes of Library and Reading Room (A2), Charcha Mandal (A3), Cultural and Recreational Activities (A4), Short Term Training Programmes (A5), Information Window (A7), Supportive Facilities (A8) and over all opinion. There is significant at difference on the themes of Organisation of Evening Classes (A1) and Games and Sports Activities (A6).

In the Preraks opinion towards organisation of the evening class (A1), Preraks belong to artisans' family background scored higher mean value of 40.0435 and Standard Deviation of 8.1323 than that of other four categories. Employed family background Preraks mean score is 27.00 and

Standard Deviation of 2.9439. Further, the 'F' test also shows that the difference between five groups of Preraks is found highly significant. The significant value is 5.881 which is significant at 0.01 level.

The table shows that the Preraks opinion towards library and reading room theme (A2), artisans' family background Preraks mean score (40.1304) is more than agriculture (35.50), others (30.1667), business (29.4615) and employed (26.50) and the 'F' test also shows that the difference between these five groups of Preraks is found highly significant different from each other in this aspect.

In the Preraks opinion towards Charcha Mandal theme (A3), the Preraks of artisans' family background scored maximum mean value of 37.5217 and Standard Deviation of 10.1393. The business family background Preraks mean score is 26.9231 and Standard Deviation of 4.8384. Further, the 'F' test also shows that the difference between the five groups if Preraks is found highly significant different from each other at 0.01 level.

The study indicates that the Preraks opinion towards cultural and recreational activity theme (A4), artisans family background Preraks mean score (37.7391) is more than the agriculture (33.9063), employed (30.00), business (28.3077) and others Preraks mean scores (27.833) and the 'F' test value is 3.369 which is significant at 0.05 levels in this aspect.

It is clearly evident from the Preraks opinion towards short duration programmes theme (A5), artisans' family background Preraks mean score (33.6957) and standard deviation (12.6435) and least minimum score of employed family background Preraks (25.25) and 'F' test also shows that the difference among these five groups of Preraks is found not significant different from each other in this aspect.

According to the Preraks opinion towards games and sports theme (A6), artisans' family background Preraks scored mean value of 32.8261 and Standard Deviation of 13.0302. The employed family background Preraks mean score is 22.50 and Standard Deviation of 4.2032. Further, the 'F' test also shows that the difference between these groups of Preraks is found highly significant difference at 0.01 level.

The findings indicate that the Preraks opinion towards information window programmes theme (A7), artisans family background Preraks scored mean value of 34.5652 and Standard Deviation of 12.2357. The business family background Preraks mean score is 28.5385 and Standard Deviation of 3.7775. Further, the 'F' test also shows that the difference between these five groups of Preraks is found highly significant difference at 0.01 level.

As per the Preraks opinion towards supportive facilities activity theme (A8), artisans' family background Preraks mean score (33.6957) is more than the agriculture (31.500), others (29.1667), employed (28.25) and business (26.5385) and the 'F' test value is 1.351 which is not significant difference even at 0.05 level in this aspect.

In the present study an attempt was made to find out the influence of personal variable i.e. family background on the opinion of Preraks towards the organisation of continuing education activities, the details of which are as shown in table 5.20. It can be observed that Preraks from artisan families group have obtained a mean opinion score of 290.21 with a standard deviation of 83.59. The Preraks from employed background have secured a least mean opinion score of 219.25 with a standard deviation of 18.99. Preraks from artisans family background group have obtained a more favourable mean attitude score in relation to their counterparts. 'F' test was employed to find out the difference between the means and the 'F' value obtained (3.117) is found to be statistically significant even at 0.05 level.

The influence of the family background of the Preraks on their opinions, it was found that there is no significant difference in the themes of Short Term Training Programmes (A5), Games and Sports Activities (A6), Information Window (A7), Supportive Facilities (A8), high level significant difference is found in Organisation of Evening Classes (A1), Library and Reading Room (A2), Charcha Mandal (A3). And remaining theme Cultural and Recreational Activities (A4) and overall opinions is found significant at 0.05 level.

Correlation Matrix

The simple correlations with dependent variable i.e., attitude of Preraks towards organisation of continuing education activities are as shown in the table 5.21.

Table 5.21: Correlation Matrix Showing the Attitude of Preraks Towards Organisation of Continuing Education Activities

Sl. No.	1	2	3	4	5	6	7	8	9	10	11	12
1.	1.00	0.16	0.02	0.27	-0.07	0.08	-0.06	0.19	0.33	0.25	-0.14	0.05
2.		1.00	0.20	-0.04	0.17	0.08	-0.09	-0.10	-0.04	-0.06	0.02	0.09
3.			1.00	-0.12	0.21	0.00	0.09	-0.17	0.03	-0.07	0.20	0.12
4.				1.00	0.10	0.03	0.18	0.32	0.35	0.27	-0.16	-0.10
5.					1.00	-0.02	0.03	0.12	0.17	0.11	0.05	-0.15
6.						1.00	0.22	0.13	-0.18	-0.16	0.00	0.14
7.							1.00	0.26	0.14	-0.02	0.08	0.16
8.								1.00	0.33	0.38	0.06	-0.10
9.									1.00	0.57	0.20	-0.06
10.										1.00	-0.13	-0.12
11.											1.00	0.08
12.												1.00

Order of Variables

1. Age
2. Sex
3. Marital Status
4. Caste
5. Nativity
6. Education
7. Experience
8. Occupation
9. Individual Income
10. Family Income
11. Family background
12. Attitude of Preraks

As per the last vertical column, the order of 1-12 variables is age, gender, marital status, caste, nativity, education, experience, occupation, individual income, family income, family background, and attitude towards the organisation of continuing education activities. The order of high correlations with attitude are age (0.05), gender (0.09), marital status (0.12), caste (-0.10), nativity (-0.15), education (0.14), experience (0.16), occupation (-0.10), individual income (-0.16), family income (-0.12), family background (0.08), and attitude towards the organisation of continuing education activities (0.08).

Influence of Personal Variables on Attitude/Opinion of Neo-Literates Towards Organisation of Continuing Education Activities

In the present investigation an attempt was made to find out the influence of personal variables on the attitude of neo-literates towards the organisation of continuing education activities.

In the neo-literates opinion towards organisation of the evening class (A1), the male neo-literates scored higher mean value of 23.3784 and maximum Standard Deviation of 9.5718 than that of female category. The female neo-literates mean score is 20.2778 and Standard Deviation of 9.4798. Further, the 't' test also shows that the difference between male and female neo-literates is found significant difference from each other. It shows that both the male and female category respondents expressed different opinion towards organisation of evening class theme.

In the neo-literates opinion towards library and reading room theme (A2), male neo-literates mean score (24.4054) is more than the female mean scores (21.4444). Standard Deviation of male and female are 11.3629 and 10.9812 respectively and the 't' test also shows that the difference between male and female neo-literates is found significant difference from each other in this aspect. From the neo-literates opinion towards Charcha Mandal theme (A3), the male neo-literates scored maximum mean value of 22.2973 and minimum Standard Deviation of 9.1260. The female neo-literates mean score is 20.7130 and Standard Deviation of 9.8759. Further, the 't' test also shows that the difference between male and female neo-literates is found not significant different from each other.

Opinion of the Neo-literates Towards Organisation of Continuing Education Centre Activity – Gender-wise

Table 5.22: Mean, Standard Deviation and 'F' Value for Various Gender Groups Respondents on the Themes of Opinions of Neo-literates Towards Continuing Education Programme

Sl. No.	Theme	Group	N	Mean	S D	't'-Value
1.	A1	Male	111	23.3784	9.5718	2.408*
		Female	108	20.2778	9.4798	
2.	A2	Male	111	24.4054	11.3629	1.96*
		Female	108	21.4444	10.9812	
3.	A3	Male	111	22.2973	9.1260	1.233
		Female	108	20.7130	9.8759	
4.	A4	Male	111	23.6577	9.5179	1.828
		Female	108	21.2407	10.0493	
5.	A5	Male	111	20.9189	8.0183	1.26
		Female	108	19.4907	8.7504	
6.	A6	Male	111	19.9730	7.2444	1.825
		Female	108	18.1759	7.3266	
7.	A7	Male	111	22.6306	9.3088	1.284
		Female	108	20.9444	10.1169	
8.	A8	Male	111	21.8468	8.2992	1.307
		Female	108	20.2870	9.3489	
	Total	Male	111	179.1081	68.4301	1.729
		Female	108	162.5741	73.0425	

** Significant at 0.01 level, * Significant at 0.05 level

As observed from neo-literates opinion towards cultural and recreational activity theme (A4), male neo-literates mean score (23.6577) is more than the female mean scores (21.2407). Standard Deviation of male and female are 9.5179 and 10.0493 respectively and the 't' test value is 1.828 which is not significantly different from each other in this aspect. As observed the neo-literates opinion towards short duration programmes theme (A5), male neo-literates mean score (20.9189) is more than the female mean scores (19.4907). Standard Deviation of male and female are 8.0183 and 8.7504 respectively and the 't' test also shows that the difference between male and female neo-literates is found not significantly different from each other in this aspect.

The neo-literates opinion towards games and sports theme (A6), the male neo-literates scored mean value of 19.9730 and Standard Deviation of 7.2444. The female neo-literates mean score is 18.1759 and Standard Deviation of 7.3266. Further, the 't' test also shows that the difference between male and female neo-literates is found not significantly different from each other.

In the neo-literates opinion towards information window programmes theme (A7), the male neo-literates scored mean value of 22.6306 and Standard Deviation of 9.3088. The female neo-literates mean score is 20.9444 and Standard Deviation of 10.1169. Further, the 't' test also shows that the difference between male and female neo-literates is found not significantly different from each other. In the neo-literates opinion towards supportive facilities activity theme (A8), male neo-literates mean score (21.8468) is more than the female mean scores (20.2870). Standard Deviation of male and female are 8.2992 and 9.3489 respectively and the 't' test value is 1.307 which is not significantly different from each other in this aspect.

It can be observed from the table 5.22 that neo-literates representing men group have obtained a mean attitude score of 179.10 with a standard deviation of 68.43. The neo-literates belonging to women group have obtained a mean attitude score of 162.57 with a standard deviation of 73.042. Men learners have exhibited a more favourable attitude than women group. 't' test was employed to find out the significance of difference between the means and the 't' value (1.729) obtained is found to be statistically not significant even at 0.05 level.

The sex of the neo-literates has no impact on their opinion towards over all opinion and the sub themes of Charcha Mandal (A3), Cultural and Recreational Activities (A4), Short Term Training Programmes (A5), Games and Sports Activities (A6), Information Window (A7), Supportive Facilities (A8). In case of Organisation of Evening Classes (A1), Library and Reading Room (A2) is significant difference at 0.05 level.

Opinion of the Neo-literates Towards Organisation of Continuing Education Centre Activity – Age-wise

In the neo-literates opinion towards organisation of the evening class (A1), the neo-literates belong to 21-35 years of age scored higher mean value of 23.3246 and minimum Standard Deviation of 9.2454 than that of other two categories. The above 36 years of age neo-literates mean score is 18.8462 and Standard Deviation of 9.6615. Further, the 'F' test also shows that the difference between three groups of neo-literates is found significant different from each other. The significant value is 3.526 which is significant at 0.05 level.

The study indicates the neo-literates opinion towards library and reading room theme (A2), 21-35 years of age neo-literates mean score (25.4912) is more than the below 20 years (21.1364) and above 36 years (18.5641). Standard Deviation of below 20 years, 21-35 years and above 36 years are 10.4055, 11.6568 and 9.5829 respectively and the 'F' test also shows that the difference between these three groups of neo-literates is found highly significant difference.

As per neo-literates opinion towards Charcha Mandal theme (A3), the 21-35 years of age neo-literates scored maximum mean value of 23.0965 and Standard Deviation of 9.1109. The above 36 years of age neo-literates mean score is 17.9231 and Standard Deviation of 9.0303. Further, the 'F' test also shows that the difference between the three groups of neo-literates is found highly significant difference from each other.

Table 5.23: Mean, Standard Deviation and 'F' Value for Various Age Groups Respondents on the Themes of Opinions of Neo-literates Towards Continuing Education Programme

Sl. No.	Theme	Group	N	Mean	S D	'F'-Value
1.	A1	Below 20	66	21.0758	9.9031	3.526*
		21-35	114	23.3246	9.2454	
		Above 36	39	18.8462	9.6615	
2.	A2	Below 20	66	21.1364	10.4055	7.108**
		21-35	114	25.4912	11.6568	
		Above 36	39	18.5641	9.5829	
3.	A3	Below 20	66	20.9091	9.9564	4.638**
		21-35	114	23.0965	9.1109	
		Above 36	39	17.9231	9.0303	
4.	A4	Below 20	66	21.3939	9.9536	4.175**
		21-35	114	24.1579	9.4696	
		Above 36	39	19.3333	9.9110	
5.	A5	Below 20	66	19.3788	8.4703	5.348**
		21-35	114	21.7895	8.3055	
		Above 36	39	17.0256	7.5967	
6.	A6	Below 20	66	18.3788	7.2828	4.258**
		21-35	114	20.3333	7.2217	
		Above 36	39	16.6410	7.0877	
7.	A7	Below 20	66	21.3485	10.2799	3.689*
		21-35	114	23.2105	9.2722	
		Above 36	39	18.4359	9.4222	
8.	A8	Below 20	66	19.9848	8.8187	4.923**
		21-35	114	22.7368	8.5983	
		Above 36	39	18.0769	8.7491	
	Total	Below 20	66	163.6061	72.1453	5.135**
		21-35	114	184.1404	68.6739	
		Above 36	39	144.8462	68.7702	

** Significant at 0.01 level, * Significant at 0.05 level.

The neo-literates opinion towards cultural and recreational activity theme (A4), neo-literates from 21-35 years of age mean score (24.1579) is more than the below 20 years (21.3939) and above 36 years mean scores (19.3333). Standard Deviation of below 20 years, 21-35 years and above 36 years are 9.536, 9.4696 and 9.911 respectively and the 'F' test value is 4.175 which is significant at 0.01 level in this aspect.

It was observed from the neo-literates opinion towards short duration programmes theme (A5), 21-35 years of age neo-literates mean score (21.7895) is more than that of below 20 years (19.3788) and above 36 years of age mean scores (17.0256). Standard Deviation of below 20 years, 21-35 years and above 36 years are 8.4703, 8.3055, and 7.5967 respectively and the 'F' test also shows that the difference among below 20 years, 21-35 years and above 36 years of neo-literates is found highly significantly different from each other in this aspect.

Neo-literates opinion towards games and sports theme (A6), 21-35 years of age neo-literates scored mean value of 20.3333 and Standard Deviation of 7.2217. The above 36 years of age neo-literates mean score is 16.6410 and Standard Deviation of 7.0877. Further, the 'F' test also shows that the difference between these groups of neo-literates is found highly significant difference from each other.

In the neo-literates opinion towards information window programmes theme (A7), 21-35 years of age neo-literates scored mean value of 23.2105 and Standard Deviation of 9.2722. The above 36 years of age neo-literates mean score is 18.4359 and Standard Deviation of 9.4222. Further, the 'F' test also shows that the difference between these three groups of neo-literates is found significant difference at 0.05 level.

Neo-literates opinion informs towards supportive facilities activity theme (A8), neo-literates from 21-35 years of age mean score (22.7368) is more than the below 20 years (19.9848) and above 36 years (18.0769) and the 'F' test value is 4.923 which is significant difference from each other at 0.01 level in this aspect.

The details relating to the influence of age on the attitude of neo-literates towards the organisation of continuing education activities reveals that the 21-35 years of age group have secured a more favourable mean attitude score than the other age groups (below 20 years and above 36 years). The mean attitude score of 21-35 years age group is 184.1404, the mean attitude score of below 20 years of age group is 163.6061 whereas the mean attitude score of 36 years and above age group is 144.8462. 'F' test was employed to find out the significance of difference among the means as the calculated 'F' value is found to be highly statistically significant at 0.01 level.

In order to understand the influence of the age of Preraks on their opinion, high level significant difference is found in the themes of Library and Reading Room (A2), Charcha Mandal (A3), Cultural and Recreational Activities (A4), Short Term Training Programmes (A5), Games and Sports Activities (A6), Supportive Facilities (A8). And remaining themes Organisation of Evening Classes (A1), Information Window (A7), and overall opinion is found significant at 0.05 level.

Opinion of the Neo-literates Towards Organisation of Continuing Education Centre Activity – Marital Status-wise

The field study indicates that the neo-literates opinion towards organisation of the evening class (A1), the unmarried neo-literates scored higher mean value of 24.6809 and Standard Deviation of 8.5494 than that of other two categories. The married neo-literates mean score is 21.0649 and Standard Deviation of 9.7476. Further, the 'F' test also shows that the difference between three groups of neo-literates is found not significant difference from each other. The significant value is 2.626 which is not significant even at 0.05 level.

Neo-literates opinion towards library and reading room theme (A2), unmarried neo-literates mean score (27.2128) is more than the widow/widower (21.8889) and married (21.7662). Standard Deviation of unmarried, married and widow/widower are 10.7257, 11.0612 and 12.0874 respectively and the 'F' test also shows that the difference between these three groups of neo-literates is found highly significant difference from each other in this aspect. The significant value is 4.444 which is significant at 0.01 level.

Table 5.24: Mean, Standard Deviation and 'F' Value for Various Marital Status Groups Respondents on the Themes of Opinions of Neo-literates Towards Continuing Education Programme

Sl. No.	Theme	Group	N	Mean	S D	'F'-Value
1.	A1	Unmarried	47	24.6809	8.5494	2.626
		Married	154	21.0649	9.7476	
		Widow/widower	18	21.1667	10.4050	
2.	A2	Unmarried	47	27.2128	10.7257	4.444**
		Married	154	21.7662	11.0612	
		Widow/widower	18	21.8889	12.0874	
3.	A3	Unmarried	47	25.0213	8.7365	4.286**
		Married	154	20.6688	9.5535	
		Widow/widower	18	19.6111	9.4130	
4.	A4	Unmarried	47	26.4043	9.0112	5.051**
		Married	154	21.4870	9.8081	
		Widow/widower	18	20.5556	9.9836	
5.	A5	Unmarried	47	23.5106	7.9833	4.9**
		Married	154	19.4221	8.3680	
		Widow/widower	18	18.3889	7.9123	
6.	A6	Unmarried	47	21.8511	6.7276	4.405**
		Married	154	18.3571	7.2452	
		Widow / widower	18	18.1111	8.1232	
7.	A7	Unmarried	47	25.5745	8.8139	5.163**
		Married	154	21.0130	9.8186	
		Widow/widower	18	18.6667	8.9902	
8.	A8	Unmarried	47	24.5106	8.1451	4.76**
		Married	154	20.2403	8.8525	
		Widow/widower	18	19.2778	8.7434	
	Total	Unmarried	47	198.7660	64.1551	4.81**
		Married	154	164.0195	71.1521	
		Widow/widower	18	157.6667	72.7914	

** Significant at 0.01 level, * Significant at 0.05 level

It was noticed from neo-literates opinion towards Charcha Mandal theme (A3), the unmarried neo-literates scored maximum mean value of 25.0213 and Standard Deviation of 8.7365. The widow/widower neo-literates mean score is 19.6111 and Standard Deviation of 9.4130. Further, the 'F' test also shows that the difference between the three groups of neo-literates is found significant difference from each other. The significant value is 4.286 which is significant at 0.01 level.

As per neo-literates opinion towards cultural and recreational activity theme (A4), unmarried neo-literates mean score (26.4043) is more than the married (21.487) and widow/ widower mean scores (20.5556). Standard Deviation of unmarried, married and widow / widower are 9.0112, 9.8081 and 9.9836 respectively and the 'F' test value is 5.051 which is significant at 0.01 level in this aspect.

In the neo-literates opinion towards short duration programmes theme (A5), unmarried neo-literates mean score (23.5106) is more than that of married (19.4221) and widow/ widower (18.3889). Standard Deviation of unmarried, married widow/widower are 7.9833, 8.3680 and 7.9123 respectively and the 'F' test also shows that the difference among married, unmarried and widow/widower of neo-literates is found significant difference from each other in this aspect.

As per the neo-literates opinion towards games and sports theme (A6), the unmarried neo-literates scored mean value of 21.8511 and Standard Deviation of 6.7276. The widow/widower neo-literates mean score is 18.1111 and Standard Deviation of 8.1232. Further, the 'F' test also shows that the difference between these three groups of neo-literates is found significant difference from each other.

In the neo-literates opinion towards information window programmes theme (A7), the unmarried neo-literates scored mean value of 25.5745 and Standard Deviation of 8.8139. The widow/widower neo-literates mean score is 18.6667 and Standard Deviation of 8.9902. Further, the 'F' test also shows that the difference between these three groups of neo-literates is found significant different from each other.

According to the neo-literates opinion towards supportive facilities activity theme (A8), unmarried neo-literates mean score (24.5106) is more than the married (20.2403) and widow/widower (19.2778) and the 'F' test value is 4.76 which is significant different from each other in this aspect.

The neo-literates of the study were categorised into three groups based on their level of martial status i.e., married, unmarried and widow/widower. It is evident from the table 5.24 that the unmarried group have obtained a more favourable mean attitude score on organisation of continuing education activities in relation to married and widow/widower group (198.76 > 164.01> 157.66). 'F' test was employed to find out the significance of difference between the means and the calculated 'F' value is found to be statistically significant at 0.01 level.

In order to estimate the influence of the marital status on the opinion of the neo-literates, neo-literate marital status expressed one and the same opinion towards Organisation of Evening Classes (A1). There is high level significant difference towards the themes Library and Reading Room (A2), Charcha Mandal (A3), Cultural and Recreational Activities (A4), Short Term Training Programmes (A5), Games and Sports Activities (A6), Information Window (A7), Supportive Facilities (A8) and over all opinion.

Opinion of the Neo-literates Towards Organisation of Continuing Education Centre activity – Caste-wise

The neo-literates opinion towards organisation of the evening class (A1), the S.C. neo-literates scored higher mean value of 23.1064 and Standard Deviation of 8.4782 than that of other two categories. The O.C neo-literates mean score is 18.717 and Standard Deviation of 9.3529. Further, the 'F' test also shows that the difference between three groups of neo-literates is found significantly different from each other. The significant value is 3.818 which is significant at 0.05 level. In the neo-literates opinion towards library and reading room theme (A2), S.C. neo-literates mean score (24.5532) is more than the B.C. (23.8739) and O.C. (19.4340). Standard Deviation of O.C., B.C. and S.C. are 10.7444, 11.5916, and 10.2677 respectively and the 'F' test also shows that the difference between these three groups of neo-literates is found highly significant different from each other in this aspect. Neo-literates opinion towards Charcha Mandal theme (A3), the S.C. neo-literates scored maximum mean value of 23.4468 and Standard Deviation of 9.0477. The B.C. neo-literates mean score is 21.7983 and Standard Deviation of 9.3913. Further, the 'F' test also shows that the difference between the three groups if neo-literates is found not significant difference even at 0.05 level in this aspect.

In the neo-literates opinion towards cultural and recreational activity theme (A4), S.C. neo-literates mean score (24.1277) is more than the B.C. (23.0336) and O.C. neo-literates mean scores (19.717). Standard Deviation of O.C., B.C. and S.C. are 10.2664, 9.8488 and 8.8407 respectively and the 'F' test value is 2.993 which is significant at 0.05 level in this aspect.

The result from the table 5.25, shows that the neo-literates opinion towards short duration programmes theme (A5), S.C. neo-literates mean score (22.00) is more than that of B.C. (20.6723) and O.C. (17.6038). Standard Deviation of O.C., B.C. and S.C. are 8.2587, 8.4323 and 7.9455 respectively and the 'F' test also shows that the difference among these three groups of neo-literates is found significant different from each other in this aspect. The significant value is 3.901 which is significant at 0.05 level.

As per the neo-literates opinion towards games and sports theme (A6), the S.C. neo-literates scored mean value of 20.6170 and Standard Deviation of 6.8193. The O.C. neo-literates mean score is 17.2264 and Standard Deviation of 7.6903. Further, the 'F' test also shows that the difference between these groups of neo-literates is found not significant difference even at 0.05 level.

It is evident from the study that the neo-literates opinion towards information window programmes theme (A7), the S.C. neo-literates scored mean value of 24.6809 and Standard Deviation of 9.1844. The O.C. neo-literates mean score is

19.0377 and Standard Deviation of 9.9052. Further, the 'F' test also shows that the difference between these three groups of neo-literates is found highly significant difference at 0.01 level.

Table 5.25: Mean, Standard Deviation and 'F' Value for Various Caste Groups Respondents on the Themes of Opinions of Neo-literates Towards Continuing Education Programme

Sl. No.	Theme	Group	N	Mean	S D	'F'-Value
1.	A1	O.C.	53	18.7170	9.3529	3.818*
		B.C.	119	22.7479	9.9467	
		S.C.	47	23.1064	8.4782	
2.	A2	O.C.	53	19.4340	10.7444	3.549*
		B.C.	119	23.8739	11.5916	
		S.C.	47	24.5532	10.2677	
3.	A3	O.C.	53	19.1698	9.8893	2.672
		B.C.	119	21.7983	9.3913	
		S.C.	47	23.4468	9.0477	
4.	A4	O.C.	53	19.7170	10.2664	2.993*
		B.C.	119	23.0336	9.8488	
		S.C.	47	24.1277	8.8407	
5.	A5	O.C.	53	17.6038	8.2587	3.901*
		B.C.	119	20.6723	8.4323	
		S.C.	47	22.0000	7.9455	
6.	A6	O.C.	53	17.2264	7.6903	2.839
		B.C.	119	19.3109	7.2366	
		S.C.	47	20.6170	6.8193	
7.	A7	O.C.	53	19.0377	9.9052	4.329**
		B.C.	119	21.8908	9.5941	
		S.C.	47	24.6809	9.1844	
8.	A8	O.C.	53	18.6792	9.2877	3.15*
		B.C.	119	21.4034	8.7006	
		S.C.	47	22.9574	8.2882	
	Total	O.C.	53	149.5849	72.9746	3.633*
		B.C.	119	174.7311	70.9514	
		S.C.	47	185.4894	64.9678	

** Significant at 0.01 level, * Significant at 0.05 level

In the neo-literates opinion towards supportive facilities activity theme (A8), S.C neo-literates mean score (22.9574) is more than the B.C. (21.4034) and O.C. (18.6792) and the 'F' test value is 3.15 which is significance at 0.05 level in this aspect.

In the present study, an attempt was made to find out whether the neo-literates belonging to different castes differ significantly in their attitude towards organisation of continuing education activities. As the table 5.25 reveals, the mean attitude scores obtained by scheduled castes group is some what better than the mean attitude score secured by the backward castes and forward castes. The mean differences are less. The calculated 'F' value also indicates that the mean differences are statistically significant at 0.05 level.

To estimate the influence of the caste of the neo-literates on their opinion, there is no significant difference in the themes of Charcha Mandal (A3), Games and Sports Activities (A6). And high significant difference is found in the theme of Information Window (A7). In case of other themes Organisation of Evening Classes (A1), Library and Reading Room (A2), Cultural and Recreational Activities (A4), Short Term Training Programmes (A5), Supportive Facilities (A8) and over all opinion is significant difference is found.

Opinion of the Neo-literates Towards Organisation of Continuing Education Centre Activity – Nativity-wise

Neo-literates opinion towards organisation of the evening class (A1), the urban neo-literates scored higher mean value of 23.9398 and minimum Standard Deviation of 9.477 than that of rural category. The rural neo-literates mean score is 20.5735 and Standard Deviation of 9.5341. Further, the 't' test also shows that the difference between rural and urban neo-literates is found significant difference at 0.05 level.

According to the neo-literates opinion towards library and reading room theme (A2), urban neo-literates mean score (25.1928) is more than the rural neo-literates mean scores (21.5735). Standard Deviation of rural and urban are 11.3442 and 10.7844 respectively and the 't' test also shows that the difference between rural and urban neo-literates is found significant difference at 0.05 level in this aspect.

Table 5.26: Mean, Standard Deviation and 'F' Value for Various Nativity Groups Respondents on the Themes of Opinions of Neo-literates Towards Continuing Education Programme

Sl. No.	Theme	Group	N	Mean	S D	't'-Value
1.	A1	Rural	136	20.5735	9.5341	2.541*
		Urban	83	23.9398	9.4770	
2.	A2	Rural	136	21.5735	11.3442	2.333*
		Urban	83	25.1928	10.7844	
3.	A3	Rural	136	20.2647	9.2426	2.522*
		Urban	83	23.5663	9.6527	
4.	A4	Rural	136	21.0735	9.5060	2.72**
		Urban	83	24.7470	9.9974	
5.	A5	Rural	136	18.7941	7.8156	3.275**
		Urban	83	22.5422	8.8391	
6.	A6	Rural	136	18.1029	7.2473	2.577*
		Urban	83	20.6988	7.2039	
7.	A7	Rural	136	20.8603	9.9942	1.838
		Urban	83	23.3373	9.1322	
8.	A8	Rural	136	20.4118	8.9753	1.429
		Urban	83	22.1687	8.5737	
	Total	Rural	136	161.6544	70.0838	2.509*
		Urban	83	186.1928	70.4346	

** Significant at 0.01 level, * Significant at 0.05 level

The views of neo-literates towards Charcha Mandal theme (A3), the urban neo-literates scored maximum mean value of 23.5663 and maximum Standard Deviation of 9.6527. The rural neo-literates mean score is 20.2647 and Standard Deviation of 9.2426. Further, the 't' test also shows that the difference between rural and urban neo-literates is found significant difference at 0.05 level from each other.

The neo-literates opinion attitude towards cultural and recreational activity theme (A4), urban neo-literates mean score (24.747) is more than the rural neo-literates mean scores (21.0735). Standard Deviation of rural and urban are 9.506 and 9.9974 respectively and the 't' test value is 2.72 which is significant different at 0.01 level from each other in this aspect.

Neo-literates opinion indicates towards short duration programmes theme (A5), urban neo-literates mean score (22.5422) is more than the rural mean scores (18.7941). Standard Deviation of rural and urban neo-literates are 7.8156 and 8.8391 respectively and the 't' test also shows that the difference between rural and urban neo-literates is found significant difference at 0.01 level from each other in this aspect. In the neo-literates opinion towards games and sports theme (A6), the urban neo-literates scored mean value of 20.6988 and Standard Deviation of 7.2039. The rural neo-literates mean score is 18.1029 and Standard Deviation of 7.2473. Further, the 't' test also shows that the difference between rural and urban neo-literates is found significant difference at 0.05 level from each other.

As per the Neo-literates opinion indication towards information window programmes theme (A7), the urban neo-literates scored mean value of 23.3373 and Standard Deviation of 9.1322. The rural neo-literates mean score is 20.8603 and Standard Deviation of 9.9942. Further, the 't' test also shows that the difference between rural and urban neo-literates is found not significantly different from each other. In the neo-literates opinion towards supportive facilities activity theme (A8), urban neo-literates mean score (22.1687) is more than the rural mean scores (20.4118). Standard Deviation of rural and urban neo-literates are 8.9753 and 8.5737 respectively and the 't' test value is 1.429 which is not significantly different from each other in this aspect.

An attempt was made to find out whether the neo-literates belonging to different nativity differ significantly in their attitude towards organisation of continuing education activities. As the table 5.26, reveals, the mean attitude scores obtained by rural nativity group is some what better than the mean attitude score secured by the urban nativity. The mean differences are very high. The calculated 't' value also indicates that the mean differences are statistically highly significant at 0.05 level.

According to the neo-literates opinion towards library and reading room theme (A2), urban neo-literates mean score (25.1928) is more than the rural neo-literates mean scores (21.5735). Standard Deviation of rural and urban are 11.3442 and 10.7844 respectively and the 't' test also shows that the difference between rural and urban neo-literates is found significant difference at 0.05 level in this aspect.

To estimate the influence of the nativity of the neo-literates on their opinion, there is high level significant difference in the themes of Cultural and Recreational Activities (A4), Short Term Training Programmes (A5), and there is significant different at 0.05 level in case of Organisation of Evening Classes (A1), Library and Reading Room (A2), Charcha Mandal (A3), Games and Sports Activities (A6) and over all opinion. There is no significant difference is found in the theme of Information Window (A7), Supportive Facilities (A8).

Opinion of the Neo-literates Towards Organisation of Continuing Education Centre Activity – Family Background

The neo-literates opinion towards organisation of the evening class (A1), business family background neo-literates scored higher mean value of 29.20 and Standard Deviation of 3.559 than that of other four categories. Artisans family background neo-literates mean score is 10.00. Further, the 'F' test also shows that the difference between five groups of neo-literates is found highly significantly different from each other. The significant value is 50.607 which is significant at 0.01 level.

In the neo-literates opinion towards library and reading room theme (A2), others family background neo-literates mean score (30.8889) is more than business (30.8), employed (26.50), agriculture (24.3535) and artisans (10.0) and the 'F' test also shows that the difference between these five groups of neo-literates is found highly significant different from each other in this aspect. The evidence indicates that the neo-literates opinion towards Charcha Mandal theme (A3), the neo-literates of employed family background scored maximum mean value of 30.00 and Standard Deviation of 1.2566. The artisans' family background neo-literates mean score is 10.00. Further, the 'F' test also shows that the difference between the five groups if neo-literates is found highly significant different from each other.

In the neo-literates opinion towards cultural and recreational activity theme (A4), business family background neo-literates mean score (30.60) is more than the employed (30.00), others (28.1852) agriculture (23.3737), artisans (10.00) neo-literates mean scores, and the 'F' test value is 60.736 which is highly significant at 0.01 level in this aspect.

It is observed that the neo-literates opinion towards short duration programmes theme (A5), employed family background neo-literates mean score (25.25) and standard deviation (3.5818) and minimum score of artisans family background neo-literates (10.00) and 'F' test also shows that the difference among these five groups of neo-literates is found highly significant different from each other in this aspect. The significant value is 50.607.As per the neo-literates opinion towards games and sports theme (A6), business family background neo-literates scored mean value of 25.6 and Standard Deviation of 4.113. The artisan's family background neo-literates mean score is 10.00. Further, the 'F' test also shows that the difference between these groups of neo-literates is found highly significant difference at 0.01 level.

Table 5.27: Mean, Standard Deviation and 'F' Value for Various Family Background Groups Respondents on the Themes of Opinions of Neo-literates Towards Continuing Education Programme

Sl. No.	Theme	Group	N	Mean	S D	'F'-Value
1	2	3	4	5	6	7
1.	A1	Agriculture	99	22.9697	9.6769	50.607**
		Business	25	29.2000	3.5590	
		Employed	20	27.0000	2.6157	
		Artisans	48	10.0000	.0000	
		Others	27	28.1852	5.4775	
2.	A2	Agriculture	99	24.3535	11.6569	39.633**
		Business	25	30.8000	7.2284	
		Employed	20	26.5000	3.7346	
		Artisans	48	10.0000	.0000	
		Others	27	30.8889	6.2347	
3.	A3	Agriculture	99	22.7172	9.8479	48.788**
		Business	25	25.0000	3.4157	
		Employed	20	30.0000	1.2566	
		Artisans	48	10.0000	.0000	
		Others	27	28.0741	4.4196	
4.	A4	Agriculture	99	23.3737	9.7798	60.736**
		Business	25	30.6000	2.4664	
		Employed	20	30.0000	3.6274	
		Artisans	48	10.0000	.0000	
		Others	27	28.1852	2.0388	
5.	A5	Agriculture	99	21.1515	8.5588	50.607**
		Business	25	24.0000	1.7078	
		Employed	20	25.2500	3.5818	
		Artisans	48	10.0000	.0000	
		Others	27	27.7037	3.9693	
6.	A6	Agriculture	99	20.0707	7.1589	52.329**
		Business	25	25.6000	4.1130	
		Employed	20	22.5000	3.7346	
		Artisans	48	10.0000	.0000	
		Others	27	23.0741	2.8946	

(Contd...)

1	2	3	4	5	6	7
7.	A7	Agriculture	99	22.1616	9.4272	58.263**
		Business	25	27.2000	4.8045	
		Employed	20	29.7500	5.4471	
		Artisans	48	10.0000	.0000	
		Others	27	30.5556	1.4233	
8.	A8	Agriculture	99	21.2929	8.4046	68.817**
		Business	25	26.8000	2.0817	
		Employed	20	28.2500	4.1279	
		Artisans	48	10.0000	.0000	
		Others	27	29.3704	2.0782	
	Total	Agriculture	99	178.0909	70.8115	61.531**
		Business	25	219.2000	17.3013	
		Employed	20	219.2500	16.8800	
		Artisans	48	80.0000	.0000	
		Others	27	226.0370	17.5816	

**: Significant at 0.01 level, * Significant at 0.05 level

It is clearly evident from the observation the neo-literates opinion towards information window programmes theme (A7), others family background neo-literates scored mean value of 30.5556 and Standard Deviation of 1.4233. The artisans' family background neo-literates mean score is 10.00. Further, the 'F' test also shows that the difference between these five groups of neo-literates is found highly significant difference at 0.01 level.

It is observed that the neo-literates opinion towards supportive facilities activity theme (A8), others family background neo-literates mean score (29.3704) is more than the employed (28.25), business (26.80), agriculture (21.2929) and artisans (10.00) and the 'F' test value is 68.817 which is significant difference at 0.01 level in this aspect.

In the present study, an attempt is made to find out the influence of family background of learners on their attitude towards organisation of continuing education activities. The neo-literates who are other occupational group have obtained a more favourable mean attitude score towards the organisation of continuing education activities in relation to employed, business, agriculture and artisans. The respective mean attitude scores of the groups are 226.03, 219.25, 219.2 and 80.0 (vide Table 5.27). 'F' test was employed to find out the significance of difference among the mean scores and the calculated 'F' value of 61.531 is statistically significant at 0.01 level.

To find out the difference among the family background on their opinions of the neo-literates there is high level significant difference in all the themes and over all opinion.

Opinion of the Neo-literates Towards Organisation of Continuing Education Centre Activity – Education-wise

The observation clearly indicates that the neo-literates opinion towards organisation of the evening class (A1), the illiterate qualification of neo-literates scored higher mean value of 30.5217 and Standard Deviation of 4.2448 than that of other two categories. The primary education of neo-literates mean score is 16.5278 and Standard Deviation of 8.0196. Further, the 'F' test also shows that the difference between three groups of neo-literates is found highly significantly different from each other. The significant value is 65.877 which is significant at 0.01 level.

Neo-literates opinion towards library and reading room theme (A2), illiterate neo-literates mean score (31.7391) is more than literate (19.0789), and primary (18.3333). Standard Deviation of illiterates, literate and primary are 6.8291, 10.7045, and 10.226 respectively and the 'F' test also shows that the difference between these three groups of neo-literates is found highly significant difference at 0.01 level from each other in this aspect.

Neo-literates expressed the opinion towards Charcha Mandal theme (A3), the illiterate neo-literates scored maximum mean value of 27.3478 and Standard Deviation of 4.1225. The literate neo-literates mean score is 18.4211 and Standard Deviation of 9.2353. Further, the 'F' test also shows that the difference between the three groups of neo-literates is found highly significant difference at 0.01 level from each other. The neo-literates opinion towards cultural and recreational activity theme (A4), illiterate neo-literates mean score (29.6232) is more than the literate (19.2193), and primary neo-literates mean scores (19.0278) and the 'F' test value is 34.998 which is significant at 0.01 level in this aspect.

Table 5.28: Mean, Standard Deviation and 'F' Value for Various Educational Groups Respondents on the Themes of Opinions of Neo-literates Towards Continuing Education Programme

Sl. No.	Theme	Group	N	Mean	S D	'F'-Value
		Illiterate	69	30.5217	4.2448	
1.	A1	Literate	114	18.2807	8.9655	65.877**
		Primary	36	16.5278	8.0196	
		Illiterate	69	31.7391	6.8291	
2.	A2	Literate	114	19.0789	10.7045	42.621**
		Primary	36	18.3333	10.2260	
		Illiterate	69	27.3478	4.1225	
3.	A3	Literate	114	18.4211	9.2353	23.34**
		Primary	36	20.1389	12.4606	
		Illiterate	69	29.6232	2.7230	
4.	A4	Literate	114	19.2193	9.9082	34.998**
		Primary	36	19.0278	11.1239	
		Illiterate	69	25.8116	3.5944	
5.	A5	Literate	114	17.4211	8.1522	28.142**
		Primary	36	18.3333	10.4335	
		Illiterate	69	23.7246	3.8229	
6.	A6	Literate	114	17.2193	7.6271	25.035**
		Primary	36	16.1111	7.4173	
		Illiterate	69	27.9855	3.9276	
7.	A7	Literate	114	18.9737	10.1793	24.811**
		Primary	36	18.8889	10.7245	
		Illiterate	69	27.6377	3.5062	
8.	A8	Literate	114	17.9298	8.5089	36.882**
		Primary	36	18.4722	10.2831	
		Illiterate	69	224.3913	19.4484	
	Total	Literate	114	146.5439	70.7058	38.204**
		Primary	36	145.8333	79.7505	

* Significant at 0.01 level, * Significant at 0.05 level

As per the opinion of neo-literates towards short duration programmes theme (A5), illiterate neo-literates mean score (25.8116) is more than that of primary (18.333), and literate (17.4211). Standard Deviation of illiterate, literate and primary are 3.5944, 8.1522, and 10.4335 respectively and the 'F' test also shows that the difference among these three groups of neo-literates is found highly significant different from each other in this aspect. In the neo-literates opinion towards games and sports theme (A6), illiterate neo-literates scored maximum mean value of 23.7246 and Standard Deviation of 3.8229. The primary neo-literates minimum means score of 16.1111 and Standard Deviation of 7.4173. Further, the 'F' test also shows that the difference between these groups of neo-literates is found highly significant difference at 0.01 level.

In the neo-literates opinion towards information window programmes theme (A7), the illiterate neo-literates scored mean value of 27.9855 and Standard Deviation of 3.9276. The primary neo-literates mean score is 18.8889 and Standard Deviation of 10.7245. Further, the 'F' test also shows that the difference between these three groups of neo-literates is found significant difference at 0.01 level. In the neo-literates opinion towards supportive facilities activity theme (A8), illiterate neo-literates mean score (27.6377) is more than the primary (18.4722), and literate (17.9298) and the 'F' test value is 36.882 which is highly significant at 0.01 level in this aspect.

The details pertaining to the influence of educational status of the neo-literates on the attitude of neo-literates towards organisation of continuing education activities reveals that the group having illiterates members have obtained a better mean attitude score towards organisation of continuing education activities in relation to their counterparts. 'F' test was employed to find out the significance of difference between the means and the calculated 'F' value of 38.204 is found to be statistically significant at 0.01 level.

In order to estimate the influence of the education of neo-literates on their opinion, it is found there is high level significant difference in all the themes and over all opinion.

Opinion of the Neo-literates Towards Organisation of Continuing Education Centre Activity – Occupation-wise

In the neo-literates opinion towards organisation of the evening class (A1), the occupation of the neo-literates doing business scored higher mean value of 28.5676 and Standard Deviation of 3.9196 than that of other three categories. The occupation of artisan neo-literates mean score is 17.7826 and Standard Deviation of 8.4381. Further, the 'F' test also shows that the difference between four groups of neo-literates is found significantly different from each other. The significant value is 13.801 which is significant at 0.01 level.

From the neo-literates opinion towards library and reading room theme (A2), business neo-literates mean score (26.9459) is more than other groups and the 'F' test also shows that the difference between these four groups of neo-literates is found significance difference at 0.01 level from each other in this aspect. The significant value is 4.144.

The opinion of the neo-literates towards Charcha Mandal theme (A3), the employed neo-literates scored maximum mean value of 30.50 and Standard Deviation of 1.5811. The artisan occupational neo-literates mean score is 17.7826 and Standard Deviation of 8.7462. Further, the 'F' test also shows that the difference between the four groups of neo-literates is found significance value is 11.701 which is significant at 0.01 level. In the neo-literates opinion towards cultural and recreational activity theme (A4), employed occupational neo-literates mean score (29.50) is more than the business (29.2973), agriculture (21.7379), and artisans (18.8696) and the 'F' test value is 12.67 which is significant at 0.01 level in this aspect.

The observation indicates that the neo-literates opinion towards short duration programmes theme (A5), employed neo-literates mean score (27.00) is more than that of business (24.4054), agriculture (19.9126), and artisans (17.4348) and the 'F' test also shows that the difference among these four groups of neo-literates is found significant different from each other in this aspect.

Table 5.29: Mean, Standard Deviation and 'F' Value for Various Occupational Groups Respondents on the Themes of Opinions of Neo-literates Towards Continuing Education Programme

Sl. No.	Theme	Group	N	Mean	S D	'F'-Value
1	2	3	4	5	6	7
1.	A1	Agriculture	103	21.5146	10.6171	13.801**
		Business	37	28.5676	3.9196	
		Employed	10	28.5000	2.6352	
		Artisans	69	17.7826	8.4381	
2.	A2	Agriculture	103	23.3981	12.5404	4.144**
		Business	37	26.9459	2.8377	
		Employed	10	26.5000	4.7434	
		Artisans	69	19.6087	11.8473	
3.	A3	Agriculture	103	21.2816	10.4304	11.701**
		Business	37	26.7027	4.2286	
		Employed	10	30.5000	1.5811	
		Artisans	69	17.7826	8.7462	
4.	A4	Agriculture	103	21.7379	10.4918	12.67**
		Business	37	29.2973	3.2392	
		Employed	10	29.5000	3.6893	
		Artisans	69	18.8696	9.5439	
5.	A5	Agriculture	103	19.9126	9.1546	8.631**
		Business	37	24.4054	3.2699	
		Employed	10	27.0000	4.2164	
		Artisans	69	17.4348	8.2524	
6.	A6	Agriculture	103	18.4660	7.8301	8.236**
		Business	37	24.0000	2.0276	
		Employed	10	20.5000	3.6893	
		Artisans	69	17.1739	7.6350	
7.	A7	Agriculture	103	21.6117	10.2309	12.536**
		Business	37	28.8108	7.0073	
		Employed	10	25.5000	4.7434	
		Artisans	69	17.7826	8.5058	

(Contd...)

1	2	3	4	5	6	7
8.	A8	Agriculture	103	20.2621	9.3010	17.736**
		Business	37	28.0000	1.8409	
		Employed	10	29.0000	5.2705	
		Artisans	69	17.4348	8.1177	
	Total	Agriculture	103	168.1845	77.6525	11.317**
		Business	37	216.7297	15.5056	
		Employed	10	217.0000	22.1359	
		Artisans	69	143.8696	68.8850	

** Significant at 0.01 level, * Significant at 0.05 level

In the neo-literates opinion towards games and sports theme (A6), business neo-literates scored maximum mean value of 24.00 and Standard Deviation of 2.0276. The artisans' neo-literates minimum means score of 17.1739 and Standard Deviation of 7.6350. Further, the 'F' test also shows that the difference between these groups of neo-literates is found significant difference at 0.01 level.

According to the opinion of neo-literates towards information window programmes theme (A7), the business neo-literates scored mean value of 28.8108 and Standard Deviation of 7.0073. The artisans occupations neo-literates mean score is 17.7826 and Standard Deviation of 8.5058. Further, the 'F' test also shows that the difference between these four groups of neo-literates is found significant difference at 0.01 level. The significant value is 12.536.

In the neo-literates opinion towards supportive facilities activity theme (A8), employed neo-literates mean score (29.00) is more than the business (28.00), agriculture (20.2621), and artisans (17.4348) and the 'F' test value is 17.736 which is significant at 0.01 level in this aspect.

In order to see the influence of occupation on the attitude, the neo-literates of the study were categorised into four groups namely, agriculture, business, employed and artisans. The details as shown in the table 5.29, indicate that the neo-literates belonging to employed group have secured a mean attitude score of 217.000 with a standard deviation of 22.13. The neo-literates, representing artisans group have secured a mean attitude score of 143.86 with a standard deviation of 68.88. The calculated 'F' value is found to be statistically significant at 0.01 level.

In order to estimate the influence of the occupation of neo-literates on their opinion, there is high level significant difference is found in all the themes and over all opinion.

As per the neo-literates opinion towards organisation of the evening class (A1), above 2000/- PM of income of neo-literates scored higher mean value of 27.625 and Standard Deviation of 3.0356 than that of other two categories. Rs. 1000/- to Rs. 2000/- PM of income of neo-literates mean score is 19.1121 and Standard Deviation of 9.8420. Further, the 'F' test also shows that the difference between three groups of neo-literates is found highly significantly different from each other. The significant value is 14.031 which is significant at 0.01 level.

The observations indicates that the neo-literates opinion towards library and reading room theme (A2), above Rs. 2000/- PM income of neo-literates mean score (27.00) is more than below Rs. 1000/- (22.2063), and Rs. 1000/- to Rs. 2000/- (21.9483). Standard Deviation of below Rs. 1000/-, Rs. 1000/- to Rs. 2000/- and above Rs. 2000/- are 9.4718, 13.4409 and 3.3589 respectively and the 'F' test also shows that the difference between these three groups of neo-literates is found significance difference at 0.05 level from each other in this aspect. The opinion expressed by neo-literates towards Charcha Mandal theme (A3), above Rs. 2000/- PM income of neo-literates scored maximum mean value of 27.375 and Standard Deviation of 3.8543. The Rs. 1000/- to Rs. 2000/- PM income of neo-literates mean score is 18.9224 and Standard Deviation of 9.6874. Further, the 'F' test also shows that the difference between the three groups of neo-literates is found highly significant difference at 0.01 level.

Opinion of the Neo-literates Towards Organisation of Continuing Education Centre Activity - Individual Income-wise

Table 5.30: Mean, Standard Deviation and 'F' Value for Various Individual Income Groups Respondents on the Themes of Opinions of Neo-literates Towards Continuing Education Programme

Sl. No.	Theme	Group	N	Mean	S D	'F'-Value
1.	A1	Below Rs. 1000/- PM	63	23.2222	10.1591	14.031**
		Rs. 1000/- to Rs. 2000 PM	116	19.1121	9.8420	
		Above Rs. 2000/- PM	40	27.6250	3.0356	
2.	A2	Below Rs. 1000/- PM	63	22.2063	9.4718	3.256*
		Rs. 1000/- to Rs. 2000 PM	116	21.9483	13.4409	
		Above Rs. 2000/- PM	40	27.0000	3.3589	
3.	A3	Below Rs. 1000/- PM	63	22.5714	9.9510	13.714**
		Rs. 1000/- to Rs. 2000 PM	116	18.9224	9.6874	
		Above Rs. 2000/- PM	40	27.3750	3.8543	
4.	A4	Below Rs. 1000/- PM	63	23.3492	10.1141	20.129**
		Rs. 1000/- to Rs. 2000 PM	116	19.4310	9.8292	
		Above Rs. 2000/- PM	40	29.8750	2.8840	
5.	A5	Below Rs. 1000/- PM	63	20.9683	8.7270	9.005**
		Rs. 1000/- to Rs. 2000 PM	116	18.3276	8.9158	
		Above Rs. 2000/- PM	40	24.5000	2.9089	
6.	A6	Below Rs. 1000/- PM	63	19.6032	7.0380	10.31**
		Rs. 1000/- to Rs. 2000 PM	116	17.4138	7.9587	
		Above Rs. 2000/- PM	40	23.1250	2.9716	
7.	A7	Below Rs. 1000/- PM	63	23.2063	10.3926	16.477**
		Rs. 1000/- to Rs. 2000 PM	116	18.8534	9.3421	
		Above Rs. 2000/- PM	40	28.1250	5.4875	
8.	A8	Below Rs. 1000/- PM	63	21.5556	8.7377	19.848**
		Rs. 1000/- to Rs. 2000 PM	116	18.4741	8.9903	
		Above Rs. 2000/- PM	40	27.8750	3.1394	
	Total	Below Rs. 1000/- PM	63	176.6825	71.4267	13.338**
		Rs. 1000/- to Rs. 2000 PM	116	152.4828	75.5264	
		Above Rs. 2000/- PM	40	215.5000	13.9688	

** Significant at 0.01 level, * Significant at 0.05 level

The neo-literates opinion towards cultural and recreational activity theme (A4), above Rs. 2000/- PM income of neo-literates mean score (29.875) is more than below Rs. 1000/- PM (23.3492), and Rs. 1000/- to 2000/- PM income of neo-literates mean scores (19.431) and the 'F' test value is 20.129 which is significant at 0.01 level in this aspect. Classified opinion of the neo-literates towards short duration programmes theme (A5), above Rs. 2000/- PM income of neo-literates mean score (24.5) is more than that of below Rs. 1000/- PM (20.9683), and Rs. 1000/- to 2000/- PM (18.3276), and the 'F' test also shows that the difference among these three groups of neo-literates is found highly significant different from each other in this aspect.

It is observed that the neo-literates opinion towards games and sports theme (A6), above Rs. 2000/- PM income neo-literates scored maximum mean value of 23.125 and Standard Deviation of 2.9716. The Rs.1000/- to 2000/- PM income neo-literates minimum mean score of 17.1438 and Standard Deviation of 7.9587. Further, the 'F' test also shows that the difference between these groups of neo-literates is found highly significant difference at 0.01 level. In relation to the opinion of neo-literates towards information window programmes theme (A7), above Rs. 2000/- PM income of neo-literates scored mean value of 28.125 and Standard Deviation of 5.4875. The Rs.1000/- to 2000/- PM income of neo-literates mean score is 18.8534 and Standard Deviation of 9.3421. Further, the 'F' test also shows that the difference between these three groups of neo-literates is found highly significant difference at 0.01 level.

In the neo-literates opinion towards supportive facilities activity theme (A8), above Rs. 2000/- PM income of neo-literates mean score (27.8750) is more than the below Rs. 1000/- PM (21.5556), and Rs.1000/- to 2000/- PM (18.4741) and the 'F' test value is 19.848 which is significant at 0.01 level in this aspect.

In the present study an attempt was made to know the influence of individual income on the attitude of neo-literates towards the organisation of continuing education activities. The details as presented in the table 5.30, reveal that the neo-literates belonging to the higher income group (Rs. 2,000/- PM) have secured a better mean attitude score in relation to the lower and middle income groups (215.5 > 176.68 >152.48). The calculated 'F' value is statistically significant at 0.01 level.

To calculate the influence of the individual income of the neo-literates on their opinion, the trend of mean opinions scores found that there is high level significant difference in the themes of Organisation of Evening Classes (A1), Charcha Mandal (A3), Cultural and Recreational Activities (A4), Short Term Training Programmes (A5), Games and Sports Activities (A6), Information Window (A7), Supportive Facilities (A8) and in case of Library and Reading Room (A2) is found significant at 0.05 level.

Opinion of the Neo-literates Towards Organisation of Continuing Education Centre Activity – Family Income-wise

The neo-literates opinion towards organisation of the evening class (A1), above Rs. 2000/- PM of family income of neo-literates scored higher mean value of 23.7263 and Standard Deviation of 8.0165 than that of other two categories. Below Rs. 1000/- PM of family income of neo-literates mean score is 20.1053 and Standard Deviation of 10.0775. Further, the 'F' test also shows that the difference between three groups of neo-literates is found significant difference from each other and the significant value is 3.281.

In the neo-literates opinion towards library and reading room theme (A2), above Rs. 2000/- PM of family income of neo-literates mean score (24.4737) is more than Rs. 1000/- to 2000/- (22.5698), and below Rs. 1000/- (19.9737). Standard Deviation of below Rs. 1000/-, Rs. 1000/- to Rs. 2000/- and above Rs. 2000/- are 10.31, 13.0911 and 9.518 respectively and the 'F' test also shows that the difference between these three groups of neo-literates is found not significance difference even at 0.05 level from each other in this aspect.

Table 5.31: Mean, Standard Deviation and 'F' Value for Various Family Income Groups Respondents on the Themes of Opinions of Neo-literates Towards Continuing Education Programme

Sl. No.	Theme	Group	N	Mean	S D	'F'-Value
1.	A1	Below Rs. 1000/- PM	38	20.1053	10.0775	3.281*
		Rs. 1000/ to Rs. 2000 PM	86	20.5465	10.7514	
		Above Rs. 2000/- PM	95	23.7263	8.0165	
2.	A2	Below Rs. 1000/- PM	38	19.9737	10.3100	2.277
		Rs. 1000/- to Rs. 2000 PM	86	22.5698	13.0911	
		Above Rs. 2000/- PM	95	24.4737	9.5180	
3.	A3	Below Rs. 1000/- PM	38	19.7632	9.9877	4.191**
		Rs. 1000/- to Rs. 2000 PM	86	19.9767	10.0282	
		Above Rs. 2000/- PM	95	23.6105	8.4794	
4.	A4	Below Rs. 1000/- PM	38	20.3947	10.2391	6.663**
		Rs. 1000/- to Rs. 2000 PM	86	20.3953	10.2765	
		Above Rs. 2000/- PM	95	25.1684	8.6352	
5.	A5	Below Rs. 1000/- PM	38	17.9211	8.0283	4.503**
		Rs. 1000/- to Rs. 2000 PM	86	19.1860	9.2374	
		Above Rs. 2000/- PM	95	22.0632	7.3829	
6.	A6	Below Rs. 1000/- PM	38	17.8158	7.7420	4.811**
		Rs. 1000/- to Rs. 2000 PM	86	17.7442	7.9249	
		Above Rs. 2000/- PM	95	20.8105	6.2216	
7.	A7	Below Rs. 1000/- PM	38	19.5789	10.9264	3.706*
		Rs. 1000/- to Rs. 2000 PM	86	20.5930	10.2227	
		Above Rs. 2000/- PM	95	23.7789	8.4137	
8.	A8	Below Rs. 1000/- PM	38	19.3158	9.0706	3.513*
		Rs. 1000/- to Rs. 2000 PM	86	19.8953	9.6711	
		Above Rs. 2000/- PM	95	22.8526	7.6700	
	Total	Below Rs. 1000/- PM	38	154.8684	73.1016	4.223**
		Rs. 1000/- to Rs. 2000 PM	86	160.9070	78.6822	
		Above Rs. 2000/- PM	95	186.4842	59.7470	

** Significant at 0.01 level, * Significant at 0.05 level.

In the neo-literates opinion towards Charcha Mandal theme (A3), above Rs. 2000/- PM of family income of neo-literates scored maximum mean value of 23.6105 and Standard Deviation of 8.4794. The below Rs. 1000/- PM of family income of neo-literates mean score is 19.7632 and Standard Deviation of 9.9877. Further, the 'F' test also shows that the difference between the three groups of neo-literates is found significant difference at 0.01 level. In the neo-literates opinion towards cultural and recreational activity theme (A4), above Rs. 2000/ - PM of family income neo-literates mean score (25.1684) is more than below Rs. 1000/- PM (20.3947), and to Rs. 1000/- to 2000/- PM of family income of neo-literates mean scores (20.3953) and the 'F' test value is 6.663 is significant at 0.01 level in this aspect.

In the neo-literates opinion towards short duration programmes theme (A5), above Rs. 2000/- PM of family income of neo-literates mean score (22.0632) is more than that of Rs. 1000/-to 2000/- PM (19.186), and below Rs. 1000/- PM (17.9211). Standard Deviation of below Rs. 1000/, Rs. 1000/- to 2000/- and above Rs. 2000/- PM are 8.0283, 9.2374 and 7.3829 respectively and the 'F' test also shows that the difference among these three groups of neo-literates is found significant difference at 0.01 level in this aspect. In the neo-literates opinion towards games and sports theme (A6), above Rs. 2000/- PM family income of neo-literates scored maximum mean value of 20.1805 and Standard Deviation of 6.2216. The Rs.1000/- to 2000/- PM family income of neo-literates minimum mean score of 17.7442 and Standard Deviation of 7.9249. Further, the 'F' test also shows that the difference between these groups of neo-literates is found significant difference at 0.01 level.

In the neo-literates opinion towards information window programmes theme (A7), above Rs. 2000/- PM family income of neo-literates scored mean value of 23.7789 and Standard Deviation of 8.4137. The below Rs. 1000/- PM family income of neo-literates mean score is 19.5789 and Standard Deviation of 10.9264. Further, the 'F' test also shows that the difference between these three groups of neo-literates is found significant difference at 0.05 level.

In the neo-literates opinion towards supportive facilities activity theme (A8), above Rs. 2000/- PM family income of neo-literates mean score (22.8526) is more than the Rs. 1000/- to 2000/- PM (19.8953), and below Rs. 1000/- PM (19.3158) and the 'F' test value is 3.513 which is significant difference at 0.05 level in this aspect.

In the present study an attempt was made to know the influence of family income on the attitude of neo-literates towards the organisation of continuing education activities. The details as presented in the table 5.31 reveal that the neo-literates belonging to the higher income group (Rs. 2,000/- PM) have secured a better mean attitude score in relation to the middle and lower income groups (186.48 > 160.90 > 154.86). The calculated 'F' value is statistically significant at 0.01 level.

To calculate the influence of the family income of the neo-literates on their opinion, the trend of mean opinions scores found that there is no significant difference in the theme of Library and Reading Room (A2) and high level significant difference in the themes of Charcha Mandal (A3), Cultural and Recreational Activities (A4), Short Term Training Programmes (A5), Games and Sports Activities (A6), and in case of Organisation of Evening Classes (A1), Information Window (A7), Supportive Facilities (A8) is found significant at 0.05 level.

Correlation Matrix

The simple correlations with dependent variable i.e., attitude of neo-literates towards organisation of continuing education activities are as shown in Table 5.32.

Table 5.32: Correlation Matrix Showing the Attitude of Neo-literates Towards Organisation of Continuing Education Activities

Sl. No.	1	2	3	4	5	6	7	8	9	10	11
1.	1.00	-0.28	0.14	-0.13	-0.04	-0.16	0.07	0.20	-0.07	0.06	-0.05
2.		1.00	-0.03	-0.20	0.02	0.08	0.14	0.02	0.00	0.13	-0.12
3.			1.00	-0.11	-0.14	0.01	-0.11	0.05	-0.24	-0.05	-0.19
4.				1.00	0.09	0.00	-0.14	-0.15	0.00	0.01	0.17
5.					1.00	-0.19	-0.03	0.16	0.19	-0.14	0.42
6.						1.00	0.00	-0.44	-0.10	-0.16	-0.44
7.							1.00	0.22	0.36	-0.19	-0.15
8.								1.00	0.26	0.21	0.14
9.									1.00	-0.14	0.18
10.										1.00	-0.17
11.											1.00

Order of Variables

1. Age
2. Sex
3. Marital Status
4. Caste
5. Nativity
6. Education
7. Occupation
8. Individual Income
9. Family Income
10. Family background
11. Attitude of Learners

In the last vertical column, the order of 1-11 variables is age, gender, marital status, caste, nativity, education, occupation, individual income, family income, family background, and attitude towards the organisation of continuing education activities. The order of correlations with attitude are age (-0.05), gender (-0.12), marital status (-0.19), caste (0.17), nativity (0.42), education (-0.44), occupation (-0.15), individual income (0.14), family income (0.18), family background (-0.17), and attitude towards the organisation of continuing education activities.

Comparison Between Preraks and Neo-Literates Opinion Towards Explanations of the Development Programme

Awareness and the necessary skills, the participants need to have desirable attitude towards education and various developmental programmes. Economic development entails not only investment but also utilisation of the facilities created as part of the programmes. If the participants do not have a favourable attitude towards the facilities created under the development projects, the goals of development will not be fulfilled. The role of awareness and attitudes is even more important for social development which may be conceived as a condition in which people are progressively integrated by means of common values as well as sharing their rights and privileges. Social awareness is an important contributor towards sustainable development because social awareness and attitudes of the participants involved in the development process play a unique role. Sustainable development can take place only if those involved in the development process not only have relevant knowledge and skills but also have the needful readiness to take to new ways of cultivation and production. Social dimension of development is very critical and non-utilisation or poor utilisation of the fruits of development programmes means a sheer wastage of resources. In the absence of knowledge about proper utilisation of increased financial assets, economic development has in a way, led to social degradation. Over population in the developing countries is to a large extent due to lack of social awareness. The masses are ignorant of the fact that economic resources cannot cope with the increasing number of people.

A large number of policies and plans for economic development have not yielded the desired results because of apathy on the part of the beneficiaries on the various developmental projects. Even in community projects, the involvement of the community is lacking inspite of a realization on the part of the planners about the need for collaboration and cooperation of all involved. Total involvement of the community members is lacking and several community projects have remained only as government projects. Keeping these things in view, the investigator enquired about the whether the Prerak explained the welfare/ development programme and same question was asked to whether new-literates has aware on programmes.

The table 5.33 revels that 72 (92.31%) of the Preraks informed that they are explained about the Jalayagnam programme. With regard to the neo-literates 185 (84.47%) of the learners are agree that they received the information from the Prerak.

In relation to the INDIRAMMA Housing programme 68 (87.18%) of the Preraks noticed that they are explained about the programme in their respective centre and 175 (79.91) of the learners information that they are learned form the Prerak.

All sample Preraks said that they are explained about the Rice for Rs. 2/- per KG for Below Poverty Line, 175 (79.91) of the sample neo-literates respondent agreed that they are came to know through the Prerak in the continuing education centre.

With regards to the Pensions for needy people 69 (88.46%) of the Preraks are explained to neo-literates and 148 (67.58%) neo-literate said that the programme is explained by the Preraks in the centre.

Majority 74 (91.03%) of the Preraks are said that they explained about the programme of Rajeev Arogya Sree to neo-literates, 198 (90.41%) of neo-literates informed that they are learned through the Preraks.

The sample Preraks 59 (75.64%) are informed they are informed to neo-literates about free electricity for Below Poverty Line programme. The sample respondents 165 (75.34 %) of neo-literates are make clear about this programme in the centre only.

Table 5.33: Comparison Between Preraks and Neo-Literates Towards Explanations of the Development Programme in the Centre

Sl. No.	Programme	Prerak	Neo-literates
1	2	3	4
1.	Jalayagnam	72	185
		92.31	84.47
2.	INDIRAMMA Houses	68	175
		87.18	79.91
3.	Rice for Rs. 2/- per KG	78	175
		100.00	79.91
4.	Pensions for needy people	69	148
		88.46	67.58
5.	Rajeev Arogya Sree	71	198
		91.03	90.41
6.	Free electricity for BPL	59	165
		75.64	75.34
7.	Indira Kranthi Pathakam	74	205
		94.87	93.61
8.	Employment Grantee Scheme	67	165
		85.90	75.34
9.	Debt recoveries for farmers	75	184
		96.15	84.02
10.	Social welfare/development	78	203
		100.00	92.69
11.	Pasu Kranthi	62	168
		79.49	76.71
12.	Debt recoveries for socially deprived	71	145
		91.03	66.21

(Contd...)

1	2	3	4
13.	Service of 104/108	75	188
		96.15	85.84
14.	Family planning	78	183
		100.00	83.56

Out of 78 Preraks, the 74 (94.87%) of sample Preraks are explained about the Indira Kranthi Pathakam to neo-literates in the centre and the neo-literates 205 (93.61 %) are correctly noticed about Indira Kranthi Pathakam from the Preraks.

From the sample 67 (85.90%), Preraks are explained about the Debt recoveries for farmers to learners. The 184 (84.02 %) neo-literates are more awareness about this programme through the Preraks in the Continuing Education Centres only.

All the Sample Preraks 78 (100.0 %) is explained about the Social / development programme to the neo-literates. Out of 219, 203 (92.69 %) sample respondents are gain more knowledge form Continuing Education Centres through the Preraks.

An attempt was made to find out the whether the Prerak has explained about the programme of Pasu Kranthi Pathakam, 62 (79.49%) sample Preraks are explained about Pasu Kranthi Pathakam to sample respondents i.e. Neo-literates. Majority of the Neo-literates 168 (76.71 %) are said the Preraks are explained about this programme.

It is very heartening to note that the Preraks 71 (91.03) are explained to Neo-literates about the Debt recoveries for socially Deprived sections. Nearly 66 percent of the sample neo-literates are said that Preraks are explained about the programme of Debt recoveries for socially Deprived.

The majority 75 (96.15%) of the Preraks are said that they are explained about the services provided by 104 / 108 to the neo-literates in Continuing Education Centres. The Neo-literates 188 (85.84 %) are learned about services provided by 104 /108 through the Preraks in the Continuing Education Centres.

All Preraks are said that they are explained about the Family Planning to the neo-literates. The majority of the 183 (83.56) of the learners are informed that they only aware of family planning through Continuing Education Centres. The comparison between the neo-literates and community towards the awareness on the literacy, functionality, health and development/welfare programmes and their utilizations are presented in the following chapter.

CHAPTER 6 Comparison of Neo-literates and Community Members

An attempt has been made in this section to project the impact of the continuing education programme on the neo-literates and community members, and community members were used as control group to find the difference among them. In doing, so the impact is analyzed with responses viz. literacy, functionality, awareness of social beliefs and welfare programmes in each area is projected with comparison to the neo-literates and community members as well as with reference to the socio-economic background of the two groups. This would enable us to understand the differential impact of the programme in general and learners who attend the centre and non-learners as well as to trace the background of the neo-literates who lag behind in utilising the programme to their benefit in particular.

Literacy Particulars

For measuring the impact of the continuing education programme on the literacy levels of the neo-literates and community members, the data are collected by enlisting responses from two groups on their ability in reading sign boards, letters, news papers, and in writing names, letters and filling of the forms and so on. The arithmetic skills are also compared between these two groups and analyse as per their ability to writing numbers, additions, subtractions, multiplications and divisions.

A total of sample members are 395 respondents were selected, out of 395 members, 219 members are neo-literates and remaining 176 members are community members were selected for the purpose of the study.

The measure of achievement in literacy is intended to estimate the level of attainment in reading, writing and arithmetic skills – 3R's – reading, writing and arithmetic. Due to limitation of the study and for the purpose of the present study, the investigator enquired about the literacy particulars.

Reading of Sign Boards

Table 6.1: Able to Read Sign Boards of Neo-literates and Community Members

Group	Yes	Some Extent	No	Total
Neo-literates	16	151	52	219
	7.3%	68.9%	23.7%	100.0%
Community	9	110	57	176
	5.1%	62.5%	32.4%	100.0%
Total	25	261	109	395
	6.3%	66.1%	27.6%	100.0%

Chi-square value = 3.996 Not Significant

With regard to the reading sign boards, 25 (6.3%) of the sample respondents are read well, out of 25 members, 16 (7.3%) neo-literates and 9 (5.1%) community members, 109 (27.6%) of the sample respondents deliberately noted that they are unable to read the sign boards, out of 109 members, 52 (23.7%) of the beneficiaries and 57 (32.4%) of the non-beneficiaries are unable to read the sign boards.

Reading of Letters

Table 6.2: Able to Read Letters of Neo-literates and Community Members

Group	Yes	Some Extent	No	Total
Neo-literates	97	90	32	219
	44.3%	41.1%	14.6%	100.0%
Community	61	63	52	176
	34.7%	35.8%	29.5%	100.0%
Total	158	153	84	395
	40.0%	38.7%	21.3%	100.0%

Chi-square value = 13.205 Significant at 0.01 level

The above table reveals that the capability of the reading letters, 158 (40.0%) of the sample respondents are read the letter well, out of 158 members, 97 (44.3%) of the beneficiaries of the continuing education programme and 61 (34.7%) of the non-beneficiaries. 153 (38.7%) of the sample respondents are read the some extent. More than one fifth of the sample respondents noticed that they are unable to read the letters.

Reading of Newspaper

Table 6.3: Able to Read Newspaper of Neo-literates and Community

Group	Yes	Some Extent	No	Total
Neo-literates	16	151	52	219
	7.3%	68.9%	23.7%	100.0%
Community	9	97	70	176
	5.1%	55.1%	39.8%	100.0%
Total	25	248	122	395
	6.3%	62.8%	30.9%	100.0%

Chi-square value = 11.833 Significant at 0.01 level

Table 6.3 reveals that the neo-literates and community members ability to read news paper skills, nearly 16 (7.3%) of beneficiaries and 9 (5.1%) of the non-beneficiaries are able to read well, 151 (68.9%) of the beneficiaries and 97 (55.1%) of the non-beneficiaries are able to some extent to read. Only 52 (23.7%) of the beneficiaries and 70 (39.8%) of non-beneficiaries are unable to read the news paper. It clearly shows that the continuing education programme is having a positive impact on learners/beneficiaries.

Writing of Letters/Words

Table 6.4: Able to Write Letters/Simple Words of Neo-literates and Community

Group	Yes	Some Extent	No	Total
Neo-literates	97	90	32	219
	44.3%	41.1%	14.6%	100.0%
Community	65	56	55	176
	36.9%	31.8%	31.3%	100.0%
Total	162	146	87	395
	41.0%	37.0%	22.0%	100.0%

Chi-square value = 15.826 Significant at 0.01 level

In writing letters and simple words, 162 (41.0%) of the sample respondents are well, out of 162 members, 97 (44.3%) of the neo-literates and 65 (36.9%) of the community are write well and 87 (22.0%) of the sample members were unable to write the letters and simple words, out of 87, 32 (14.6%) of the beneficiaries and 55 (31.3%) of the non-beneficiaries and the chi-square value is 15.826 which is significant at 0.01 level.

From the table 6.5, 116 (29.4%) of the sample respondents are able to write their names and simple sentences. Majority 232 (58.7%) of the members are able write to the some extent and only 47 (11.9%) of the respondents are unable to write their names and simple sentences, and chi-square value is 17.252 which is significant at 0.01 level.

Writing of Names/Sentences

Table 6.5: Able to Write Names/Simple Sentences of Neo-literates and Community

Group	Yes	Some Extent	No	Total
Neo-literates	83	113	23	219
	37.9%	51.6%	10.5%	100.0%
Community	33	119	24	176
	18.8%	67.6%	13.6%	100.0%
Total	116	232	47	395
	29.4%	58.7%	11.9%	100.0%

Chi-square value = 17.252 Significant at 0.01 level

Filling of Forms

Table 6.6: Able to Write Fill Forms of Neo-literates and Community Members

Group	Yes	Some Extent	No	Total
Neo-literates	59	124	36	219
	26.9%	56.6%	16.5%	100.0%
Community	40	98	38	176
	22.7%	55.7%	21.6%	100.0%
Total	99	222	74	395
	25.1%	56.2%	18.7%	100.0%

Chi-square value = 15.044 Significant at 0.01 level

The respondents agreed that they are in a position to filling the forms are 99 (25.1%). Out of 99 members 59 (26.9%) of the neo-literates and 40 (22.7%) of the community members are able to write well and 74 (18.7%) of sample members are unable to fill the bills/forms because they are unable to write properly. 222 (56.2%) of the sample members are able to write to some extent, out of 222 respondents, 124 (56.6%) are neo-literates and 98 (55.7%) are community members. The results show that the number of neo-literates who can fill the forms is comparatively greater than that of community members.

Reading and Writing the Numbers

Table 6.7: Able to Reading and Writing the Numbers of Neo-literates and Community

Group	Yes	Some Extent	No	Total
Neo-literates	51	134	34	219
	23.3%	61.2%	15.5%	100.0%
Community	39	89	48	176
	22.2%	50.6%	27.3%	100.0%
Total	90	223	82	395
	22.8%	56.5%	20.8%	100.0%

Chi-square value = 8.491 Significant at 0.05 level

With regard to the reading and writing the numbers, 90 (22.8%) of the sample respondents are able to read and write well, out of 90 members, 51 (23.3%) are neo-literates and 39 (22.2%) are community members, only 82 (20.8%) of the sample respondents are unable to read and write numbers, out of 82 members, 34 (15.5%) of them are beneficiaries and 48 (27.3%) are non-beneficiaries and chi-square value is 8.491 which is significant at 0.05 level.

Adding and Subtraction of Numbers

Table 6.8: Ability to Add and Subtract of Neo-literates and Community

Group	Yes	Some Extent	No	Total
Neo-literates	59	124	36	219
	26.9%	56.6%	16.4%	100.0%
Community	36	85	55	176
	20.5%	48.3%	31.3%	100.0%
Total	95	209	91	395
	24.1%	52.9%	23.0%	100.0%

Chi-square value = 12.277 Significant at 0.01 level

About the capability of add and subtract, 95 (24.1%) of the sample respondents are able to do add and subtract the numbers. Out of 95 members 59 (26.9%) of the neo-literates and 36 (20.5%) of the community members and 91 (23.0%) of sample members are unable to do the additions and subtractions. 209 (52.9%) of the sample members are do the some extent to do the additions and subtractions, out of 209 members, 124 (56.6%) of the learners and 85 (48.3%) of the community members and chi-square value is 12.277 which is significant at 0.01 level.

Multiplication and Division of Numbers

Table 6.9: Ability to Multiply and Division of Neo-literates and Community

Group	Yes	Some Extent	No	Total
Neo-literates	51	135	33	219
	23.3%	61.6%	15.1%	100.0%
Community	31	77	68	176
	17.6%	43.8%	38.6%	100.0%
Total	82	212	101	395
	20.8%	53.7%	25.6%	100.0%

Chi-square value = 28.532 Significant at 0.01 level

With regard to the multiplication and divisions, 82 (20.8%) of the sample respondents are doing the multiplication and divisions well, out of the 82 members, 51 (23.3%) of neo-literates and 31 (17.6%) of community members. Only 33 (15.1%) of the beneficiaries and 68 (38.6%) of the non-beneficiaries are unable to do the multiplication and divisions and chi-square value is 28.532 which is significant at 0.01 level.

Functionality Particulars

In order to find out the awareness of functionality aspects both target and control group were enquired in the following aspects.

Occupation

Table 6.10: Information Regard to your Occupation of Neo-literates and Community Members

Group	Yes	Some Extent	No	Total
Neo-literates	51	140	28	219
	23.3%	63.9%	12.8%	100.0%
Community	25	99	52	176
	14.2%	56.3%	29.5%	100.0%
Total	76	239	80	395
	19.2%	60.5%	20.3%	100.0%

Chi-square value – 18.668 Significant at 0.01 level

From the table it was noticed that the neo-literates and community members, only 76 (19.2%) are aware about their occupations, information skills, out of 76 members, 51 (23.3%) of beneficiaries and 25 (14.2%) of the non-beneficiaries, 140 (63.9%) neo-literates and 99 (56.3%) community members are to some extent are unaware. Only 28 (12.8%) of the beneficiaries and 52 (29.5%) of non-beneficiaries are unable to know their occupational information. The chi-square value is 18.668 which is significant at 0.01 level.

Occupational Information

Table 6.11: Occupational Information of Neo-literates and Community Members

Group	Yes	Some Extent	No	Total
Neo-literates	51	140	28	219
	23.3%	63.9%	12.8%	100.0%
Community	27	99	50	176
	15.3%	56.3%	28.4%	100.0%
Total	78	239	78	395
	19.7%	60.5%	19.7%	100.0%

Chi-square value = 16.133 Significant at 0.01 level

Only 51 (23.3%) of the neo-literates and 27 (15.3%) of the community members are aware the occupational information, 239 (60.5%) of the sample respondents have to know their occupational information to some extent, out of 239 members, 140 (63.9%) of neo-literates and 99 (56.3%) of community members have to know their occupational information to some extent, and chi-square value is 16.133 which is significant at 0.01 level.

Agricultural Information

Table 6.12: Awareness of Agriculture Information of Neo-literates and Community

Group		Yes	Some Extent	No	Total
Neo-literates		63	122	34	219
		28.8%	55.7%	15.5%	100.0%
Community		35	77	64	176
		19.9%	43.8%	36.4%	100.0%
Total		98	199	98	395
		24.8%	50.4%	24.8%	100.0%

Chi-square value = 22.951 Significant at 0.01 level

With regard to the knowledge on agriculture information, 98 (24.8%) of the sample respondents are able to know the information in time. Out of 98 members, 63 (28.8%) of the neo-literates and 35 (19.9%) of them were community members and 98 (24.8%) of sample members do not know the agriculture information. 199 (50.4%) of the sample members know the agriculture information to some extent, out of 199, 122 (55.7%) of them are learners and 77 (43.8%) of the community members and chi-square value is 22.951 which is significant at 0.01 level.

Awareness on Functions of the Bank

Table 6.13: Awareness of Functions of the Bank

Group	Yes	Some Extent	No	Total
Neo-literates	50	137	32	219
	22.8%	62.6%	14.6%	100.0%
Community	38	111	27	176
	21.6%	63.1%	15.3%	100.0%
Total	88	248	59	395
	22.3%	62.8%	14.9%	100.0%

Chi-square value = 0.106 Not Significant

With regard to knowing the functions of the bank, 88 (27.3%) of the sample respondents are knows the functions of banks. Out of 88 members 50 (22.8%) of then are neo-literates and 38 (21.6%) of them are community members and 59 (14.9%) of sample members do not know the functions of the bank. 248 (62.8%) of the sample members have know ledge to some extent, out of 248, 137 (62.6%) of the learners and 111 (63.1%) of them are community members and chi-square value is 0.106 which is not significant.

Habit of Savings

Table 6.14: Savings of Neo-literates and Community

Group	Yes	Some Extent	No	Total
Neo-literates	61	123	35	219
	27.9%	56.2%	16.0%	100.0%
Community	53	94	29	176
	30.1%	53.4%	16.5%	100.0%
Total	114	217	64	395
	28.9%	54.9%	16.2%	100.0%

Chi-square value = 0.322 Not Significant

With regard to the habit of savings, 114 (28.9%) of the sample respondents are having the habit of saving. Out of 114 members, 61 (27.9%) of them are neo-literates and 53 (30.1%) of them are community members and 64 (16.2%) of the sample members are unable to save the money. And chi-square value is 0.322 which is not significant even at 0.05 level.

Social Awareness Particulars

A. Institutional Membership

Membership in Youth Clubs

Table 6.15: Membership of Neo-literates and Community in Youth Clubs

Group	Yes	No	Total
Neo-literates	153	66	219
	69.9%	30.1%	100.0%
Community	125	51	176
	71.0%	29.0%	100.0%
Total	278	117	395
	70.4%	29.6%	100.0%

Chi-square value = 0.063 Not Significant

The analysis of the table shows that the member ship in youth clubs of neo-literates and community members, 153 (69.9%) of them are beneficiaries and 125 (71.0%) of the non-beneficiaries are having membership in youth clubs, 66 (30.1%) of the beneficiaries and 51 (29.0%) of the non-beneficiaries are not a members of any youth club and the chi-square value is 0.063 which is not significant.

With regard to the membership in self help groups, 277 (70.1%) of the sample respondents are the members of the any one of the self help groups. Out of 277 members 153 (69.9%) of them are neo-literates and 124 (70.5%) of them are community members and are having the membership and 118 (29.9%) of sample members are not having membership in any self help group and chi-square value is 0.016 which is not significant.

Membership in Self-help Groups

Table 6.16: Membership of Neo-literates and Community in Self-help Group

Group		Yes	No	Total
Neo-literates		153	66	219
		69.9%	30.1%	100.0%
Community		124	52	176
		70.5%	29.5%	100.0%
Total		277	118	395
		70.1%	29.9%	100.0%

Chi-square value = 0.016 Not Significant

Membership in Co-operative Societies

Table 6.17: Membership of Neo-literates and Community in Co-operative Societies

Group		Yes	No	Total
Neo-literates		145	74	219
		66.2%	33.8%	100.0%
Community		110	66	176
		62.5%	37.5%	100.0%
Total		255	140	395
		64.6%	35.4%	100.0%

Chi-square value = 0.587 Not Significant

Association with co-operative societies, 255 (64.6%) of the sample respondents are the members are associated with co-operative societies. Out of 255 members 145 (66.2%) of them are neo-literates and 110 (62.5%) of them are community members and 140 (35.4%) of sample members are not having membership in co-operative societies. And chi-square value is 0.587 which is not significant.

Membership in Political Bodies

Table 6.18: Membership of Neo-literates and Community in Political Bodies

Group		Yes	No	Total
Neo-literates		154	65	219
		70.3%	29.7%	100.0%
Community		120	56	176
		68.2%	31.8%	100.0%
Total		274	121	395
		69.4%	30.6%	100.0%

Chi-square value = 0.21 Not Significant

Membership in political bodies, 274 (69.4%) of the sample respondents are having the membership. Out of 274 members 154 (70.3%) of them are neo-literates and 120 (68.2%) of them are community members and 121 (30.6%) of sample members have not a members in political bodies and chi-square value is 0.21 which is not significant.

B. Social Taboos

Widow Marriages

Table 6.19: Opinion of the Neo-literates and Community Towards Widow Marriages

Group	Agree	Don't know	Disagree	Total
Neo-literates	51	134	34	219
	23.3%	61.2%	15.5%	100.0%
Community	32	100	44	176
	18.2%	56.8%	25.0%	100.0%
Total	83	234	78	395
	21.0%	59.2%	19.7%	100.0%

Chi-square value = 5.961 Significant at 0.05 level

Regarding the opinion on the widow marriages the investigator enquired about the widow marriages whether they are encouraged or not, majority 234 (59.2%) of the sample respondents are having no idea, out 234 members 134 (61.2%) of the neo-literates and 100 (56.8%) of the community members are available. 83 (21.0%) of the sample members have agreed and 78 (19.7%) of the members are disagreed and the chi-square value is 5.961 which is significant at 0.05 level.

Dowry System

Table 6.20: Opinion of the Neo-literates and Community Towards Abolition of Dowry System

Group	Agree	Don't know	Disagree	Total
Neo-literates	29	149	41	219
	13.2%	68.0%	18.7%	100.0%
Community	41	109	26	176
	23.3%	61.9%	14.8%	100.0%
Total	70	258	67	395
	17.7%	65.3%	17.0%	100.0%

Chi-square value = 7.019 Significant at 0.05 level

With regard to the abolition of dowry system, 70 (17.7%) of the sample members have agreed. Out of 70 members, 29 (13.2%) of them are neo-literates and 41 (23.3%) of them are community members and only 67 (17.0%) of the sample respondents have disagreed with this regard, out of 67 members, 41 (18.7%) members are neo-literates and 26 (14.8%) members are community members and chi-square value is 7.019 which is significant at 0.05 level.

Majority 217 (54.9%) of the sample respondents reported that they have no idea about inter caste marriages because of rural back ground of the sample. Out of 217 members, 123 (56.2%) of them are neo-literates and 94 (53.4%) of them are community, 111 (28.1%) of the sample respondents informed that they are agree with inter caste marriages and the chi-square value is 0.636 which is not significant even at 0.05 level.

Inter Caste Marriage

Table 6.21: Opinion of the Neo-literates and Community Towards Inter Caste Marriage

Group		Agree	Don't know	Disagree	Total
Neo-literates		58	123	38	219
		26.5%	56.2%	17.4%	100.0%
Community		53	94	29	176
		30.1%	53.4%	16.5%	100.0%
Total		111	217	67	395
		28.1%	54.9%	17.0%	100.0%

Chi-square value = 0.636 Not Significant

Child Marriage

Table 6.22: Opinion of the Neo-literates and Community Towards Child Marriage

Group		Agree	Don't know	Disagree	Total
Neo-literates		50	137	32	219
		22.8%	62.6%	14.6%	100.0%
Community		38	111	27	176
		21.6%	63.1%	15.3%	100.0%
Total		88	248	59	395
		22.3%	62.8%	14.9%	100.0%

Chi-square value = 0.106 Not Significant

The above table reveals that the sample respondents are exposed on child marriage aspects more than one fifth i.e. 88 (22.3%) of the sample members are agreed, out of 88 members, 50 (22.8%) of them are neo-literates and 38 (21.6%) of them are community members, only 59 (14.9%) of the sample members are disagreed with this regard, and chi-square value is 0.106 which is not significant.

Bad Habits

Table 6.23: Opinion of the Neo-literates and Community Towards Bad Habits

Group		Agree	Don't know	Disagree	Total
Neo-literates		123	61	35	219
		56.2%	27.9%	16.0%	100.0%
Community		94	53	29	176
		53.4%	30.1%	16.5%	100.0%
Total		217	114	64	395
		54.9%	28.9%	16.2%	100.0%

Chi-square value – 0.322 Not Significant

Majority 217 (54.9%) of the sample respondents have acquired the knowledge towards the problems of the bad habits, out of 217 sample respondents 123 (56.2%) of the members are neo-literates and 94 (53.4%) of the members are community members. Only 64 (16.2%) of the sample respondents reported that they have not acquired necessary information in this regard. The chi-square value is 0.322 which is not significant even at 0.05 level.

Habit of Alcohol

Table 6.24: Opinion of the Neo-literates and Community Towards the Habit of Alcohol

Group		Agree	Don't know	Disagree	Total
Neo-literates		137	53	29	219
		62.6%	24.2%	13.2%	100.0%
Community		110	45	21	176
		62.5%	25.6%	11.9%	100.0%
Total		247	98	50	395
		62.5%	24.8%	12.7%	100.0%

Chi-square value = 0.206 Not Significant

The investigator carried out on the opinion on habit of alcohol, 247 (62.5%) of the sample respondents informed that they are agree consuming of alcohol is a bad habit, out of 247 members, 137 (62.6%) of them are neo-literates and 110 (62.5%) of them are community members. Only 50 (12.7%) of the sample members have disagreed in this regard and 98 (24.8%) of the members have expressed they have no idea and the chi-square value is 0.206 which is not significant.

Reservation System

Table 6.25: Opinion of the Neo-literates and Community Towards Reservation

Group	Agree	Don't know	Disagree	Total
Neo-literates	59	125	35	219
	26.9%	57.1%	16.0%	100.0%
Community	49	98	29	176
	27.8%	55.7%	16.5%	100.0%
Total	108	223	64	395
	27.3%	56.5%	16.2%	100.0%

Chi-square value = 0.077 Not Significant

With regard to the provision of reservation to certain social groups, 108 (27.3%) of the sample respondents have agreed. Out of 108 members 59 (26.9%) of the neo-literates and 49 (27.8%) of the community members and 223 (56.5%) of sample members are having no idea in this regard, out of 223, 125 (57.1%) are neo-literates and 98 (55.7%) are community and 64 (16.2%) of the sample members are disagreed with this aspect. Chi-square value is 0.077 which is not significant.

With regard to the female literacy, 211 (53.4%) of the sample respondents are agreed, out of 211, 120 (54.8%) of the neo-literates and 91 (51.7%) of the community member and 112 (28.4%) of the sample members are having no idea with regard to women education, out 112, 60 (27.4%) of the beneficiaries and 52 (29.5%) of the non-beneficiaries and the chi-square value is 0.381 which is not significant.

Female Literacy

Table 6.26: Opinion of the Neo-literates and Community Towards Female Literacy

Group	Agree	Don't know	Disagree	Total
Neo-literates	120	60	39	219
	54.8%	27.4%	17.8%	100.0%
Community	91	52	33	176
	51.7%	29.5%	18.8%	100.0%
Total	211	112	72	395
	53.4%	28.4%	18.2%	100.0%

Chi-square value = 0.381 Not Significant

C. Point of Views on Social Beliefs

Belief of God

Table 6.27: Opinion of the Neo-literates and Community Towards Belief of God

Group	Agree	Don't know	Disagree	Total
Neo-literates	63	122	34	219
	28.8%	55.7%	15.5%	100.0%
Community	53	94	29	176
	30.1%	53.4%	16.5%	100.0%
Total	116	216	63	395
	29.4%	54.7%	15.9%	100.0%

Chi-square value = 0.21 Not Significant

With regard to belief of the god, 116 (29.4%) of the sample respondents are believed. Out of 116 members 63 (28.8%) of the neo-literates and 53 (30.1%) of the community members and 63 (15.9%) of sample members have disagreed. 216 (54.7%) of the sample members are believe in the god to some extent, out of 216, 122 (55.7%) of the learners and 94 (53.4%) of the community members and chi square value is 0.21 which is not significant.

Belief of Evil Spirits/Bad Omens

Table 6.28: Opinion of the Neo-literates and Community Towards Devil

Group		Agree	Don't know	Disagree	Total
Neo-literates		50	137	32	219
		22.8%	62.6%	14.6%	100.0%
Community		38	110	28	176
		21.6%	62.5%	15.9%	100.0%
Total		88	247	60	395
		22.3%	62.5%	15.2%	100.0%

Chi-square value = 0.176 Not Significant

With regard to belief of the evil spirits, 88 (22.3%) of the sample respondents have belief. Out of 88 members 50 (22.8%) of the neo-literates and 38 (21.6%) of the community members and 60 (15.2%) of sample members have disagreed. 247 (62.5%) of the sample members have believed the evil spirits to some extent, out of 247 members, 137 (62.6%) of the learners and 110 (62.5%) of the community members and chi square value is 0.176 which is not significant.

Religious Rigidity

Table 6.29: Opinion of the Neo-literates and Community Towards Religious Rigidity

Group		Agree	Don't know	Disagree	Total
Neo-literates		55	137	27	219
		25.1%	62.6%	12.3%	100.0%
Community		45	110	21	176
		25.6%	62.5%	11.9%	100.0%
Total		100	247	48	395
		25.3%	62.5%	12.2%	100.0%

Chi-square value = 0.021 Not Significant

With regard to religious rigidity, 100 (25.3%) of the sample respondents believed of religion. Out of 100 members 55 (25.1%) of the neo-literates and 45 (25.6%) of the community members and 48 (12.2%) of sample members are disagreed. 247 (62.5%) of the sample members are believed the religious rigidity some extent, out of 247 members, 137 (62.6%) of the learners and 110 (62.5%) of the community members and chi square value is 0.021 which is not significant.

Caste Rigidity

Table 6.30: Opinion of the Neo-literates and Community Towards Caste Rigidity

Group	Agree	Don't know	Disagree	Total
Neo-literates	59	125	35	219
	26.9%	57.1%	16.0%	100.0%
Community	49	98	29	176
	27.8%	55.7%	16.5%	100.0%
Total	108	223	64	395
	27.3%	56.5%	16.2%	100.0%

Chi-square value = 0.077 Not Significant

With regard to caste rigidity, 108 (27.3%) of the sample respondents are believes of the caste system. Out of 108 members 59 (26.9%) of the neo-literates and 49 (27.8%) of the community members and 64 (16.2%) of sample members have disagreed. 223 (56.5%) of the sample members have believed in the caste rigidity some extent, out of 223 members, 125 (57.1%) of the learners and 98 (55.7%) of the community members and chi square value is 0.077 which is not significant.

With regard to witch crafts, 96 (24.3%) of the sample respondents have shown response that they believed. Out of 96 members 52 (23.7%) of the neo-literates and 44 (25.0%) of the community members and 57 (14.4%) of sample members are disagreed. 242 (61.3%) of the sample members are believers of the witch crafts some extent, out of 242 members, 135

(61.6%) of the learners and 107 (60.8%) of them are community members and chi-square value is 0.086 which is not significant.

Witch Crafts

Table 6.31: Opinion of the Neo-literates and Community Towards Witch Crafts

Group	Agree	Don't know	Disagree	Total
Neo-literates	52	135	32	219
	23.7%	61.6%	14.6%	100.0%
Community	44	107	25	176
	25.0%	60.8%	14.2%	100.0%
Total	96	242	57	395
	24.3%	61.3%	14.4%	100.0%

Chi-square value = 0.086 Not Significant

Medical Awareness

Health is one of the important aspects that deserve proper attention of all. Health is wealth and if health is lost in this condition everything is lost. So people have to pay more attention towards keeping up good health. The rural people should basically possess knowledge about medical aspects, so that they will be able to pay necessary attention towards the health of the family member. In the context of adult education, attention is paid towards literacy, functionality and awareness. Further, to strengthen the awareness aspects post – literacy and continuing education materials are provided on health and other aspects. With all these efforts the health knowledge of the people in rural areas is lagging behind. Hence it is necessary to probe into the health knowledge of rural people.

Good health, habits and practices always makes people to think in right direction and act. This one way helps to lead better family life to be responsible citizens and also do their duty with vision and utility. This will help in national development. Health has an impact on the socio-psychological factors of human being.

Facilities Provided by the Government

Table 6.32: Opinion of the Neo-literates and Community Members Towards Facilities Provided by the Government

Group	Yes	Some Extent	No	Total
Neo-literates	140	61	18	219
	63.9%	27.9%	8.2%	100.0%
Community	108	42	26	176
	61.4%	23.9%	14.8%	100.0%
Total	248	103	44	395
	62.8%	26.1%	11.1%	100.0%

Chi-square value = 4.46 Not Significant

The investigator carried out on the awareness on medical facilities provided by the government, 248 (62.8%) of the sample respondents noticed that they are aware of medical facilities, out of 248 members, 140 (63.9%) of them are neo-literates and 108 (61.4%) of them are community members, only 44 (11.1%) of the sample members are not aware of the medical facilities provided by the government and 18 (8.2%) of the members are neo literates and 26 (14.8%) are community members and they have no idea and the chi-square value is 4.46 which is not significant.

Using the Facilities

Table 6.33: Opinion of the Neo-literates and Community Members Towards Using the Facilities

Group	Yes	Some Extent	No	Total
Neo-literates	201	6	12	219
	91.8%	2.7%	5.5%	100.0%
Community	120	50	6	176
	68.2%	28.4%	3.4%	100.0%
Total	321	56	18	395
	81.3%	14.2%	4.6%	100.0%

Chi-square value = 52.957 Significant at 0.01 level

With regard to the using the facilities, 321 (81.3%) of the sample respondents are utilized. Out of 321 members, 201 (91.8%) of the neo-literates and 120 (68.2%) of the community members and 18 (4.6%) of sample members are having no idea in this regard. Out of 18, 12 (5.5%) are neo-literates and 6 (3.4%) are community members and 56 (14.2%) of the sample members are to some extent able to use the medical facilities provided by the government. Chi-square value is 52.957 which is significant at 0.01 level.

Vaccination

Table 6.34: Awareness of the Neo-literates and Community Members Towards Vaccination

Group	Yes	No Idea	No	Total
Neo-literates	159	45	15	219
	72.6%	20.5%	6.8%	100.0%
Community	104	46	26	176
	59.1%	26.1%	14.8%	100.0%
Total	263	91	41	395
	66.6%	23.0%	10.4%	100.0%

Chi-square value = 9.9 Significant at 0.01 level

With regard to the vaccination, 263 (66.6%) of the sample members are vaccinated, out of 263 members, 159 (72.6%) of them are neo-literates and 104 (59.1%) of them are community members and only 41 (10.4%) of the sample respondents are not vaccinated, out of 41 members, 15 (6.8%) members are neo-literates and 26 (14.8%) members are community members and chi-square value is 9.9 which is significant at 0.01 level.

Regard to the vaccination, 263 (66.6%) of the sample members are vaccinated, further the investigator enquired about who are the advised to you to vaccination, 35 (22.0%) of the neo-literates and 20 (19.2%) of the community members are noticed that they are self advised, in case of 61 (38.4%) of the neo-literates and 37 (35.6%) of community members are informed that the Prerak has advised, 6 (3.8%) of the neo-literates informed the health department officials are also advised.

Advisor

Table 6.35: Advisor of Neo-literates and Community Members Towards Vaccination

Sl. No.	Person (N=263)	Neo-literates		Community	
		N	%	N	%
1.	Self	35	22.0	20	19.2
2.	Prerak of the CEC	61	38.4	37	35.6
3.	Elders in the house	34	21.4	35	33.7
4.	Caste/village elders	23	14.5	12	11.5
5.	Health department officials	6	3.8	0	0.0

Awareness and Benefits of Rural Development Programmes of Neo-Literates and Community Members

In India, development, definitional and conceptually, denotes progress-social, economic, educational, cultural, scientific and technological-brought about by planned programmed efforts to inaugurate an era of orderly and peaceful transformation of a society in a constitutionally desired direction. The unfortunate fact, however, is that despite considerable progress, there have emerged marked disparities in income and in the poor people's access to resources, economic opportunities and social services. While everyone considers economic development as a priority condition and as essential instrument of social trans-function, nobody thinks that it alone can bring about social transformation and a desired vision of development. The social tensions that we are faced with are largely the result of our single-minded pursuit to economic growth model of development, putting the broader mandate of social transformation- with social justice, equity, equality of opportunity and poor people's empowerment and participation in developmental efforts as its salient characteristics in to the background.

Jalayagnam

Jalayagnam, as the word speaks is a ritual for water utilisation. It has been implemented by Hon. Chief Minister of Andhra Pradesh Dr. Y.S. Rajasekhar Reddy as an election promise to the cultivating people of state to bring 73 lakh acres under irrigation in five years. This project accords the highest priority for the development of irrigation infrastructure, particularly in backward and drought prone areas by taking up this programme in a big way. Jalayagnam includes a number of irrigation projects by construction of reservoirs and lift irrigation systems for lifting water from major rivers, particularly from Godavari to provide immediate irrigation benefits.

Awareness of Jalayagnam

Table 6.36: Awareness of the Neo-literates and Community Members Towards Jalayagnam Programme

Group	Yes	Some Extent	No	Total
Neo-literates	139	53	27	219
	63.5%	24.2%	12.3%	100.0%
Community	98	38	40	176
	55.7%	21.6%	22.7%	100.0%
Total	237	91	67	395
	60.0%	23.0%	17.0%	100.0%

Chi-square value = 7.496 Significant at 0.01 level

With regard to the awareness of the programme Jalayagnam of the both beneficiaries and non-beneficiaries, majority 237 (60.0%) of the of the sample respondents reported that they knew about the programme, out of 237 members, 139 (63.5%) of them are neo-literates and 98 (55.7%) of them are community members, 91 (23.0%) of the members got the information some extent and 67 (17.0%) of the sample respondents are not aware of the programme and the chi-square value is 7.496 which is significant at 0.01 level.

Benefits of Jalayagnam

Table 6.37: Benefits of the Neo-literates and Community Members Towards Jalayagnam

Group		Benefited	On Process	Not Benefited	Total
Neo-literates		183	26	10	219
		83.6%	11.9%	4.6%	100.0%
Community		126	38	12	176
		71.6%	21.6%	6.8%	100.0%
Total		309	64	22	395
		78.2%	16.2%	5.6%	100.0%

Chi-square value = 8.364 Significant at 0.1 level

An attempt has been made to identify the benefits derived from programmes. With regard to the benefit of the Jalayagnam programme, 309 (78.2%) of the sample respondents have benefited. Out of 309 members, 183 (83.6%) of them are neo-literates and 126 (71.6%) of them are community members. And 64 (16.2%) of sample members are in the process of benefit. 22 (5.6%) of the sample members are do not benefited and chi-square value is 8.364 which is significant at 0.01 level.

INDIRAMMA House

The INDIRAMMA scheme (Integrated Development In Rural Areas and Model Municipal Areas) which involves all villagers and aims at integrated rural development covering the various facets of the main stream development process by providing basic infrastructure. Bringing various welfare schemes like housing, drinking water, link roads, medical care, primary education, nutrition and old age pensions under one roof is the main objective of the scheme. The uniqueness of this scheme lies in the reach it has to individuals as well as groups.

Awareness of INDIRAMMA Houses

Table 6.38: Awareness of the Neo-literates and Community Members Towards INDIRAMMA Houses

Group	Yes	Some Extent	No	Total
Neo-literates	140	51	28	219
	63.9%	23.3%	12.8%	100.0%
Community	108	36	32	176
	61.4%	20.5%	18.2%	100.0%
Total	248	87	60	395
	62.8%	22.0%	15.2%	100.0%

Chi-square value = 2.328 Significant at 0.05 level

With regard to the awareness of the INDIRAMMA Houses programme of the both neo-literates and community, majority 248 (62.8%) of the of the sample respondents reported that they knew about the programme, out of 248 members, 140 (63.9%) of them are neo-literates and 108 (61.4%) of them are community members, 87 (22.0%) of the members got the information some extent and 60 (15.2%) of the sample respondents are not aware of the programme and the chi-square value is 2.328 which is significant at 0.05 level.

Benefits of INDIRAMMA Houses

Table 6.39: Benefits of the Neo-literates and Community Members Towards INDIRAMMA Houses

Group	Benefited	On Process	Not Benefited	Total
Neo-literates	140	40	39	219
	63.9%	18.3%	17.8%	100.0%
Community	92	28	56	176
	52.3%	15.9%	31.8%	100.0%
Total	232	68	95	395
	58.7%	17.2%	24.1%	100.0%

Chi-square value = 10.535 Significant 0.01 level

With regard to the benefit of INDIRAMMA house, 232 (58.7%) of the sample respondents are benefited. Out of 232 members 140 (63.9%) of the neo-literates and 92 (52.3%) of the community members are benefited and 95 (24.1%) of sample members are not benefited. 68 (17.2%) of the sample members are in the process of the benefit, out of 68 members, 40 (18.3%) of the learners and 28 (15.9%) of the community members and the chi-square value is 10.535 which is significant at 0.01 level.

Rice for Rs. 2/- per KG

The objective was to reduce poverty levels in rural villages by providing staple food at prices below market prices. It was felt that such an initiative helped the poorest of the poor and destitute families by providing them at least two morsels of food every day while they strived for livelihood wages as farm labour. As part of the effort the AP government is providing rice at Rs. Two per kg to 1.72 crore BPL card holders, nearly 22 lakh APL (above poverty level) pink card holders and beneficiaries of the AAY (Antyodaya Anna Yojana) scheme.

Awareness of Rs. 2/- per KG

Table 6.40: Awareness of the Neo-literates and Community Members Towards Rice for Rs. 2/- per KG

Group	Yes	Some Extent	No	Total
Neo- literates	122	61	36	219
	55.7%	27.9%	16.4%	100.0%
Community	79	40	57	176
	44.9%	22.7%	32.4%	100.0%
Total	201	101	93	395
	50.9%	25.6%	23.5%	100.0%

Chi-square value = 13.79 Significant 0.01 level

With regard to the awareness of the rice for Rs. 2/- per KG programme of the both participants and non-participants, majority 201 (50.9%) of the sample respondents reported that they knew about the programme, out of 201 members, 122 (55.7%) of them are neo-literates and 79 (44.9%) of them are community members, 101 (25.6%) of the members got the information to some extent and 93 (23.5%) of the sample respondents are not aware of the programme and the chi-square value is 13.79 which is significant at 0.01 level.

Benefits of Rs. 2/- per KG

Table 6.41: Benefits of the Neo-literates and Community Members Towards Rice for Rs. 2/- per KG

Group	Benefited	On Process	Not Benefited	Total
Neo-literates	208	8	3	219
	95.0%	3.7%	1.4%	100.0%
Community	149	11	16	176
	84.7%	6.3%	9.1%	100.0%
Total	357	19	19	395
	90.4%	4.8%	4.8%	100.0%

Chi-square value = 14.611 Significant 0.01 level

With regard to the benefit of rice for Rs. 2/- per KG, 357 (90.4%) of the sample respondents are benefited with this regard, out of 357 sample members, 208 (95.0%) of them are neo-literates and 149 (84.7%) of them are community members are fully benefited, 19 (4.8%) of the sample respondents are in the process of benefit and same number of respondents are not benefited and chi-square value 14.611 which is significant at 0.01 level.

Pensions for Needy People

The Government of India introduced National Social Assistance Programme (NSAP) with effect from 15th August 1995 with a view to support minimum needs of the poor destitute having little or no regular means of subsistence from their own source of income or through financial support from their family members. One of the components is National Old

Age Pension scheme. Under the scheme poor destitute old aged persons of 65 and above are extended support at the rate of Rs.75/- per pensioner per month.

The Government of Andhra Pradesh decided to bring the disbursement of all pensions under one umbrella by transferring the widow pensions from Social Welfare Department and disabled pensions from Disabled Welfare Department to the Rural Development Department with effect from 1st April 2006. Old Age, Weavers, Widows and Disabled pensions are major criteria.

Awareness of Pensions for Needy People Programme

Table 6.42: Awareness of the Neo-literates and Community Members Towards Pensions for Needy People

Group	Yes	Some Extent	No	Total
Neo-literates	107	96	16	219
	48.9%	43.8%	7.3%	100.0%
Community	101	8	67	176
	57.4%	4.5%	38.1%	100.0%
Total	208	104	83	395
	52.7%	26.3%	21.0%	100.0%

Chi-square value = 102.506 Significant at 0.01 level

With regard to the awareness of the pensions for needy people programme of the both beneficiaries and non-beneficiaries, majority 208 (52.7%) of the sample respondents reported that they knew about the programme, out 208 members, 107 (48.9%) of them are neo-literates and 101 (57.4%) of them are community members, 104 (26.3%) of the members got the information to some extent and 83 (21.0%) of the sample respondents are not aware of the programme and the chi-square value is 102.506 which is significant at 0.01 level.

From table 6.43, 242 (61.3%) of the sample respondents are noticed that the benefit of pensions for needy people are benefited, and 57 (14.4%) of the members are in the process of benefit and only 96 (24.3%) of the respondents are not yet benefited, and chi-square value is 12.236 which is significant at 0.01 level.

Benefits of Pensions for Needy People

Table 6.43: Benefits of the Neo-literates and Community Members Towards Pensions for Needy People

Group		Benefited	On Process	Not Benefited	Total
Neo- literates		149	31	39	219
		68.0%	14.2%	17.8%	100.0%
Community		93	26	57	176
		52.8%	14.8%	32.4%	100.0%
Total		242	57	96	395
		61.3%	14.4%	24.3%	100.0%

Chi-square value = 12.236 Significant 0.01 level

Rajeev Arogya Sree

The name of the scheme shall be "Rajiv Aarogya Sri Community Health Insurance Scheme". The State government of Andhra Pradesh to provide medical assistance to families living below poverty line for the treatment of serious ailments such as cancer, kidney failure, heart and neurosurgical diseases etc., requiring hospitalization and surgery. Available network of government hospitals do not have the requisite equipment or the facility or the specialist pool of doctors to meet the state wide requirement for the treatment of such diseases. Large proportions of people, especially below poverty line borrow money or sell assets to pay for hospitalization. Presently many people suffering from such diseases are approaching the Government to provide financial assistance to meet hospitalization expenses for surgical procedures.

With regard to the awareness of the Rajeev Arogya Sree programme of the both neo-literates and community members, majority 195 (49.4%) of the of the sample respondents reported that they knew about the programme, out of 195 members, 167 (76.3%) of them are neo-literates and 28 (15.9%) of them are community members, 57 (14.4%) of the members got the information to some extent and 143 (36.2%) of the sample respondents are not aware of the programme and the chi-square value is 159.42 which is significant at 0.01 level.

Awareness of Rajeev Arogya Sree Programme

Table 6.44: Awareness of the Neo-literates and Community Members Towards Rajeev Arogya Sree

Group	Yes	Some Extent	No	Total
Neo-literates	167	28	24	219
	76.3%	12.8%	11.0%	100.0%
Community	28	29	119	176
	15.9%	16.5%	67.6%	100.0%
Total	195	57	143	395
	49.4%	14.4%	36.2%	100.0%

Chi-square value = 159.42 Significant at 0.01 level

Benefits of Rajeev Arogya Sree

Table 6.45: Benefits of the Neo-literates and Community Members Towards Rajeev Arogya Sree

Group	Benefited	On Process	Not Benefited	Total
Neo-literates	140	61	18	219
	63.9%	27.9%	8.2%	100.0%
Community	108	42	26	176
	61.4%	23.9%	14.8%	100.0%
Total	248	103	44	395
	62.8%	26.1%	11.1%	100.0%

Chi-square value = 4.46 Not Significant

With regard to the benefit of the Rajeev Arogya Sree programme, 248 (62.8%) of the sample respondents are benefited. Out of 248 members 140 (63.9%) of them are neo-literates and 108 (61.4%) of them are community members are benefited and 103 (26.1%) of sample members are in the process of benefit. 44 (11.1%) of the sample members are do not benefited and chi-square value is 4.46 which is not significant.

Free Electricity

To mitigate hardship faced by farmers in the State of Andhra Pradesh, the State Government has announced Free Power Policy to all the agricultural consumers on 14th May 2004. This policy not only ensures economic sustenance of the needy farmers but it also encourages more efficient usage of power through adoption of energy conservation measures by the agricultural consumers.

Awareness of Free Electricity

Table 6.46: Awareness of the Neo-literates and Community Members Towards Free Electricity for BPL (Agricultural)

Group	Yes	Some Extent	No	Total
Neo-literates	96	107	16	219
	43.8%	48.9%	7.3%	100.0%
Community	9	112	55	176
	5.1%	63.6%	31.3%	100.0%
Total	105	219	71	395
	26.6%	55.4%	18.0%	100.0%

Chi-square value = 90.008 Significant at 0.01 level

With regard to the awareness of the free electricity for bellow poverty line for agricultural occupants programme of the both participants and non-participants, 105 (26.6%) of the sample respondents reported that they knew about the programme, out 105 members, 96 (43.8%) of them are neo-literates and 9 (5.1%) of them are community members, 219 (55.4%) of the members got the information some extent and 71 (18.0%) of the sample respondents are not aware of the programme and the chi-square value is 90.008 which is significant at 0.01 level.

Benefits of Free Electricity

Table 6.47: Benefits of the Neo-literates and Community Members Towards Free Electricity for BPL (Agricultural)

Group		Benefited	On Process	Not Benefited	Total
Neo-literates		201	6	12	219
		91.8%	2.7%	5.5%	100.0%
Community		120	50	6	176
		68.2%	28.4%	3.4%	100.0%
Total		321	56	18	395
		81.3%	14.2%	4.6%	100.0%

Chi-square value = 52.957 Significant 0.01 level

With regard to the benefit of free electricity for BPL, 321 (81.3%) of the sample respondents are benefited with this regard, out of 321 sample members, 201 (91.8%) of them are neo-literates and 120 (68.2%) of them are community members are fully benefited, 56 (14.2%) of the sample respondents are in the process of benefit and 18 (4.6%) of the sample respondents are not yet benefited and chi-square value 52.957 which is significant at 0.01 level.

Indira Kranthi Patham (Rs. 0.25 ps interest rate)

The main objective of Indira Kranthi Patham (IKP) is to eradicate abject poverty in the rural areas of the State and to enable the poor in 22 rural districts of Andhra Pradesh to improve their livelihoods and quality of life. This objective is sought to be achieved through the active participation of the poor women and through their self-help groups and their federations. The Project gives special focus to 29.86 lakh poorest of the poor families. After formation of new government in 2004, Dr. Y.S. Rajasekhar Reddy became a chief minister of Andhra Pradesh then he reduced the interest rate to three per cent. This is known as Pavala Vaddi.

Awareness of Indira Kranthi Pathakam

Table 6.48: Awareness of the Neo-literates and Community Members Towards Indira Kranthi Pathakam

Group	Yes	Some Extent	No	Total
Neo-literates	113	96	10	219
	51.6%	43.8%	4.6%	100.0%
Community	130	20	26	176
	73.9%	11.4%	14.8%	100.0%
Total	243	116	36	395
	61.5%	29.4%	9.1%	100.0%

Chi-square value = 54.053 Significant at 0.01 level

With regard to the awareness of the Indira Kranthi Pathakam programme of the both neo-literates and community, majority 243 (61.5%) of the of the sample respondents reported that they knew about the programme, out of 243 members, 113 (51.6%) of them are neo-literates and 130 (73.9%) of them are community members, 116 (29.4%) of the members got the information to some extent and 36 (9.1%) of the sample respondents are not aware of the programme and the chi-square value is 54.053 which is significant at 0.01 level.

With regard to the benefit of Indira Kranthi Pathakam, 263 (66.6%) of the sample respondents are benefited. Out of 263 members 159 (72.6%) of the neo-literates and 104 (59.1%) of the community members are benefited and 91 (23.0%) of sample members are in the process benefit. 41 (10.4%) of the sample members are not yet benefited, out of 41 members, 15 (6.8%) of the learners and 26 (14.8%) of the community members and the chi-square value is 9.9 which is significant at 0.01 level.

Benefits of Indira Kranthi Pathakam

Table 6.49: Benefits of the Neo-literates and Community Members Towards Indira Kranthi Pathakam

Group	Benefited	On Process	Not Benefited	Total
Neo-literates	159	45	15	219
	72.6%	20.5%	6.8%	100.0%
Community	104	46	26	176
	59.1%	26.1%	14.8%	100.0%
Total	263	91	41	395
	66.6%	23.0%	10.4%	100.0%

Chi-square value = 9.9 Significant 0.01 level

Employment Guarantee Scheme

National Rural Employment Guarantee Act (MGNREGA). The Act aims at enhancing livelihood security of households in rural areas of the country by providing at least one hundred days of guaranteed wage employment in a financial year to every household whose adult members volunteer to do unskilled manual work. This a historic initiative mounted by the present central Government. Government of India contributes 90% and the balance 10% is contributed by the State Government. It guarantees employment for 100 days in a year to every rural household near their habitation. The guaranteed employment to anyone and every one across the country has been attempted for the first time since independence in our country. Guaranteed manual employment to unskilled labour , equal wages for equal work for men, as well as women, elimination of middlemen as well as heavy machinery from the works so executed and tracking every rupee from the headquarters all the way up to the worksite so as to maximize transparency and minimize leakages are the avowed objectives of the programme.

Awareness of MGNREGP

Table 6.50: Awareness of the Neo-literates and Community Members Towards Employment Guarantee Scheme (MGNREGP)

Group	Yes	Some Extent	No	Total
Neo-literates	74	119	26	219
	33.8%	54.3%	11.9%	100.0%
Community	23	128	25	176
	13.1%	72.7%	14.2%	100.0%
Total	97	247	51	395
	24.6%	62.5%	12.9%	100.0%

Chi-square value = 22.751 Significant at 0.01 level

With regard to the awareness of the Employment guarantee sachem programme of the both beneficiaries and non-beneficiaries, 97 (24.6%) of the of the sample respondents reported that they knew about the programme, out of 97 members, 74 (33.8%) of them are neo-literates and 23 (13.1%) of them are community members, 247 (62.5%) of the members got the information to some extent and 51 (12.9%) of the sample respondents are not aware of the programme and the chi-square value is 22.751 which is significant at 0.01 level.

With regard to the benefit of the employment guarantee scheme, 294 (74.4%) of the sample respondents are benefited. Out of 294 members 185 (84.5%) of the neo-literates and 109 (61.9%) of the community members are benefited and 52 (13.2%) of sample members are in the process of benefit. 49 (12.4%) of the sample members are do not benefited and chi-square value is 40.553 which is significant at 0.01 level.

Debt Waiver for Farmers

Debt waiver package may not benefit cash crop farmers The Rs 60,000-crore farm loan waiver package may not bring cheer to all farmers. Those growing plantation crops like coffee and engaging in agriculture-allied activities like weaving, processing of food materials and floriculture, may not get any benefit from the package. Long-duration crops, including plantation crops, are covered under investment credit and are not eligible for the 7% subsidized interest rate. They attract normal rate of interest, of about 10-11%, a National Bank for Agriculture and Rural Development (NABARD) official said. In addition, a farmer often avails non-farm credit for allied activities to supplement his livelihood. This loan component again would not be waived off as per the new package, sources said.

Benefits of Employment Guarantee Scheme

Table 6.51: Benefits of the Neo-literates and Community Members Towards Employment Guarantee Scheme (NREGP)

Group	Benefited	On Process	Not Benefited	Total
Neo-literates	185	8	26	219
	84.5%	3.7%	11.9%	100.0%
Community	109	44	23	176
	61.9%	25.0%	13.1%	100.0%
Total	294	52	49	395
	74.4%	13.2%	12.4%	100.0%

Chi-square value = 40.553 Significant 0.01 level

With regard to the awareness of the debt waiver for farmers programme of the both participants and non-participants, majority 235 (59.5%) of the sample respondents reported that they knew about the programme, out of 235 members, 137 (62.6%) of them are neo-literates and 98 (55.7%) of them are community members, 107 (27.1%) of the members got the information to some extent and 53 (13.4%) of the sample respondents are not aware of the programme and the chi-square value is 3.056 which is not significant.

Awareness of Debt Waiver for Farmers

Table 6.52: Awareness of the Neo-literates and Community Members Towards Debt Waiver for Farmers

Group	Yes	Some Extent	No	Total
Neo-literates	137	58	24	219
	62.6%	26.5%	11.0%	100.0%
Community	98	49	29	176
	55.7%	27.8%	16.5%	100.0%
Total	235	107	53	395
	59.5%	27.1%	13.4%	100.0%

Chi-square value = 3.056 Not significant

Benefits of Debt waiver for farmers programme

Table 6.53: Benefits of the Neo-literates and Community Members Towards Debt Waiver for Farmers

Group	Benefited	On Process	Not Benefited	Total
Neo-literates	135	60	24	219
	61.6%	27.4%	11.0%	100.0%
Community	99	50	27	176
	56.3%	28.4%	15.3%	100.0%
Total	234	110	51	395
	59.2%	27.8%	12.9%	100.0%

Chi-square value = 1.966 Not Significant

With regard to the benefit of debt waiver for farmers, majority 234 (59.2%) of the sample respondents are benefited. Out of 234 members 135 (61.6%) of the neo-literates and 99 (56.3%) of the community members are benefited and 51 (12.9%) of sample members are not benefited. 110 (27.8%) of the sample members are in the process of the benefit, out of 110 members, 60 (27.4%) of the learners and 50 (28.4%) of the community members and the chi-square value is 1.966 which is not significant.

Social Welfare/Rural Development

The main objectives of the Social Welfare Department are Educational advancement, Socio-Economic development, Welfare and Protection of Scheduled Castes and implementation of programmes of Social Security like Homes for orphan children, rehabilitation of jogins, bonded labourers and scavengers, pensions to poor widows and house-sites to weaker sections.

Awareness of Social Welfare/Rural Development

Table 6.54: Awareness of the Neo-literates and Community Members Towards Social Welfare/Rural Development

Group	Yes	Some Extent	No	Total
Neo-literates	76	125	18	219
	34.7%	57.1%	8.2%	100.0%
Community	44	107	25	176
	25.0%	60.8%	14.2%	100.0%
Total	120	232	43	395
	30.4%	58.7%	10.9%	100.0%

Chi-square value = 6.465 Significant at 0.05 level

With regard to the awareness of the social welfare/rural development programme of the both neo-literates and community, 120 (30.4%) of the sample respondents reported that they knew about the programme, out of 120 members, 76 (34.7%) of them are neo-literates and 44 (25.0%) of them are community members, 232 (58.7%) of the members got the information to some extent and 43 (10.9%) of the sample respondents are not aware of the programme and the chi-square value is 6.456 which is significant at 0.05 level.

With regard to the benefit of social welfare/rural development programmes, 283 (71.6%) of the sample respondents have benefited in this regard, out 284 sample members, 174 (79.5%) of them are neo-literates and 109 (61.9%)

of them are community members are fully benefited, 62 (15.7%) of the sample respondents are in the process of benefit and 50 (12.7%) of the sample respondents not yet benefited and chi-square value 21.729 which is significant at 0.01 level.

Benefits of Social welfare/Rural Development

Table 6.55: Benefits of the Neo-literates and Community Members Towards Social Welfare/Rural Development

Group		Benefited	On Process	Not Benefited	Total
Neo-literates		174	18	27	219
		79.5%	8.2%	12.3%	100.0%
Community		109	44	23	176
		61.9%	25.0%	13.1%	100.0%
Total		283	62	50	395
		71.6%	15.7%	12.7%	100.0%

Chi-square value = 21.729 Significant 0.01 level

Pasu Kranthi

In order to improve the economic status of the BPL families who have access to land, 'Pashu Kranthi Pathakam' was launched in 2007-08. In this programme, two high yielding milch animals at one year are provided on subsidy to the BPL families with special reference to farmers belonging to scheduled castes schedules tribes and backward classes. In this programme *sheep insurance programme* is highly populated to cushion the adverse impact upon the livelihood during epidemics - i.e. Sheep reared by poorer sections of the society belonging to backward classes, Government have been taken up Sheep Insurance Programme since 2006-07.

With regard to the awareness on the Pasu Kranthi programme of the both beneficiaries and non-beneficiaries, 157 (39.7%) of the sample respondents reported that they knew about the programme, out 157 members, 108 (49.3%) of them are neo-literates and 49 (27.8%) of them are community members, 201 (50.9%) of the members got the information some extent and 37 (9.4%) of the sample respondents are not aware of the programme and the chi-square value is 29.888 which is significant at 0.01 level.

Awareness of Pasu Kranthi Programme

Table 6.56: Awareness of the Neo-literates and Community Members Towards Pasu Kranthi

Group	Yes	Some Extent	No	Total
Neo-literates	108	103	8	219
	49.3%	47.0%	3.7%	100.0%
Community	49	98	29	176
	27.8%	55.7%	16.5%	100.0%
Total	157	201	37	395
	39.7%	50.9%	9.4%	100.0%

Chi-square value = 29.888 Significant at 0.01 level

Benefits of Pasu Kranthi Programme

Table 6.57: Benefits of the Neo-literates and Community Members Towards Pasu Kranthi

Group	Benefited	On Process	Not Benefited	Total
Neo-literates	186	25	8	219
	84.9%	11.4%	3.7%	100.0%
Community	112	41	23	176
	63.6%	23.3%	13.1%	100.0%
Total	298	66	31	395
	75.4%	16.7%	7.8%	100.0%

Chi-square value = 25.129 Significant 0.01 level

With regard to the benefit of the Pasu Kranthi programme, 298 (75.4%) of the sample respondents have been benefited. Out of 298 members 186 (84.9%) of the neo-literates and 112 (63.6%) of the community members are benefited and 66 (16.7%) of sample members are in the process of benefit. 31 (7.8%) of the sample members are not benefited and chi-square value is 25.129 which is significant at 0.01 level.

Debt Waiver for Socially Deprived Programme

This programme is movement for artisans/skilled workers/farm sector by helping to uplift their sills, supply of equipment and waiving loans. The proposed loan waiver and debt relief package provides for complete write-off of all outstanding debt held on December 31, 2007 to scheduled commercial banks and co-operative societies, of small and marginal farmers, that is those holding less than 2 hectares of land. For all other farmers, there will be a one-time settlement for the outstanding debt, whereby 25 per cent will be written off if the farmer repays 75 per cent. It should be noted that currently the amount of unpaid loans of small and marginal farmers currently held by the scheduled commercial banks is estimated to be around 20,500 corers.

Awareness of Debt Waiver for Socially deprived

Table 6.58: Awareness of the Neo-literates and Community Members Towards Debt Waiver for Socially Deprived

Group	Yes	Some Extent	No	Total
Neo-literates	161	40	18	219
	73.5%	18.3%	8.2%	100.0%
Community	107	44	25	176
	60.8%	25.0%	14.2%	100.0%
Total	268	84	43	395
	67.8%	21.3%	10.9%	100.0%

Chi-square value = 7.62 Significant at 0.05 level

With regard to the awareness on debt waiver for socially deprived programme of the both beneficiaries and non-beneficiaries, majority 268 (67.8%) of the sample respondents reported that they knew about the programme, out 268 members, 161 (73.5%) of them are neo-literates and 107 (60.8%) of them are community members, 84 (21.3%) of the members got the information to some extent and 43 (10.9%) of the sample respondents are not aware of the programme and the chi-square value is 7.62 which is significant at 0.05 level.

Benefits of Debt Waiver for Socially Deprived

Table 6.59: Benefits of the Neo-literates and Community Members Towards Debt Waiver for Socially Deprived

Group		Benefited	On Process	Not Benefited	Total
Neo-literates		200	8	11	219
		91.3%	3.7%	5.0%	100.0%
Community		110	45	21	176
		62.5%	25.6%	11.9%	100.0%
Total		310	53	32	395
		78.5%	13.4%	8.1%	100.0%

Chi-square value = 51.008 Significant 0.01 level

With regard to the benefit of the debt waiver for socially deprived programme, 310 (78.5%) of the sample respondents are benefited. Out of 310 members 200 (91.3%) of the neo-literates and 110 (62.5%) of the community members are benefited and 53 (13.4%) of sample members are in the process of benefit. 32 (8.1%) of the sample members have not yet benefited and chi-square value is 51.008 which is significant at 0.01 level.

Service of 104/108

The introduction of innovative programmes like the Rajiv Aarogyasri augurs well for the state as such initiatives will help in making healthcare delivery system of the state more efficient and effective in the years to come. Since Rajiv Aarogyasri covers emergency ambulance services like 104, 108 and community health insurance, it offers all the critical healthcare services meant for the poor families in remote, interior and tribal areas all over the state. Since the community health insurance scheme involves corporate hospitals significantly & the EMRI & HMRI are public private partnership institutes, one unnoticed major gain from Rajiv Aarogyasri is that the respective strengths of the public, private & non-profit sectors are synergized in the healthcare domain to the benefit of all, particularly the vulnerable sections of the population dwelling below the poverty line

Awareness of 104/108 Service Programme

Table 6.60: Awareness of the Neo-literates and Community Members Towards Service of 104/108

Group	Yes	Some Extent	No	Total
Neo-literates	85	126	8	219
	38.8%	57.5%	3.7%	100.0%
Community	44	119	13	176
	25.0%	67.6%	7.4%	100.0%
Total	129	245	21	395
	32.7%	62.0%	5.3%	100.0%

Chi-square value = 9.857 Significant 0.01 level

With regard to the awareness on services of 104/108 programme of the both participants and non-participants, 129 (32.7%) of the sample respondents reported that they knew about the programme, out of 129 members, 85 (38.8%) of them are neo-literates and 44 (25.0%) of them are community members, 245 (62.0%) of the members are got the information to some extent and 21 (5.3%) of the sample respondents are not aware of the programme and the chi-square value is 9.857 which is significant at 0.01 level.

With regard to the benefit of services of 104 and 108, 302 (76.5%) of the sample respondents are benefited, out of 302 members 181 (82.6%) of the neo-literates and 121 (68.8%) of the community members are benefited and 93 (23.5%) of sample members are not yet benefited, out of 93 members, 38

(17.4%) of the learners and 55 (31.3%) of the community members and the chi-square value is 10.471 which is significant at 0.01 level.

Benefits of 104/108 Service Programme

Table 6.61: Benefits of the Neo-literates and Community Members Towards Service of 104/108

Group	Benefited	Not Benefited	Total
Neo-literates	181	38	219
	82.6%	17.4%	100.0%
Community	121	55	176
	68.8%	31.3%	100.0%
Total	302	93	395
	76.5%	23.5%	100.0%

Chi-square value = 10.471 Significant 0.01 level

Family Planning

The Government of India, created a separate Department of family planning in the year 1966 in the ministry of Health, Family planning and urban development. The programme is being implemented through the state Governments as centrally sponsored scheme with full financial assistance. At present the programme is being implemented from the centre and the state level down to the village communities as a part of normal health services. The programme envisages free distribution of Nirodh (Condom) and oral pills, besides sterilization of males (Vasectomy) and females (tubectomy) are done through Government hospitals and private practitioners. The persons undergoing sterilization are given rewards in cash. Besides these a broad – based programme of education and motivation is in operation all over the country through mass media and other channels of communication. Family planning pamphlets and leaflets are distributed free in towns as well as in villages.

Awareness of Family Planning Programme

Table 6.62: Awareness of the Neo-literates and Community Members Towards Family Planning

Group	Yes	Some Extent	No	Total
Neo-literates	165	40	14	219
	75.3%	18.3%	6.4%	100.0%
Community	123	46	7	176
	69.9%	26.1%	4.0%	100.0%
Total	288	86	21	395
	72.9%	21.8%	5.3%	100.0%

Chi-square value = 4.246 Not Significant

With regard to the awareness on the family planning programme of the both beneficiaries and non-beneficiaries, majority 288 (72.9%) of the sample respondents reported that they knew about the programme, out of 288 members, 165 (75.3%) of them are neo-literates and 123 (69.9%) of them are community members, 86 (21.8%) of the members got the information to some extent and 21 (5.3%) of the sample respondents are not aware of the programme and the chi-square value is 4.246 which is not significant.

With regard to the benefit of family planning, 293 (74.2%) of the sample respondents are benefited with this regard, out of 293 sample members, 199 (90.9%) of them are neo-literates and 94 (53.4%) of them are community members are fully benefited, 61 (15.4%) of the sample respondents are in the process of benefit and 41 (10.4%) of respondents are not yet benefited and chi-square value is 74.07 which is significant at 0.01 level.

Mode of Accession

Awareness is the key for human resource development and awareness facilitates accessing information. In view of this, enquiry has been made regarding the mode of accessing information. Source of information is one of the factor to development for individuals, in this regard the investigator enquired about how they are able acquire the knowledge, the multiple answers are gathered for the purpose of the study, the investigator has given six options and they are 1. Prerak, 2. Sarpanch, 3. Village Elders, 4. Political Leaders, 5.Family Members and 6. Government officials.

Benefits of Family Planning Programme

Table 6.63: Benefits of the Neo-literates and Community Members Towards Family Planning

Group	Benefited	On Process	Not Benefited	Total
Neo-literates	199	8	12	219
	90.9%	3.7%	5.5%	100.0%
Community	94	53	29	176
	53.4%	30.1%	16.5%	100.0%
Total	293	61	41	395
	74.2%	15.4%	10.4%	100.0%

Chi-square value = 74.07 Significant 0.01 level

With regard to the Jalayagam Programme, Majority 250 (63.29) of the sample respondent reported that they learned through the Preraks, out of 250 members, 200 (91.32%) are neo-literates and 50 (28.41%) are community members, 210 (53.16%) of the sample respondents reported that the political leaders have also propagated about this programme. In this case of 140 (35.44%) of the sample respondents it was noticed that the Government Officials are also involved and have propagated to this programme, out of 140 members, 68 (31.05%) of them are neo-literates and 72 (40.91%) of them are community members.

Majority 300 (75.95%) of the sample respondents noticed that the Prerak of the Continuing Education Programme explained about IDIRAMMA Housing Programme, 275 (69.62%) of the sample respondents noticed that the political leaders have also explained about this programme. In case of 250 (63.29%) of the sample respondents reported that they learned through village panchayat Sarpanch.

Table 6.64: Mode of Accession on the Details on Development/ Welfare Schemes

Sl.No.	Programmes	Respondent	1	2	3	4	5	6
1.	Jalayagnam	Neo-literate	200	100	125	95	100	68
			91.32	45.66	57.08	43.38	45.66	31.05
		Community	50	100	50	115	90	72
			28.41	56.82	28.41	65.34	51.14	40.91
2.	INDIRAMMA Houses	Neo-literate	189	110	135	99	140	97
			86.30	50.23	61.64	45.21	63.93	44.29
		Community	111	140	126	176	70	98
			63.07	79.55	71.59	100.00	39.77	55.68
3.	Rice for Rs. 2/- per KG	Neo-literate	200	102	89	142	109	148
			91.32	46.58	40.64	64.84	49.77	67.58
		Community	150	173	106	97	139	124
			85.23	98.30	60.23	55.11	78.98	70.45
4.	Pensions for needy people	Neo-literate	198	178	177	144	175	110
			90.41	81.28	80.82	65.75	79.91	50.23
		Community	123	58	68	85	49	109
			69.89	32.95	38.64	48.30	27.84	61.93

(Multiple responses are recorded)

With regards to the Rice for Rs. 2/- per KG, Majority 350 (88.61) of the sample respondents reported that they have learned through the Prerak, 195 (49.37%) Village elders also propagated about this programme. In some cases the sample respondents reported that they have learned through the political leaders.With regards to the Pensions for needy people, majority of the sample respondents noticed that the Preraks have created awareness about this programme. The Government officials 321 (81.27%) have shown awareness about the Pensions for needy people and also 229 (57.97%) of the sample respondents noticed that the political leaders also explained about this problem.

Table 6.65: Mode of Accession on the Details on Development/ Welfare Schemes

Sl. No.	Programmes	Respondent	1	2	3	4	5	6
1.	Rajeev Arogya Sree	Neo-literate	211	99	112	124	208	87
			96.35	45.21	51.14	56.62	94.98	39.73
		Community	154	157	145	145	92	123
			87.50	89.20	82.39	82.39	52.27	69.89
2.	Free electricity for BPL	Neo-literate	198	204	197	207	177	68
			90.41	93.15	89.95	94.52	80.82	31.05
		Community	157	117	168	105	112	57
			89.20	66.48	95.45	59.66	63.64	32.39
3.	Indira Kranthi Pathakam	Neo-literate	173	199	208	204	44	36
			79.00	90.87	94.98	93.15	20.09	16.44
		Community	127	126	92	161	101	89
			72.16	71.59	52.27	91.48	57.39	50.57
4.	NREGP	Neo-literate	205	65	101	99	87	64
			93.61	29.68	46.12	45.21	39.73	29.22
		Community	139	60	124	123	140	128
			78.98	34.09	70.45	69.89	79.55	72.73
5.	Debt waiver for farmers	Neo-literate	201	187	149	111	95	88
			91.78	85.39	68.04	50.68	43.38	40.18
		Community	156	61	147	125	153	123
			88.64	34.66	83.52	71.02	86.93	69.89

(Multiple responses are recorded)

The opinion of the Rajeev Arogya Sree programme, majority 365 (92.41%) of the respondents are aware of this programme through Prerak and also the Government officials 210 (53.16%) involved to create awareness of this programme.

With regard to the free electricity for Below Poverty Line (BPL) of neo-literates and Community members, the majority 365 (92.41%) of the Village Elders explained about this programme, 312 (78.99) of the sample respondents have informed that the political leaders have explained about this programme.In regard to the Indira Kranthi Pathakam majority of the sample respondents noticed that the political leaders 365 (92.41) have shown awareness about this programme. In this case of 125 (31.65%) of the sample respondents noticed that the Government Officials are also propagated of this programme.

Table 6.66: Mode of Accession on the Details on Development/ Welfare Schemes

Sl. No.	Programmes	Respondent	1	2	3	4	5	6
1.	Social welfare	Neo-literate	210	165	174	98	37	87
			95.89	75.34	79.45	44.75	16.89	39.73
		Community	167	89	95	40	138	161
			94.89	50.57	53.98	22.73	78.41	91.48
2.	Pasu Kranthi	Neo-literate	204	99	103	114	96	140
			93.15	45.21	47.03	52.05	43.84	63.93
		Community	129	116	148	117	152	85
			73.30	65.91	84.09	66.48	86.36	48.30
3.	Debt waiver for deprived	Neo-literate	178	145	105	93	81	60
			81.28	66.21	47.95	42.47	36.99	27.40
		Community	80	91	109	92	66	50
			45.45	51.70	61.93	52.27	37.50	28.41
4.	Service of 104/108	Neo-literate	178	142	132	99	176	109
			81.28	64.84	60.27	45.21	80.37	49.77
		Community	121	136	134	115	82	105
			68.75	77.27	76.14	65.34	46.59	59.66
5.	Family planning	Neo-literate	212	137	112	119	147	97
			96.80	62.56	51.14	54.34	67.12	44.29
		Community	113	122	135	100	142	168
			64.20	69.32	76.70	56.82	80.68	95.45

(Multiple responses are recorded)

About the MGNREGP, Majority 344 (88.61) of the sample respondents have reported that they learned through the

Prerak, 195 (49.37%) Village elders also propagated about this programme. In this case of the sample respondents they have reported that they learned through the political leaders.

In case of the Debt waiver for farmers, Majority 357 (90.38%) of the sample respondents reported that they learned through the Prerak, 211 (53.42%) Government Officials have also propagated about this programme.With regard to the Social Welfare Programmes, Majority 377 (95.44) of reported that they learned through the Preraks. 138 (34.94%) political leaders were also reported that they learned.

With regard to the Pasu Kranthi Programme, Majority 333 (84.30%) of sample respondent reported that they learned by the Prerak, 215 (54.43%) of the sample respondents reported that the Sarpanch were also propagated about this programme.

With regards to the Debt waiver for deprived, Majority 258 (65.32) of the sample respondents reported that they have learned through the Prerak, 110 (27.85%) Village elders are also propagated about this programme. With regards to the Services of 104/108, Majority 299 (75.70%) of the sample respondents reported that they learned by the Prerak, 214 (54.18%) government officials have also propagated about this programme.

The family planning programme, majority 325 (82.28%) of the sample respondents have reported that they learned through the Prerak, 219 (55.44%) sample respondents have expressed that the political leaders also propagated about this programme.

In providing information about the welfare/ development programmes, in all most all aspects Preraks has a significant role in providing necessary information not only to the neo-literates but also to the community and villagers. The key role of Preraks is to be noted.

In dissemination of to people, the role of Preraks is highly recognizable followed by village elders, Saupanch, family members, political leaders and government officials, except in the case of family planning. The government official's involvement is observed because target fixed up by the government. Hence, there is a need of the government to act as in the case of family planning in all other welfare/ development programmes.

The impact of the continuing education programme on the neo-literates is following analysis chapter.

Impact of Continuing Education Programme on Neo-literates

In order to identify the learners based on their benefits acquired, and neo-literates are enquired about the benefits by attending the continuing education programme. The benefits were categorized into six areas as 1. Participation, 2. Capacity Building, 3.Awareness, 4. Strengths acquired, 5. Benefits, and 6. Empowerment, for the purpose of the analysis the mean scores were calculated.

In order to measure the benefit of the literacy to attending the continuing education centre, a 5-point rating scale questionnaire was administered to the learners identify the level.

The neo-literates obtained mean scores on recognition among the family members 4.076, maintaining community hygiene 4.018, member in village level committees (3.552), motivating the other learners to form into an association for the benefit (3.525). In case of participation in Palle Bata programmes (3.456) and Carrying out financial transactions without others help (2.465). With regard to the participation theme neo-literates have got the above average mean scores.

The benefit acquired in capacity building and self sustenance from attending Continuing Education Centre, the neo-literates shows the better in admitting children in schools

(4.4566) and membership in DWCRA/village committees (4.2374). A good impact on able to recognize the difference between interest from money lenders and bankers (3.4292), reading a message of the family planning and followed small family norms. In the other items there is low impact on talking to claim the wages on par with others (2.3562) and developing reading habit regularly.

Area – 1: Participation

Table 7.1: Items Relating to Participation Theme and Their Respective Mean Values Checked by the Neo-literates

Sl. No.	Statement	Mean
1.	Receiving recognition among the family members	4.076
2.	Better in maintaining community hygiene	4.018
3.	Became member in village level committees.	3.552
4.	Motivating the other Learners to form into an association for the benefit.	3.525
5.	Participating in Palle Bata programme launched by the government very actively.	3.456
6.	Carrying out financial transactions without others help.	2.465

Area – 2: Capacity Building

Table 7.2: Items Relating to Capacity Building Theme and Their Respective Mean Values Checked by the Neo-literates

Sl. No.	Statement	Mean
1.	Capable in admitting the children in schools	4.4566
2.	Taking membership in DWCRA/Village committees	4.2374
3.	Able to recognize the difference between interest from moneylenders and bankers.	3.4292
4.	Reading the message of the family planning and followed small family norms.	3.2877
5.	Talking to claim the wages on par with others.	2.3562
6.	Developing reading habit regularly.	1.4886

Area – 3: Awareness

Table 7.3: Items Relating to Awareness Theme and Their Respective Mean Values Checked by the Neo-literates

Sl. No.	Statement	Mean
1.	Sending the children to school regularly.	4.2511
2.	Trying to improve girl child enrolment in schools.	4.0639
3.	Able to move with others freely.	3.3379
4.	Approaching the officials without hesitation to express the problems.	3.1461
5.	Understand vote value	3.0320
6.	Taking care of women in Pre & Post natal condition	3.0183

On enquiry about the awareness created by attending the centres the neo-literates having better awareness mean scores in the aspects like regular schooling of their children (4.2511), trying to improve girl child enrolment in schools (4.0639), move with others freely (3.3379), approaching the officials without hesitation to express the problems (3.1461), vote value (3.0320), and taking care of women in pre and post natal condition (3.0183). It shows that there is a great impact of the continuing education programme in this aspect.

Neo-literates obtained their strengths to attending the continuing education centre, the following aspects viz. they are trying to wipeout the social evils (child marriage, superstition etc.,) mean scores is 4.0502, they are very capable in claiming the difference of change given by the conductor/ grosser mean score is 3.9589, they very through participating in tree plantation programme mean score is 3.7352, a good impact on encouragement to girl child in the family (3.5662) and claiming the right wage for the work (3.4521) and very poor impact on collecting the ration regularly (1.4716).

Area – 4: Strengths Acquired

Table 7.4: Items Relating to Strengths Acquired Theme and Their Respective Mean Values Checked by the Neo-literates

Sl. No.	Statement	Mean
1.	Trying to wipe out the social evils (child marriage, superstition etc.)	4.0502
2.	Capable in claiming the difference of change given by the conductor/grosser.	3.9589
3.	Participating in tree plantation programme regularly.	3.7352
4.	Giving encouragement to girl child in the family.	3.5662
5.	Claiming the right wage for the work.	3.4521
6.	Collecting of ration items regularly.	1.3653

Area – 5: Benefits

Table 7.5: Items Relating to Benefits Theme and Their Respective Mean Values Checked by the Neo-literates and Community Members

Sl. No.	Statement	Mean
1.	Motivating the illiterates to go to center to learn.	4.0776
2.	Encouraging the child for immunization.	4.0685
3.	Checked wrong quality weights in fair price shop.	3.8904
4.	Freeness from alcoholism.	3.5023
5.	Developing the habit of saving money.	3.4064
6.	Able to read the names of agricultural crops & fertilizers	3.3379

The respondents were asked of their acquired benefits on the above relating to their daily happening in family and society. The neo-literates are obtained mean scores, the items relating to motivating the illiterates to go to centre to learn (4.0776) and encouraging the child for immunization (4.0685) is high impact. The neo-literates are very care full in measuring the quality weight in fair price shop (3.8904) freeness from alcoholism (3.5023). most of the neo-literates are developing the habit of saving money (3.4064) and also able to read the names of agricultural crops and fertilizers (3.3379). There is a significant impact item like identification of agricultural crops, fertilizers, motivating others to join the centre child immunization and checking weights in ration shops. It was hearting to note continuing education programme has impact in changing life style of neo-literates.

Area – 6: Empowerment

Table 7.6: Items Relating to Empowerment Theme and Their Respective Mean Values Checked by the Neo-literates

Sl. No.	Statement	Mean
1.	MGNREGP's benefit	4.3881
2.	Avoidance of middlemen	4.1689
3.	Able in checking the accounts maintained by the SHGs	4.0594
4.	Participated in Panchayat elections.	3.4566
5.	Interested in helping others to read and write.	3.3790
6.	Able to do things confidently.	3.0913

The investigator enquired about the empowerment aspect to neo-literates, there is a significant impact on neo-literates towards benefit of MGNREGP (4.3881), avoidance of middlemen (4.1689) good knowledge on checking the accounts maintained by SHGs (4.0594), excellent impact on participating in Panchayat election (3.4566), helping the others to read and write mean score is 3.379 and able to do things confidently (3.0913).

In the aspects participation, capacity building, awareness, strengths acquired, benefits and empowerment. Except in the few cases the neo-literates agreed that they are developed because of attending the continuing education centre in areas like respect in the family, enrolment of children in formal schooling, in particular girl children, positive change of attitude towards child marriage and superstitions believes and immunization to children.

Socio-Economic and Demographic Background of Neo-literates and Impact of Continuing Education Programme

In order to find out the background of the successful beneficiaries and to trace the characteristics of the neo-literates who are lagging behind the following analysis is made with reference the sex, age, marital status, social class, nativity, family background, educational standards, occupation, both family and individual incomes. A discussion of this sort will permit us to fix point the neo-literate who are generally lag behind in repairing the benefits of continuing education centre and who need some specialized attention, if the programme should become more successful in producing the expected impact.

Benefit V/s Sex

The aim of the programme is to provide quality of life and creating awareness to all the sections of the community. As a result of this, both sex groups participated in continuing education centre activities. The mean benefit scores of the two groups are calculated and 't' test is applied to study the differences if any between these two groups. The calculated mean benefit score of men and women indicates that female learners found to be more benefit than the men learners. The 't' value is 1.895which indicates that the difference is not significant.

Benefit V/s Age

Variation in age of the target group is associated with differential effectiveness of the programme. In order to study the influence of age of learners on their benefits, the learners categorized into three age groups viz., below 20, 21-35and 36 years and above and respective mean benefit scores demonstrates that the learners of below 20 years age group are found to be getting more benefit than the other two groups. On the other hand, 'F' value shows that the mean difference between the three groups of learners is significant at 0.05 level and the value is 3.253.

Table 7.7: Mean Benefit Scores, SDs Obtained by the Neo-literates Belonging to Different Groups and Their Respective t/F Values

Sl. No.	Variable	Group	*N*	Mean	Standard Deviation	*'t/F'-Value*
1.	Sex	Male	111	124.8198	10.7384	1.895
		Female	108	127.5278	10.3999	
2.	Age	Below 20	66	128.8939	10.1256	3.253*
		21-35	114	125.1404	10.9147	
		Above 36	39	124.4872	10.0154	
3.	Marital Status	Married	47	128.2340	12.1444	1.148
		Unmarried	154	125.5649	10.2721	
		Widow	18	125.7778	9.3025	
4.	Caste	O.C.	53	125.6792	11.1438	0.124
		B.C.	119	126.4790	10.5307	
		S.C.	47	125.8723	10.5163	
5.	Nativity	Rural	136	125.7794	11.0230	0.669
		Urban	83	126.7711	10.0028	
6.	Family background	Agriculture	105	126.2095	10.4951	0.048
		Business	34	126.6471	10.5655	
		Employed	27	125.6667	12.2192	
		Artisans	53	125.9811	10.3969	
7.	Education	Illiterate	69	127.3043	10.3616	1.122
		Literate	114	125.1228	10.8889	
		Pri. Education	36	127.2222	10.2904	
8.	Occupation	Agriculture	103	126.2330	10.6119	0.258
		Business	37	125.0270	9.2421	
		Employed	10	128.1000	10.4291	
		Artisans	69	126.3623	11.5236	
9.	Individual income	Below Rs. 1000/-	63	127.2381	8.6168	0.533
		Rs. 1000/- 2000 /-	116	125.9138	11.5612	
		>Rs. 2000/- PM	40	125.1500	10.8168	
10.	Family income	Below Rs. 1000/-	38	122.5526	10.2975	3.341*
		Rs. 1000/- 2000/-	86	125.9767	10.8682	
		>Rs. 2000/- PM	95	127.7579	10.2912	

Benefit V/s Marital Status

The marital status of the neo-literates is found to have variety of influences on the receiving benefits. The sample learners are categorized into three groups viz., married, unmarred and widow/widower, their respective mean benefit scores are calculated to understand the influence of marital status on benefits in attending continuing education centres. The trend of the mean benefits scores are presented in the Table 7.7 and shows that unmarried learners are found to be getting lesser benefits than their counterparts. Further, the calculated 'F' value is 1.148 and also indicates that the difference between the mean benefits scores of the married, unmarried and widow/widower learners is found not significant.

Benefit V/s Caste

In order to understand the influence of caste on the benefits of the learners, the learners are categorized into three groups as Other Castes/Forward Castes, Backward Castes, and Scheduled Castes. The trend of the mean benefit scores illustrates that backward castes are getting higher benefits than the other groups. The calculated 'F' value indicates that the mean benefits scores of all these three groups are not significantly different from each other.

Benefit V/s Native Place

The results presented in the table 7.7 clearly shows that the influences of the native place viz., Rural and Urban areas, on the benefits of learners. The trend of the mean benefit scores obtained by learners of urban, clearly indicates that the learners from urban native place are getting higher benefits than the learners belongs to other native place. However, the obtained 't' value is 0.669, which is not significant.

Benefit V/s Family Background

The results relating to the influence of the family background on the benefits got by the learners in attending the continuing education centres, the trend of the mean benefit scores show that the learners employed getting fewer benefits than the other groups. The calculated 'F' value is 0.048 also shows that the difference between these groups is not significant.

Benefit V/s Education

Based on their education, the learners are categorized into three groups i.e. illiterates, literates and primary education and their benefit scores are calculated and presented in the table 7.7. The trend of the mean benefit scores shows that the learners with literacy background expressed their acquired benefit in the centre is less than their counterparts. The 'F' value indicates that difference between these three groups is not significant even at 0.05 level.

Benefit V/s Occupation

The results relating to the influence of the occupation on the benefits acquired by the learners in attending the continuing education centres, the trend of the mean benefit scores show that the learners business getting fewer benefits than the other groups. The calculated 'F' value is 0.258 also shows that the difference between these groups is not significant. The analysis of occupation was made with a view in what extent the neo-literates are intended to learn and time available to attend the centre.

Benefit V/s Individual Income

Based on level of individual income, the learners are categorized into three groups i.e. below Rs. 1000/-, Rs. 1000/ - to 2000/- and above Rs. 2000/- PM and their benefit scores are calculated and presented in the table 7.7. The trend of the mean benefit scores shows that the learners with above Rs. 2000/- PM of income are getting fewer benefits than the other groups. The 'F' value indicates that difference between these three groups is not significant even at 0.05 level.

Benefit V/s Family Income

Based on their family income, the learners are categorized into three groups i.e. below Rs. 1000/-, Rs. 1000/- to 2000/-

and above Rs. 2000/- PM and their benefit scores are calculated and presented in the table 7.7. The trend of the mean benefit scores shows that the learners with below Rs. 1000/- PM of income are getting fewer benefits than the other groups. The 'F' value indicates that difference between these three groups is significant even at 0.05 level.

On enquiry about benefits received by attending continuing education centre is relation to socio-economic background of neo-literates show that the most of the neo-literates belongs to female sex, below 20 years of age, married, backward social class, urban nativity, agricultural and business family occupation groups, literates, employed category, lower income of Rs. 1000/- per month than their counterparts and high family income group neo-literates expressed that they are benefited to attending the centre.

The summary and conclusions of the study are presented in the following chapter.

CHAPTER 8 Outlook of the Continuing Education Programme

Introduction

Literacy is a process which dispels and promotes rational thinking and moulds human beings into responsible citizens. The absence of literacy directly and indirectly retards the development of individuals, society, community and the country as a whole. For the success of any programme, people should be motivated by providing necessary congenial environment, socio-economic conditions and committed efforts on the part of implementing bodies should be seen. In spite of number of efforts made by central and state governments in India, still illiteracy remains as challenging for a country.

Literacy is one of the key aspects of human resource development. In order to quantify the human resources of the country, the State and Central Governments have launched a number of educational (both formal and non-formal) programmes for the promotion of literacy. As a result, large pools of illiterates were made literates. However, a vast majority of the illiterates still exist, particularly among females.

Eradication of illiteracy has been one of the major national concerns of the Government of India since independence. The need for literate population and universal education for all children in the age group 6-14 years was recognized as a crucial input for nation building and was given due consideration in the constitution as well as in the successive five year plans. A number of significant programmes have been taken up since independence to eradicate illiteracy among adults viz. social education, Gram Shikshan Mohim, Farmers' Functional Literacy Programme, Non-formal Education, Polyvalent Adult Education Centers, Education Commission, Functional Literacy for Adult women, National Adult Education Programme, Rural Functional Literacy Project, State Adult Education Programme, Adult Education Through Voluntary Agencies, Review National Adult Education Programme, National Literacy Mission, Improved Pace and Content of Learning, Mass Campaign Approach, Total Literacy Campaigns, Post Literacy Campaigns and Continuing Education Programme.

Relapse into illiteracy is a serious problem in adult education. This is due to lack of adequate usage of the limited literacy skills acquired by adult learners in their daily life. With the introduction of total literacy campaigns in India millions of illiterates are acquiring basic literacy skills and joining the class of neo-literates each year. They require activities to strengthen literacy skills and to improve their living conditions. Without a meaningful scheme of post-literacy and continuing education the neo-literates may most likely relapse into illiteracy.

Government of India has initiated a new scheme of continuing education for neo-literates from 1995 onwards keeping in view the past experiences in organizing adult and continuing education programmes. The main objectives of the scheme and the activities aimed retention of literacy skills, functional literacy for improvement of living conditions, Dissemination of information on development programmes, Creation of awareness about national concerns, Improvement of economic conditions, library and reading rooms and Organisation of cultural and recreational activities with effective community participation.

Continuing education centres are started at the grass root level and Preraks are appointed to carry out the activities of the centres. Neo-literates are the main beneficiaries of the programme. The State Resource Centre happens to be the main agency to prepare and supply the post-literacy and continuing education materials and to arrange for the training of Preraks to carry out the different activities like organisation of evening classes, library and reading room, charcha mandal, simple and short duration programmes, recreational activities etc., at the centres.

Continuing Education Programme influences rural Development in three ways. Firstly, it increases the awareness of rural people about on-going activities in society. The anti-arrack movement by the women folk of our State is a notable illustration of the impact of adult education programme. Secondly education facilities social and occupational mobility among the members of the society. Educational achievements, to a large extent determine the nature and type of opportunities that become available to the rural people. Thirdly, education provides an insight to the rural folk bout intricacies and complexities or bureaucratic administration. It prepares them to accept and cooperate with the bureaucrats or implementing agencies

With reference to Rural Development programme, the initial emphasis was on community rather than the rural areas as such. This led to emergence of Community Development programmes and Community Block concept in the beginning. Later on, the emphasis of rural development programmes was shifted to integrated approach, popularly known as Integrated Rural Development Programme (IRDP) wherein an integrated approach with a rural family as a base unit, was taken up to translate the policy issues into programmes. Income generation programmes too gained prominence during this phase. During this period the Farmer's Functional Literacy Programme, Rural Functional Literacy Programme, Non-Formal Education for school drop-outs, Adult Education for Women and other literacy programmes were started to impart literacy skills, so that the target group can participate in the developmental initiative of the Government without exploitation of middlemen and vested groups. Later in 1978, the National Adult Education Programme was started with the objectives promoting Literacy, Functionality and Awareness to the illiterate population. Then the National Literacy Mission was launched in 1988 in three stages as Total Literacy Campaigns, Post-Literacy Programme and Continuing Education Programme. All the adult education programmes were designed to strengthen the masses in Literacy and Social Awareness so that they can utilise the Government Welfare Programmes independently and benefits may be reach them directly.

Review of Related Literature

Research studies, which focus their attention on different aspects of the functioning of post-literacy and continuing education may throw light on the ways and means of organizing continuing education centres effectively. A few research studies conducted by the researchers (Berke (1970), Simmons (1972), Dixit Asha (1975), Pillai (1976), Vekataiah (1977), Sivadasan Pillai (1979), NAEP in Tajasthan in (1979), Singh and Singh (1979),Social Education and Development Society (1980), Muthuswamy (1980), Pestonjee (1980), Madana Mohana Reddy (1980), Pillai K. Sivadasan (1980), Muthayya and Hemalatha (1981), Umayaparvathi (1982), Chouhan and Rai (1984), Savitha Markanda (1985), David (1988),Mistry (1988), Vasudeva Rao BS (1988), Aram (1989), Bhasin (1992), Kumaraswamy (1992), Nair, Omanna and Rehim (1992), Adilakshmi (1993), Sardhar Patel Institute of Economic and Social Research (1993), Shah S.Y. (1993), Department of Adult and Continuing Education (1994), Reddy P.A and Reddeppa (1995), Shirley Walters (1995), Parthasarathy (1996), Radha Krishna Murthy C (1996), Jagannadha Sarma (1998), Pandy (1998), Vasudeva Rao (1999), Mastan (2000), Viswanadha Gupta and Janardhana Reddy (2000), Reddeppa (2001), Egbule, Patrick E. and Njoku, Edna-Matheswa C (2001), Akanisi Kedrayate (2002), Jagannada Rao D (2202), Schweigert,

Thomas F (2002), Surapa Raju S (2002), Vasantha Kumari and Sudha Rani (2002), Baby Sarojini (2003), Bharathi (2003), Bhola (2003), Reddeppa Reddy (2003), Srinivasa Rao G (2004), Vasudeva Rao BS and Viswanadha Gupta P (2004), Bhat, R.L. and Sharma, Namita (2005), Kulasekhar (2005), Niranjan Reddy (2005), Robert Devadoss (2005), Sikligar PC (2005), Vasudeva Rao, Viswanadha Gupta and Srinivasa Rao (2005), Viswanadha Gupta, Adinarayana Reddy Vasudeva Rao (2006), Rodriguez, Liza M (2007), Adinarayana Reddy P (2007), Padma Kumari (2007), Chaudhury, Sahadat H (2008), Mamata Das (2008), Sabine Strassburg (2008) have been identified and presented with a view to get better insight into the research problem to be attempted.

Though the concept of Continuing Education in India is unique as compared with the foreign countries programmes but the basic objective is to enlighten peoples' minds, hence some studies abroad also included.

The Major Findings of the Study

Socio-demographic Background of Sample Respondents

Profile of the Preraks

- Out of the total 78 Preraks, 17 (21.8%) Preraks are females and remaining 61 (78.2%) Preraks are males.
- The age of the Preraks ranged from below 20 years to above 36 years of age, 31 (39.7%) of Preraks were above 36 years while the 20 (25.6%) are below 20 years.
- Majority 55 (70.5%) are married, 17 (21.8%) unmarried Preraks.
- More than one fifth are from upper castes and 16 (20.5%) are from schedule castes and 45 (57.7%) are from the backward classes.
- Our data shows that 48 (51.3%) Preraks are native of rural areas, and 30 (38.5%) from urban nativity.
- Nearly half of the Preraks (46.2%) had intermediate education. 19 (24.4%) graduates and only 4 (5.1%) Preraks are having post graduations.

- Preraks 29 (37.2%) are occupied with agricultural occupation and 23 (29.5%) are from artisan. Only 7 (9.0%) are employed. The business people 14 (17.9%) are also involved in this activity.
- Only 15 (19.2%) of the Preraks are having monthly come of Rs. 2000/- above. Preraks 34 (43.6%) has income ranging between Rs. 1000/- to Rs. 2000/- per month. The remaining 29 (37.2%) Preraks with monthly income of below Rs. 1000/- per month.
- Majority 38 (48.7%) of the sample Preraks family income is above Rs. 2000/- per month and remaining 31 (39.7%) Preraks are earning Rs. 1000/- to 2000/- income per month.
- Majority 40 (51.3%) of them has less than 2 years of experience followed by 2-4 years are 25 (28.2%) and remaining 13 (16.7%) of the sample Preraks are having more than 4 years experience in the continuing education programme.
- 32 (41.0%) Preraks are belong to agriculture family background and 23 (29.5%) of the Preraks are artisans. 13 (16.7%) are doing business followed by 6 (7.7%) engaged in other works and only 4 (5.1%) of the Preraks are employed.

Profile of the Neo-literates

- With regard to neo-literates profile, 111 (50.7%) are males and 108 (49.3%) are females.
- Only 39 (17.8%) of neo-literates are above 35 years, while 30% are below 20 years and remaining 114 (52.1%) respondents are between 21-35 years. However, most of the neo-literates 82.1% belonged to productive age group.
- Majority 154 (70.3%) of the neo-literates are married and 47 (21.5%) of them are unmarried.
- Majority 119 (54.3%) of the neo-literates are from Backward Castes followed by the forward/other castes 53 (24.2%) and Scheduled Castes 47 (21.5%).

- Majority 136 (62.1%) of the neo-literates are from rural background and remaining 83 (37.9%) of them are from urban background.
- Nearly half of the neo-literates, 99 (45.2%) of the sample are from the agricultural family background followed by artisans 48 (21.9%), others 27 (12.3%), business 25 (11.4%) and employed 20 (9.1%).
- More than half of the neo-literates, 114 (52.1%) of the sample are found to be literates and 69 (31.5%) of them are illiterates. The remaining 36 (16.4%) of them are having primary education.
- Majority 103 (47.0%) of the neo-literates are from the agricultural and allied occupations followed by artisans 69 (31.5%), business 37 (16.9%) and employed 10 (4.6%).
- Majority 116 (53.0%) of the sample members are earning Rs. 1000 to Rs. 2000/- PM, 63 (28.8%) of the members are earning below Rs. 1000/- PM and only 40 (18.3%) of the members are earning above Rs. 2000/- PM.
- More than two fifth, 95 (43.4%) of the sample neo-literates are from above Rs. 2000/- PM of family income, and followed by 86 (39.3%) sample learners are between Rs. 1000/- to 2000/- PM income group.

Profile of the Community Members

- The sex wise representation of the community members of the sample shows that 84 (47.7%) of them are females and 92 (52.3%) are males.
- About 85 (48.3%) of the community members are between 21-35 years of age followed by below 20 years (33.0%), and 33 (18.8%) of respondents are above 36 years of age.
- Majority 127 (72.2%) of the sample are married and 37 (21.0%) of them are unmarried.
- More than half of the community members i.e. 97 (55.1%) respondents are belongs to Backward Castes, followed by 40 (22.7%) from Others Castes and 39 (22.2%) are scheduled castes.

- Nearly two third, 108 (61.4%) of the community members are with rural background and remaining 68 (38.6%) are urban background.
- Nearly half of the sample i.e. 79 (44.9%) of the community members belong to agriculture background, artisans 40 (22.7%), 21 (11.9%) belongs to other works business 20 (11.4%) and employed 16 (9.1%).
- About 92 (52.3%) of the community members are literates and 55 (31.3%) of them are illiterates and remaining 29 (16.5%) are up to primary level.
- Majority 83 (47.2%) of the respondents are doing agriculture and allied works, 57 (32.4%) community members are artisans, 28 (15.9%) business occupation and 8 (4.5%) of them are employees.
- With regard to income, 95 (54.0%) of the community members are earning between Rs. 1000 to Rs. 2000/- PM, 49 (27.8%) of the members are earning below Rs. 1000/- PM.
- Regarding the family income, 79 (44.9%) of the community members are earning above Rs. 2000/- PM, 69 (39.2%) of members are earning between Rs. 1000/- to Rs. 2000, only 28 (15.9%) of the members are earning below Rs. 1000/- PM.

Attitude/Opinion of the Preraks and Neo-literates Towards Organisation of the Continuing Education Centre Activities – Theme-wise

Preraks and learners opinions towards the following aspects were gathered and divided into eight themes as follows, Organisation of Evening Classes, Library and Reading Room, Charcha Mandal, Cultural and Recreational Activities, Short Term Training Programmes, Games and Sports Activities, Information Window Programmes, Supportive Facilities. Analysis was made on the eight themes and the mean value scores of the total responses were calculated.

- There is difference of opinion between Preraks and neo-literates and in all items; Preraks obtained better mean scores than the neo-literates. The more difference is observed in the case of assessment leads to dissatisfaction (0.677), timing of the centre (0.6052), dual teaching (0.6052) responsible for assistance (0.504). The analysis shows that the neo-literates are mostly depended upon Preraks about the centre.

- Preraks have obtained better mean scores than the neo-literates in the items relating to library and reading room.
- The Preraks and neo-literates suggested that the Charcha Mandal discussion should be organized in the presence of women, self help group leaders and people representatives.
- Neo-literates have differed with the views of Preraks about the cultural programmes helps neo-literates, regular planning in advance and Preraks knowledge in culture activities. Regular organising of recreational activities and taking help of community is some extent necessary according Preraks and neo-literates? The mean score difference different is insignificant in the case of other items.
- The Preraks are better opined that proper planning in visits, training for neo-literates in income generating activities compare to neo-literates. There is no significant difference among them in consideration of local needs presence of developmental department officials is not necessary in organizing training.
- There is high degree of opinion expressed by Preraks and neo-literates in views of participation by neo-iterates in games and sports and prizes for winners. The difference of mean scores is low in case of Preraks should be trained in sports and games, necessity of playing foot ball, cricket and knowledge of Preraks on rules and regulation of games sports.
- The difference of mean scores is high between Preraks and neo-literates in items like provide information and coordination with developmental officials and public about literacy levels and SHG leaders.

- The Preraks feels that for effective running the centre more financial provision is necessary and there is not much of impact due to continuing education centre on life conditions of neo-literates. Further, he/she want full time appointment as Prerak. But neo-literates regarded with the Preraks. There is no significant difference about the role of press and media to develop under functioning.

Attitude/Opinion Comparison of Preraks and Neo-Literates Towards Organisation of Continuing Education Activities

- Information pertaining to the opinion of Preraks and neo-literates towards the organisation of continuing education activities, Preraks have more mean scores.
- Organisation of library and reading room activities (A2) Preraks have obtained a better mean opinion score in relation to neo-literates.
- Information about the organisation of Charcha Mandal (A3) reveals that the Preraks have obtained a mean opinion score of 32.76 and neo-literates have obtained a mean opinion score is 21.51.
- Preraks mean opinion score is better than the neo-literates towards thc organisation of short term training programmes.
- Preraks (30.2308) and neo-literates (20.2146) have obtained opinion on the organisation of cultural and recreational activities.
- Preraks obtained more mean scores then neo-literates towards games and sports activities.
- Preraks have obtained a mean opinion of 32.10 where the mean opinion obtained by neo-literates is 21.79 for information window theme.
- Preraks and neo-literate differed significantly in their opinion on the supportive facilities.
- With regard to total opinions, the Preraks have secured a mean score of 257.33, whereas the neo-literates have secured a mean opinion score of 170.95. Preraks have more favourable opinion towards organisation of continuing education activities, when compared to neo-literates.

Influence of Personal Variables on Attitude/Opinion of Preraks towards Organisation of Continuing Education Centre Activities

- The sex of the Preraks has no impact on their opinion towards over all opinion and the sub themes Organisation of Evening Classes (A1), Library and Reading Room (A2), Charcha Mandal (A3), Cultural and Recreational Activities (A4), Short Term Training Programmes (A5), Games and Sports Activities (A6), Information Window (A7), Supportive Facilities (A8).
- This finding informs that the age has no impact on the organisation of the centre. The Preraks in the age category of above 36 years of age are better than the other two age groups in all eight themes which reveal that the age has no influence to cater to the needs of centre.
- In order to estimate the influence of the marital status on the opinion of the Preraks, the different backgrounds of Preraks marital status expressed one and the same opinion towards Library and Reading Room (A2), Charcha Mandal (A3), Short Term Training Programmes (A5), Games and Sports Activities (A6), Information Window (A7), Supportive Facilities (A8) and over all opinion, in case of Organisation of Evening Classes (A1), Cultural and Recreational Activities (A4) has significant difference at 0.05 level.
- To estimate the influence of the caste of the Preraks on their opinion, there is high level significant difference in the themes of Organisation of Evening Classes (A1), Library and Reading Room (A2), Charcha Mandal (A3), Short Term Training Programmes (A5), Information Window (A7), Supportive Facilities (A8) and over all opinion. And in the remaining two themes a significant difference is found.
- The results clearly shows that the influence of the native place i.e. rural and urban on the opinions of the Preraks. There is no significant difference in the over all opinion and eight sub themes.

- To estimate the influence of the educational qualification of the Preraks on their opinion, the difference categories of respondents expressed same opinion towards the themes Library and Reading Room (A2), Cultural and Recreational Activities (A4), Short Term Training Programmes (A5), Supportive Facilities (A8) and over all opinion. There is a significant difference in Organisation of Evening Classes (A1), Charcha Mandal (A3), Games and Sports Activities (A6), Information Window (A7).
- In order to understand the differential opinions of the different occupation groups, the trend of the mean opinion scores illustrates that there is no significant difference in Short Term Training Programmes (A5), Games and Sports Activities (A6), Information Window (A7), Supportive Facilities (A8). There is high level significant difference is found in the themes of Organisation of Evening Classes (A1), Library and Reading Room (A2), Charcha Mandal (A3). And remaining the theme Cultural and Recreational Activities (A4) and over all opinion is found significant at 0.05 level.
- To calculate the influence of the individual income of the Preraks on their opinion, the trend of mean scores found that there is no significant in the theme of Cultural and Recreational Activities (A4). There is high level significant difference in the themes of Organisation of Evening Classes (A1), Library and Reading Room (A2) and remaining all sub themes and over all opinion is found significant at 0.05 level.
- To calculate the influence of the family income of the Preraks on their opinion, the trend of mean scores found that there is no significant in the themes of Organisation of Evening Classes (A1), Library and Reading Room (A2), Charcha Mandal (A3), Cultural and Recreational Activities (A4), Short Term Training Programmes (A5), Games and Sports Activities (A6), Information Window (A7), Supportive Facilities (A8) and over all opinion.

- To calculate the influence of the experience of the Preraks on their opinion, the trend mean opinions scores found that there is no significant difference on the themes of Library and Reading Room (A2), Charcha Mandal (A3), Cultural and Recreational Activities (A4), Short Term Training Programmes (A5), Information Window (A7), Supportive Facilities (A8) and over all opinion. There is significant at difference on the themes of Organisation of Evening Classes (A1) and Games and Sports Activities (A6).
- The influence of the family background of the Preraks on their opinions, it was found that there is no significant difference in the themes of Short Term Training Programmes (A5), Games and Sports Activities (A6), Information Window (A7), Supportive Facilities (A8), high level significant difference is found in Organisation of Evening Classes (A1), Library and Reading Room (A2), Charcha Mandal (A3). And remaining theme Cultural and Recreational Activities (A4) and overall opinion is found significant at 0.05 level.

Influence of Personal Variables on Attitude/Opinion of Neo-Literates towards Organisation of Continuing Education Activities

- The sex of the neo-literates has no impact on their opinion towards over all opinion and the sub themes of Charcha Mandal (A3), Cultural and Recreational Activities (A4), Short Term Training Programmes (A5), Games and Sports Activities (A6), Information Window (A7), Supportive Facilities (A8). In case of Organisation of Evening Classes (A1), Library and Reading Room (A2) is significant difference at 0.05 level.
- In order to understand the influence of the age of Preraks on their opinion, high level significant difference is found in the themes of Library and Reading Room (A2), Charcha Mandal (A3), Cultural and Recreational Activities (A4), Short Term Training Programmes (A5),

Games and Sports Activities (A6), Supportive Facilities (A8). And remaining themes viz. Organisation of Evening Classes (A1), Information Window (A7), and overall opinion is found significant at 0.05 level.

- In order to estimate the influence of the marital status on the opinion of the neo-literates, neo-literate marital status expressed one and the same opinion towards Organisation of Evening Classes (A1). There is high level significant difference towards the themes Library and Reading Room (A2), Charcha Mandal (A3), Cultural and Recreational Activities (A4), Short Term Training Programmes (A5), Games and Sports Activities (A6), Information Window (A7), Supportive Facilities (A8) and over all opinion.
- To estimate the influence of the caste of the neo-literates on their opinion, there is no significant difference in the themes of Charcha Mandal (A3), Games and Sports Activities (A6). And high significant difference is found in the theme of Information Window (A7). In case of other themes Organisation of Evening Classes (A1), Library and Reading Room (A2), Cultural and Recreational Activities (A4), Short Term Training Programmes (A5), Supportive Facilities (A8) and over all opinion a significant difference is found.
- To estimate the influence of the nativity of the neo-literates on their opinion, there is high level significant difference in the themes of Cultural and Recreational Activities (A4), Short Term Training Programmes (A5), and there is significant different at 0.05 level in case of Organisation of Evening Classes (A1), Library and Reading Room (A2), Charcha Mandal (A3), Games and Sports Activities (A6) and over all opinion. There is no significant difference is found in the theme of Information Window (A7), Supportive Facilities (A8).
- To find out the difference among the family background on their opinions of the neo-literates there is high level significant difference in all the themes and the overall opinion.

- In order to estimate the influence of the education of neo-literates on their opinion, there is high level significant difference is found in all the themes and the overall opinion.
- In order to estimate the influence of the occupation of neo-literates on their opinion, there is high level significant difference is found in all the themes and the overall opinion.
- To calculate the influence of the individual income of the neo-literates on their opinion, the trend of mean opinions scores found that there is high level significant difference in the themes of Organisation of Evening Classes (A1), Charcha Mandal (A3), Cultural and Recreational Activities (A4), Short Term Training Programmes (A5), Games and Sports Activities (A6), Information Window (A7), Supportive Facilities (A8) and in the case of Library and Reading Room (A2) found significant at 0.05 level.
- To calculate the influence of the family income of the neo-literates on their opinion, the trend of mean opinions scores found that there is no significant difference in the theme of Library and Reading Room (A2) and high level significant difference in the themes of Charcha Mandal (A3), Cultural and Recreational Activities (A4), Short Term Training Programmes (A5), Games and Sports Activities (A6), and in case of Organisation of Evening Classes (A1), Information Window (A7), Supportive Facilities (A8) is found significant at 0.05 level.

Comparison Between the Neo-literates and Community Members Towards Different Aspects

The study has been made to assess the impact of the continuing education programme on the neo-literates and community members, and community members were used as control group to find the difference among them. In doing, so the impact is analysed with responses viz. literacy, functionality, awareness of social beliefs and welfare programmes.

Literacy Particulars

- Regarding the reading sign boards only 25 (6.3%) of the sample respondents are able. Out of 25 members, 16 (7.3%) are neo-literates and 9 (5.1%) are community members; it shows that the impact of continuing education programme.
- The sample respondents of 158 (40.0%) are able to read the letter and, out of 158 sample members, 97 (44.3%) are neo-literate and 61 (34.7%) are community members
- With regard to the 16 (7.3%) of neo-literates and 9 (5.1%) of community members are able to read the News paper.
- Majority 162 (41.0%) of the sample respondents are able to write the letter and words, out of 162 members, 97 (44.3%) are neo-literates and 65 (36.9%) are community members.
- Only 116 (29.4%) of the members are writing the names and sentences well, out of 116 members, 83 (37.9%) are neo-literates and 33 (18.3%) are community members, it shows that the impact of continuing education programme.
- About one fourth 99 (25.1%) of the sample respondents able to fill the forms well, and only 74 (18.7%) of the members are unable to fill the forms.
- One fifth (22.8%) of the members are reading and writing numbers, out of 90 members, 51 (23.3%) are neo-literates and 39 (22.2%) are community members.
- More or less one fourth (24.1%) of the members are doing the adding and subtracting the numbers, one fifth (20.8%) of the sample respondents are doing the multiplication and divisions of the numbers.

Functionality Particulars

- Only 76 (19.2%) of the sample respondents are aware about their occupation, information skills, out of 76 members, 51 (23.3%) are beneficiaries and 25 (14.2%) are community members.
- A few of 51 (23.3%) of the neo-literates and 27 (15.3%) of the community members are aware the occupational information.

- About 98 (24.8%) of the sample respondents are able to know the information in time. Out of 98 members 63 (28.8%) of the neo-literates and 35 (19.9%) of them were community members and 98 (24.8%) of sample members do not know about the agriculture information.
- With regard to the awareness on the functions of the bank, 88 (27.3%) of the sample respondents knows the functions of banks. Out of 88 members 50 (22.8%) of them are neo-literates and 38 (21.6%) of them are community members and 59 (14.9%) of sample members do not know the functions of the bank.
- Nearly 64 (16.2%) of the sample members are unable to save the money.

Social Awareness Particulars

- Majority 153 (69.9%) of the beneficiaries and 125 (71.0%) of the community members (non-beneficiaries) are having a membership in youth clubs.
- With regard to SHG membership 277 (70.1%) of the sample respondents are the members in any one of the self help groups. Out of 277 members 153 (69.9%) of them are neo-literates and 124 (70.5%) of them are community members.
- More than half of the sample members, 255 (64.6%) of the members are associated with co-operative societies. Out of 255 members 145 (66.2%) of them are neo-literates and 110 (62.5%) of them are community members.
- Majority 274 (69.4%) of the sample respondents are having the membership in political bodies. Out of 274 members 154 (70.3%) of them are neo-literates and 120 (68.2%) of them are community members.
- With regard to the encouragement of widow marriages, 83 (21.0%) of the sample members have agreed and 78 (19.7%) of the members are disagreed.
- Regard to the abolition of dowry system, 70 (17.7%) of the sample members have agreed out of 70 members, 29 (13.2%) of them were neo-literates and 41 (23.3%) of them are community members.

- Majority 217 (54.9%) of the sample respondents reported that they have no idea about inter caste marriages, out of 217 members, 123 (56.2%) of them are neo-literates and 94 (53.4%) of them are community.
- Sample respondents were exposed on child marriage aspects more than one fifth (22.3%) of the sample members are agreed out of 88 members, 50 (22.8%) of them are neo-literates and 38 (21.6%) of them are community members.
- Only 64 (16.2%) of the sample respondents informed that they have not acquired necessary information about bad habits.
- Majority 247 (62.5%) of the sample respondents informed that they are agree consuming of alcohol is a bad habit out of 247 members, 137 (62.6%) of them are neo-literates and 110 (62.5%) of them are community members.
- The provision of reservation to certain social groups, 108 (27.3%) of the sample respondents have agreed. Out of 108 members 59 (26.9%) of the neo-literates and 49 (27.8%) of the community members.

• More than half of the 211 (53.4%) sample respondents are agreed with regard to development of female literacy, out of 211, 120 (54.8%) are neo-literates and 91 (51.7%) are community member.

Point of Views on Social Beliefs

- Majority 216 (54.7%) of the sample members have believes in the god to some extent, out of 216, 122 (55.7%) of them are learners and 94 (53.4%) of the community members.
- Regard to belief in the evil spirits, 88 (22.3%) of the sample respondents have belief. Out of 88 members 50 (22.8%) of them are neo-literates and 38 (21.6%) of the community members and 60 (15.2%) of sample members have disagreed.
- Only 100 (25.3%) of the sample respondents believed of religion, out of 100 members 55 (25.1%) of the neo-literates and 45 (25.6%) of the community members and 48 (12.2%) of sample members have disagreed.

- With regard to caste rigidity, 108 (27.3%) of the sample respondents believed in the caste system. Out of 108 members 59 (26.9%) of them are neo-literates and 49 (27.8%) of the community members and 64 (16.2%) of sample members have disagreed.
- 96 (24.3%) of the sample respondents have shown response that they believed in witch crafts.

Medical Awareness

- More than half 248 of the (62.8%) sample respondents noticed that they are aware of the available medical facilities, out of 248 members, 140 (63.9%) of them are neo-literates and 108 (61.4%) of them are community members.
- Majority, 321 (81.3%) of the sample respondents are utilized. Out of 321 members 201 (91.8%) of them are neo-literates and 120 (68.2%) of the community members.
- With regard to the vaccination, 263 (66.6%) of the sample members are vaccinated, out of 263 members, 159 (72.6%) are neo-literates and 104 (59.1%) are community members.

Awareness on Development/Welfare Programmes

All the schemes analysed in the following lines are open to all people who are in the below poverty line. Whether the activity of the centre and preraks made any contribution in enhancing the knowledge on development/welfare programmes and as a facilitator in acquiring the scheme benefits, a comparison was made with the people who are not enrolled in the continuing education centre.

With regard to Jalayagnam programme, majority percentage neo-literates (63.5%) are well aware than the community members (55.7%).

INDIRAMMA houses programme, a total of 62.8% of respondents agreed that they are well aware about the scheme. The classification shows 63.9% of neo-literates aware than 62.1% of community members. The degree of difference of awareness is meagre.

Rice for Rs. 2/- per KG programme, from the total sample 50.9% of the respondents have full knowledge about distribution of rice for Rs. 2/- K.G. by government. The neo-literates (55.7%) are well aware compared to community members (44.9%). This informs majority percentage (10.8%) neo-literates are well aware.

Table 8.1: Awareness of Rural Development Programmes of Neo-Literates and Community Members

Sl. No.	Theme	Group	Percentage
1	2	3	4
1.	Jalayagnam	Neo-literates	63.5%
		Community	55.7%
2.	INDIRAMMA Houses	Neo-literates	63.9%
		Community	61.4%
3.	Rice for Rs. 2/- per KG	Neo-literates	55.7%
		Community	44.9%
4.	Pensions for needy people	Neo-literates	48.9%
		Community	57.4%
5.	Rajeev Arogya Sree	Neo-literates	76.3%
		Community	15.9%
6.	Free electricity for BPL	Neo-literates	43.8%
		Community	5.1%
7.	Indira Kranthi Pathakam	Neo-literates	51.6%
		Community	73.9%
8.	Employment Grantee Scheme	Neo-literates	33.8%
		Community	13.1%
9.	Debt recoveries for farmers	Neo-literates	62.6%
		Community	55.7%

(Contd...)

1	2	3	4
10.	Social welfare/development	Neo-literates	34.7%
		Community	25.0%
11.	Pasu Kranthi	Neo-literates	49.3%
		Community	27.8%
12.	Debt recoveries for socially deprived	Neo-literates	73.5%
		Community	60.8%
13.	Service of 104/108	Neo-literates	38.8%
		Community	25.0%
14.	Family planning	Neo-literates	75.3%
		Community	69.9%

Pension for need people, a total of 52.7 per cent of the sample have complete awareness on this scheme. Coming to group wise the community members (57.4%) are well aware than 48.9% of neo-literates. But a total of 92.7% of neo-literates have an idea either fully or some extents, in the case of community members only 61.9% have some degree of awareness

With regard to Rajiv Arogya Sree, the degree difference awareness of Rajiv Aryoga Sree programme gives a notable picture. The neo-literates (76.3%) are aware about this programme, only 15.9% of community members positively responded. High percentage difference of 60.4 was recorded in this aspect.

Coming to providing free electricity for farmers, majority (43.8%) of people who are attending the centre aware compare to their counter parts (5.1%).

Indira Kranthi Pathakam programme, more percentage of community members (73.9%) are complete awareness about the scheme compare to neo-literates (51.6%).

MGNREGP, about 88 per cent of neo-literates and 75.8% of community members has some kind of knowledge about this scheme, but in comparison neo-literates are well aware than the community members.

On Debt waiver for farmer programme, the difference of awareness between neo-literates and community members is 6.9 percent which has marginal difference.

With regard to Social welfare/Rural Development, the neo-literates (91.8%) and community members (85.8%) are have either complete or some extent knowledge on the schemes provided by the Government, which will help them to change their life pattern towards positive side.

From the Pasu Kranthi programme, in village situation majority depend on raring milchi-animals for additional income. Hence 94.3 per cent of neo-literates and 83.5% of community members well ware about this programme which initiated by the elected government.

Debit waiver for Socially Deprived Sections, only 8.2 per cent of neo-literates and 14.2 per cent of community members have no idea about the scheme. The remaining respondents have an undertaking the scheme among them there is marginal difference.

With regard to Services of 104/108, now-a-days people are more aware about health aspects and in many cases health personnel are out of their reach. Regarding the scheme individual only 38.8 per cent of neo-literates and 25.1 per cent community members well aware about the procedure and how to contact them, but in total around 95 per cent of rural people have some idea about the schemes. Among both groups neo-literates are better aware than community members.

In case of family planning programme, respondents from neo-literates are marginal aware than community members. But only 5.3 per cent respondents have no idea because these are form young unmarried category. The general observation is people are well aware about small family norms.

Benefits of Development/Welfare Programmes

With regard to Jalayagnam, neo-literates (83.6%) are benefited compare to community members (71.6%), this shows neo-literates enjoyed maximum benefit than the counterparts.

INDERAMM houses programme, more percentage of neo-literates (63.9%) is benefited than community (52.3%) which indicates the centre activity helps to neo-literates.

With regard to Rice for Rs. 2/- per KG programme, about 95 per cent of neo-literates are utilizing the facility compared to community members (84.7%). Through both groups are enjoying maximum utilization of the scheme, the neo-literates are more benefited.

Pension for need people programme, majority of the neo-literates (68%) are getting sanctioned (Individual or Family Members) than 52.8% of community members. The efforts of Preraks are fruitful.

Coming to utilizing of Rajiv Arogya Sree programme the benefits difference of percentage is 12.5% only meagre. Neo-literates (63.9%) are to some extent are better than community members (61.4%). Health is very imparting for human life and the people are conscious about this. Hence, the difference is very meagre.

Free electricity programme, from the analysis it is observed that the neo-literate about 91.8% have benefited than 68.2% of community members, though the programme was propagated by peoples representatives and Governmental Officials. the community members are lagging in following the rules and norms to get the benefit. The neo-literates are utilizing more benefits due to exposure in the Continuing Education Centre.

With regard to Indira Kranthi Pathakam, the benefit derived from the scheme, the result indicates that the neo-literates (72.6%) are in majority than their counter parts (59.1%) it is to be noted here, the majority of the community members well aware than neo-literates. But in utilization aspect more percentage of neo-literates (13.5%) got benefit there, which gives us an understanding that the centre has an impact on neo-literates.

MGNREGP, the opinion regarding benefit derived form the NREGP scheme, only 22.6% of neo-literates are utilizing the facility than their counterparts (community members).

Table 8.2: Benefits of Rural Development Programmes of Neo-Literates and Community Members

Sl. No.	Theme	Group	Percentage
1	2	3	4
1.	Jalayagnam	Neo-literates	83.6%
		Community	71.6%
2.	INDIRAMMA Houses	Neo-literates	63.9%
		Community	52.3%
3.	Rice for Rs. 2/- per KG	Neo-literates	95.0%
		Community	84.7%
4.	Pensions for needy people	Neo-literates	68.0%
		Community	52.8%
5.	Rajeev Arogya Sree	Neo-literates	63.9%
		Community	61.4%
6.	Free electricity for BPL	Neo-literates	91.8%
		Community	68.2%
7.	Indira Kranthi Pathakam	Neo-literates	72.6%
		Community	59.1%
8.	Employment Grantee Scheme	Neo-literates	84.5%
		Community	61.9%
9.	Debt recoveries for farmers	Neo-literates	61.6%
		Community	56.3%
10.	Social welfare/development	Neo-literates	79.5%
		Community	61.9%
11.	Pasu Kranthi	Neo-literates	84.9%
		Community	63.6%

(Contd...)

1	2	3	4
12.	Debt recoveries for socially deprived	Neo-literates	91.3%
		Community	62.5%
13.	Service of 104/108	Neo-literates	82.6%
		Community	68.8%
14.	Family planning	Neo-literates	90.9%
		Community	53.4%

Debt waiver for farmer programme, Out of total benefited by the government welfare schemes more neo-literates 61.6% benefited then the community members their percentage is 56.3%. Tax benefit and awareness are inter-linked.

Social welfare/Rural Development, higher percentages of neo-literates (79.5%) is benefited from the schemes than their control group (61.9%). Perhaps in explaining the norms and conditions to apply for the scheme, centre activity may be helped the neo-literates.

For Pasu Kranthi programme, in this aspect of deriving benefit from Pasu Kranthi Programme higher degrees of neo-literates (84.9%) are benefited than their counterparts (63.6%) and the difference is 21.3 per cent. The influence of continuing education programmes may be the reason for more numbers of neo-literates utilizing the Pasu Kranthi Programme.

. Debit waiver for Socially Deprived Sections, there is a higher range of 28.8% benefit derived by neo-literates than their counter parts for applying and to receive the sanction of the scheme, most like may be the Preraks and are other officials actively helped and involved both in technical and general aspects.

With regard to the services of 104/108, majority of the neo-literates (84.9%) are benefited by the health schemes than community members (63.6%). The difference of benefit is high.

Family Planning, the result shows that the neo-literates are adopting family planning practices in higher degree than only 50 per cent by the control group. There is a need to educate the community members in this aspect.

Problems

The Preraks and neo-literates were enquired about constrains faced at the centre level functioning.

1. Lack of separate building facility and electricity in many centres.
2. Collection of member ship fee from neo-literates and corpus fund from the public.
3. Extensive area of operation due to distance location of centres.
4. Delay in supply of Broad sheet (weekly newspaper)meant for neo-literates.
5. Meagre salary for Preraks and delay in the payment of honorarium.
6. Main problem is that the beneficiaries are living below poverty line they are occupied with daily earnings. The second problem is during the agricultural season attendance of learners decreasing to centres.
7. Lack of provision for buying new games materials in the place of worn out materials.
8. Improper accommodation at the centre for literacy activity.
9. Inadequate support from the officials to conduct developmental programmes.
10. Lack of expected cooperation from the village level committee.
11. Apathy of the neo literates to attend the centres.
12. Lack of understanding and awareness among the public about the importance of CEC.
13. Low level education on nodal Preraks and Preraks. This has impact on:
    (a) Understanding of programme policies.
    (b) Maintenance of records and register.
    (c) Dissemination of information to the neo-literates.

14. Improper supply of new and relevant reading materials periodically.
15. Inadequate training for nodal Prerak and Prerak.
16. Absence of vocational training programmes.
17. Maintenance of too many records and registers.

Suggestions for Better Implementation of the Programme

For successful running the centre and reaching the objectives of the continuing education programme to the target group, the respondents were requested to give their suggestions. The Preraks is main key functionary, the direct beneficiary is neo-literates and community, who are indirectly, observes the situation because the rural people have homogeneous nature. Hence, their suggestions were taken for future benefit of the programme.

1. Intensive training for nodal Preraks and Preraks both pre-service and in-service.
2. Regular supply of simple relevant and diversified reading materials.
3. Frequent visits to the centres by the CEC functionaries.
4. Supply of public address system and Television sets.
5. Timely release of funds to the centre.
6. Raising the minimum level of education for nodal preraks and Preraks.
7. Identification and organising of vocational training need according to the of learners.
8. Sensitization and awareness programmes for CEC committee members, general public and village level staffs.
9. Preraks involvement is necessary for identification of beneficiaries under IRDP, ITDA, SC Corporation and other economic supported schemes.
10. Proper and adequate infrastructural facilities to be arranged by ZSS before initiating the programme.
11. All government departments should conduct their welfare programmes in the CE centre only to motivate learners.

12. Increase of honorarium and conveyance charges to be paid to the Preraks for better functioning.
13. Strict instructions to be issued to Preraks not to do other work than the continuing education programme because it was noticed many Preraks are working for local leaders.
14. Most of the learners belong to agricultural background, priority to be given in imparting new skills in that field and allied fields.
15. Establishment of training centres in the areas of vocational training like tailoring, wiring, bee keeping and so on at least in the centre place for cluster of centres.
16. Awareness and motivation campaigns should be arranged by utilising audio visual aids and involvement of development and welfare departments is necessary to sustain neo-literates in the continuing education centres.
17. Though the government of India implemented gigantic programme in macro level, coming to micro-level operation they neglecting some important elements as the responses of the field functionaries.

Suggestions

The researcher, while collecting the data observed the daily functioning of the centre, neo-literates participation and opinions of the community. The suggestions were derived by participatory observation and enlisted.

1. Provide importing of literacy should be placed in the context of the developmental needs of the adult and should be accompanied by wide range of measures relating of health, hygiene nutrition, housing and employment needs.
2. In view of the vital functions of the preraks, their minimum qualification should be raised to graduation.
3. For eradication of residual illiteracy, intensive literacy drives should be organised on mission based approach.
4. The district authority should instruct all development

departments to utilize the continuing education centers as their platform for dissemination of information, selection of target to elicit the participation in the programme implementation.

5. The centers should organize at least two vocational training programmes for every batch to increase the human resources and to create inspirations on new socio-economic developments.
6. The centers should discharge the function of media center as a single window for information at community level.
7. Special efforts should be initiated to organize the target specific programmes, equivalence, quality of life improvement, and individual interest promotion programmes, to attract all sections of the society.
8. The training curriculum of the Preraks should be restricted to equip them to discharge their functions effectively.
9. The field functionaries should identify the local talents for organizing cultural and recreational programmes regularly.
10. Organise the programme to create awareness on welfare/development Programme among the learners.
11. Steps should be taken to understand and create awareness to solve the problems among Preraks and Neo-literates.
12. The literacy centre had to be run in convenient times for the neo-literates with their consultation because they may be tired physically after work in their occupational field. The need for effective environment building and motivational strategies are to be created.
13. Self-realization and self-acceptance greatly help to overcome various problems and contribute to better adjustment in society. Voluntary efforts will have higher impact in this respect. Factors relating to change of attitude are to be studied and identified and measures taken up accordingly.

14. Occupational and skill development training programs for neo-literates in particular and community in general are aimed at improving income status to be organised.
15. Neo literates who regularly attend and successfully completed the three primers be given preference while sanctioning housing allotment. This will help permanent stay and reduce migration.
16. Awareness process should be a continuous process, not time-bound, short-term or on and off.
17. Information and communication for rural development programmes must be highlighted through village level functionaries. This will result in mass participation in learning activity.
18. The investigator noted that efforts are being made to create environments through the Jathas, Street Plays etc., but the suggestion is that any one-off effort is not sufficient to sustain the interest of neo-literates. Therefore, with the assistance of local voluntary organisations, environment building should be a continuous process, so that the motivation of neo-literates is sustained through to the completion of an education activity. It further emphasises that local talent should be utilised to create a need-based environment.
19. There is an urgent need to prepare more and more success stories through the print and audio-visual media so that both the neo-literates and community can be inspired to participate in the national Endeavour.
20. The print and electronic media, particularly television, can be utilised in the most effective manner. This media should create a congenial learning environment so that the society and the neo-literates and community members join in and recognize the importance of education. This suggestion is very important because, from the observations, it was noted that the women are more interested in watching television serials.
21. Continuing Education Centre activity should not be introduced in isolation. It should go hand in hand with

health, economic and social development, small savings, micro-finance and above all communal harmony. It should give people an immediate benefit, however small.

The results from the analysis of the study shows that the continuing education programme has a direct impact in creating awareness on the welfare/development on neo-literates and indirect influence on the village and community. The beneficiaries expressed their satisfaction in the case of centre activity. Coming to benefits received from welfare/ development programmes. The neo-literates are having more access than community members. In a nut shell, the favorable environment of the centre has helped to enlighten the neo-literates in participation, receiving and achieving the objectives of the continuing education programme.

The findings of external evaluation of Literacy Campaigns revealed that women after attending the literacy classes are in a position to meet the authorities without fear and also in a position to explain and demand their social needs. Another, benefits they are achieved about awareness of Welfare Programmes. Participate in village development activities, decision-making in home affairs, political participation, demand of appropriate wages from employees, savings, formation of SHG's, child care and children education. Taken together, education determines the social and political perception of rural people, their patterns of interaction with Government functionaries and their role in rural development.

The Government has success rate in implementation of family welfare, pulse-polio programme anti-Malaria campaigns and control age old practices such as 'Sati', Animal Sacrifice and even to some extent in formal education and so on. When previous experiences were taken into consideration, then only any programme will yield fruitful results. The failure of implementing agencies to adopt outcome results of the evaluation studies, research observation and also lack of political and social will on the part of the people's representative and educated persons were responsible even to-day, the presence of Twenty Six percentage of illiterate people in India.

The experiences of development initiatives in rural areas, especially in the last decade or so, has been indeed metamorphosed the priorities and pattern of rural development trends. It is not only the strong emergence of Panchayati Raj Institutions but also the Self Help Groups, Peoples' Participation and Partnership etc. are the issues dominating the map of rural development in the country. Since development is a continuous process and change is inevitable, it is the conceptual clarity and sound strategy behind the philosophy of Rural Development that matters the most in ensuring sustainable as well as equity in development. Given the high incidence of poverty in rural areas, as well as existence of typical social atmosphere, ensuring sustainable and equity in development may gain further importance. The task is formidable, and is of unprecedented magnitude, innumerable challenges and possible failures, but there is no redoubled vigorous passion and professionalism to realise our dreams come true in Rural Development. Alternative to this we cannot also postpone this agenda except pursuing with dogged determination.

Literacy Campaigns can be considered as an effective tool for transformation of ideas, values, behavioural change, conventions and more specially is an agent of change. Hence, if the adult education programme is organised on set objectives, change the task according to the needs of target group, creation of congenial environment then the attitude of the learner is to be changed towards positive participation. Then only the sustainable development of life can be achieved great extent through literacy programmes as expected by the Government and Planners.

Literacy is a process which dispels and promotes rational thinking and moulds human being becomes a responsible citizen. The absence of literacy, directly and indirectly refers the development of individuals, society, community and the country. For the success of any programme, people should be motivated by providing necessary congenial environment to develop their socio-economic conditions, also committed efforts of implementing agencies and positive efforts of the elected representatives. In a democratic society people cannot remain silent spectators to the vast changes that are taking place in the society. But they have to participate effectively not only in the decision-making process, but also in the formulation and implementation of the developmental programmes. To achieve this objective, all the citizens need to be educated for desirable participation and reap the benefits of rural development programmes. In other words, 'Literacy is the Tool for the Development'.

A strong commitment on the part of implementing agencies, strong will on the part of the functionaries and the strong zeal on the part of beneficiaries towards Literacy campaigns and Rural Development programmes will be the factors for the successful implementation of the programmes and yields better results as expected by the planners and Government of India.

Suggestions for Further Research

1. A study may be carried out on continuing education programme where total literacy campaigns were successful and unsuccessful with a view to suggest remedial measures.
2. In depth studies touching upon policy implications, materials, training and administration may have to be undertake.
3. A study on the influence of supervision and community support on the performance of Preraks may be taken up.
4. A study may be carried out on the performance of other functionaries like Nodal Preraks, Mandal Literacy organizers and project officers.

"All knowledge that the world has ever received comes from the mind; the infinite library of the universe is in our own mind"

–Swami Vivekananda

Bibliography

Adinarayana Reddy, P, and Uma Devi, D., (2006) "Current Trends in Adult Education" (ed), Published by Sarup and Sons, Ansari Road, New Delhi.

Adinarayana Reddy, P. & Umadevi, D., (Ed.) (2006) Total Literacy Campaigns and Women Empowerment "Current Trends in Adult Education" Sarup and Sons, Ansari Road, New Delhi.

Adult Education Development the NAEP, (1980) Published by: Indian Adult Education Association, New Delhi, Report of the 32nd All India Adult Education Conference, Amritsar, October 7-9, 1979.

Anusuya Devi, K., (2009) "Continuing Education – Trends, Issues and Future Perspectives", (Ed. Vol.), Published by Dept. of Adult, Continuing Education Extension Work and Field Outreach, Ahcarya Nagarjuna University, Guntur (A.P).

Arasm, M. (1989) Micro-planning at Village Level, National Institute of Educational Planning and Administration, New Delhi.

Baby Sarojini. K., (2006) Women Empowerment Self-helps Group, The Associated Publishers Ambala Cantt, New Delhi.

Bhalba Vibhute (2006) "Essential Pre-conditions for Successful Working of Adult Education Programme", (Ed. Vol.) Sarup & Sons, New Delhi.

Bordia Anil (1975) "A Review of Farmers Functional Literacy Programme – 1969 – 1974", Indian Adult Education Association, New Delhi.

Bordia Anil, (1973) Adult Education during the British and After Independence in Bordia et al (ed), Adult Education in India, Nachikata Publications, Bombay.

Bordia Anil., (1973) "Literacy in India: An Analytical Study in Bordia" (ed. Vol), Adult Education in India, Nachiketa Publication, Bombay.

Bordia Anil., (1975) A Review Farmers Functional Literacy Programme 1969-74, IAEA, New Delhi.

Bordia, Anil, et al (1973) "Adult Education in India – A Book of Readings", Nichiketa Publication, Bombay.

Borg W.R., (1965) "Educational Research – An Introduction" New York; David Mc Kay Company, Inc.

Buch, M.B. (Ed), : Second Survey of Research in Education, (Baroda Society for Educational Research and Development, 1979).

Buch, M.B. (Ed), A Survey of Research in Education, (Baroda: Centre of Advance Study in Education, M.S. University of Baroda, 1974).

Buch, M.B. (Ed),: Third Survey of Research in Education, (New Delhi: National Council of Educational Research and Training, 1986).

Buch, M.B. (Ed.),: Fourth Survey of Research in Education, Volume I and II (New Delhi: National Council of Educational Research and Training, 1991)

Census of India, (2001), Andhra Pradesh, Provisional Population Tables, Paper 1 of 2001, Directorate of Census Operation, Andhra Pradesh, Hyderabad.

Chaudhury, Sahadat H (2008) Choices and Voices of Adult Illiterate: Exploring Their Literacy Needs in Rural Bangladesh, Unpublished Ph.D. Dissertation, University of Massachuseetts Amherst.

Department of Adult and Continuing Education (1994), "Concurrent Evaluation of Srikakulam District", Unpublished Evaluation Report, Andhra University, Visakhapatnam.

Dixit Asha (1975) "A Study of Educational Need Patterns of Adults in the Urban, Rural and Tribal Communities of Rajasthan", Indian Journal of Adult Education, Vol. 36.

Dixit P.S., Vasudeva Rao B.S., and Joga Rao SDA., (2000), "Development and People's Participation – Role of Literacy", (Ed) Atlantic Publishers and Distributors, New Delhi. pp. 212.

Dixit P.S., Vasudeva Rao B.S., and Joga Rao SDA (2000) "Development and Peoples Participation – Role of Literacy" Published in Edited Volume Entitled "Development with Human Touch" Published by Atlantic Publishers and Distributors, Delhi.

Dubey, J.P., (2006) "Continuing Education: Need of a Wider Perspective", Published in Current trends in Adult Education, (Ed) Sarup & Sons, New Delhi. p. 276.

Egbule, Patrick E., & Njoku, Edna-Mathews C., Mass Media Support for Adult Education in Agriculture in Southern Nigeria, Published by DVV, 56, 2001, 179-186.

Five-years Plan Reports, Govt. of India.

Gopinadhan Pillai and S.S. Rekha (1997), "Continuing Education the Kerala Experiment, The Associated Publishers Ambala, Cantt.

Gopinath Reddy M., (2000) "Rural Development Administration and the Poor: Some Emerging Issues" (Ed.) Atlantic Publishers and Distributors, New Delhi. pp. 31.

Grabowski. S.M., (1976) "Training Teachers of Adults: Models and Innovative Programmes". Occasional Paper No. 46, Syracuse University.

Hand Book for Continuing Education for Colleges (1994), Department of Continuing and Adult Education Bombay, S.N.D.T. Women's University, p. 24.

Jagannada Rao. D., (2002) "The Problems Faced by Neo-Literates to Attend Continuing Education Centres in Tirupati Rural Mandal of Chittoor District". M.A. Unpublished Dissertation, S.V. University, Tirupati.

Kumarswamy, T., (2005) "Total Literacy Campaigns Problems and Issues", Sonali Publications, New Delhi.

Lakshminarayana, P. Ch and Prakasa Rao MVSS (2006) "Literacy and the Other Developmental Indicators: The Key Factors for Sustainable Development" (Ed) Sarup & Sons, New Delhi. pp. 154.

Literacy – Facts (2001) at a Glance National Literacy Mission, New Delhi.

Literacy Mission., (1995) Directorate of Adult Education, MHRD, Govt. of India, Vol. XIX, No. 4, May.

Madana Mohana Reddy, C. (1980) "Attitude of Adult Learners Towards National Adult Education Programme", M.A. Dissertation, Department of Adult Education, S.V. University, Tirupati.

Mohanty and Jagannath (1987), "Adult Education and Development", Himalaya Publishing Company, New Delhi.

Mohanty B.B (1994), Total Literacy in the Context of Education, for All by 2000, Indian Journal of Adult Education, Vol. 55, No. 2, , p. 24.

Mohanty. S.C (1991), "National Adult Education Programme in India", Chugh Publications, Allahabad.

Muthuswamy. N., (1980) "The Attitude of Adult Education Instructors Towards the National Adult Education Programme in Srikalahasthi Block", M.A. Dissertation, Department of Adult Education, S.V. University, Tirupati.

NAEP (1978), "An Outline Directorate of Adult Education", Ministry of HRD, Government of India, New Delhi.

National Literacy Mission - Challenges and Achievements.

National Literacy Mission (1988) "Annual Report", Directorate of Adult Education, Government of India, New Delhi.

National Policy on Education – (1986) Ministry of HRD, Government of India, 1986.

Nimbalkar M.R., (1987) Adult Education and its Evaluation System,. Mittal Publications Delhi.

NIPEA, (1990) Development of Education, 1988-89, National Report of India, NIPEA, Government of India, New Delhi.

Nurullah S. and Naik J.P., (1951) A History of Education in India, Mac Millan & Co. Ltd., Delhi.

Padma Kumari (2007), "Rural Development Challenges and Role of Community: An Educational Perspectives" (Ed) Published in Rural Development Strategies & Role of Institutions by Associated Publishers, Ambala Cannt, New Delhi.

Patil., (1970) "A Critical Study of Social Education in the State of Gujarat, Ph.D. unpublished thesis, Sardal Patel University.

Prasad, H., (1971) "Literacy and Development", Gandhian Institute of Studies, Varanasi.

Rajesh., (2006) "Research in Adult Continuing Education: Critical Assessment of the Past and the Strategies for the 21st Century" A Case Study" (Ed) Sarup & Sons, New Delhi. pp. 374.

Ramabrahmam, I., (1988) "Adult Education Policy and Perspectives", Gian Publishing House, Delhi.

Reddeppa Reddy, M.C., (2003), "Continuing Education: Participation and performance of Continuing Education Committees in Tirupati (Rural) Mandal, Chittor District. Published in Evaluation Studies (Ed. Vol), The Associated Publishers, Ambala Cannt.

Reddeppa Reddy., (2006) " Continuing Education Institutions in Professional Development" Published in Current trends in Adult Education, (Ed) Sarup & Sons, New Delhi. p. 286.

Reddy, P.A, Umadevi, D., & Mahadev Reddy., (2007) "Rural Development through Continuing Education Programmes", Published in Rural Development & Empowerment of Weaker Sections (Ed. Vol.), The Associated Publishers, Ambala Cannt, New Delhi.

Reddy, P.A., (1996) "A Study of the Functioning of Jana Sikshana Nilayams", A Unpublished Report of the Project Sponsored by ICSSR, New Delhi.

Reddy, P.A., (2005) "Adult Education Role of Volunteers" Sarup & Sons, New Delhi.

Rodriguez, Liza M (2007) Adult Learning for Social Action in a Latino Community: Integrating and Sustaining Skills Development, Community Organising and Advocacy in a Grassroots Organisation, Unpublished Ph.D. Dissertation, Temple University.

Roy, Nikhil Ranjan (1967) "Adult Education in India and Abroad", S.Chand & Co., Delhi.

Sabine Strassburg (2008) Adult Education and Poverty Alleviation – What can be Learnt from Practice? Four Case Studies from South Africa, Published in Adult Education and Development DVV International Vol. 70, 2008.

Saini, R.K., (1992) "National Literacy Mission - Present Status and Strategies -from the Turning Point some Thoughts on Adult Education", Directorate of Adult Education, MHRD, Government of India.

Saini, RK., (1962) "National Literacy Mission – Present Status and Strategies – from the Turning Point – Some Thoughts on Adult Education", Directorate of Adult Education, MHRD, Government of India.

Sanjay Moon., (2007) "Socio-Economic and Cultural Aspects of Education and Inter-linking the Education with the livelihood of Rural People". Adult Education and Development, Kolkata, Vol. 20, No. 1-4.

Schweigert, Thomas F (2002) the Effect of Selected Predictor Variables Upon Adult Learning Style with in Functional Chaplaincy Training, Unpublished Ph.D. Dissertation, Touro University International.

Seeni Natrajan, V., (2007) "Education for Sustainable Livelihoods in Rural Areas – Basic Education – A Gandhian Approach" Adult Education and Development, Kolkata, Vol. 20, No. 1-4.

Selltiz Claire., (1959) "Research Methods in Social Relations" Methuen & Co. Ltd., New York.

Shah S.Y., (1999). "An Encyclopedia of Indian Adult Education", Published by National Literacy Mission, New Delhi.

Sivadasan Pillai, K., (1980) "Adult/Non-formal Education Programme in India - Legislative Connectional and Evaluation Analysis", Indian Journal of Adult Education, Vol. 41, No. 5, May 1980.

Street, Brain, V., (1984) "Literacy in Theory and Practice", Cambridge University Press.

Subba Rao D., (1978), "New Dimension to Adult Literacy", Social Welfare 25 (9), December.

Subba Rao, D., & Vasudeva Rao, B S., (1984) "Adult and Continuing Education: Some Perspectives", Rural Development Publications, Andhra Pradesh.

Subba Rao, D., (1993) "Continuing Education in India" The Associate Publishers, Ambala Cannt.

Sudha Rani, K., & Vasantha Kumari P., (2006) " Teaching/ Learning Materials for Adult Learners Neo-Literates" Published in Current trends in Adult Education, (Ed) Sarup & Sons, New Delhi. pp. 220.

Sunder Raj D., (2000) "Rural Development and People's Participation" (Ed) Atlantic Publishers and Distributors, New Delhi.

Sunder Raj, D., (2007) "People Centered Development: An Overview", (Ed. Vol.) The Associated Publishers, Ambala Cantt.

Surapa Raju, S. (2002), "Akshara Sankranthi Programme and Evaluation" Indian Journal of Adult Education, Vol. 63, No. 4. Oct-Dec 2002. pp. 43-46.

Surendra, G., (2004) "Perspectives of Continuing Education Programme", Sonali Publications, New Delhi.

Tataji, U., (2004) "Five Decades of Development Experience in India" Published by Director, Andhra University Press, Visakhapatnam.

Vandana Chakrabarti., (2004) "Life Long Learning: Innovations and Experiments in Lifelong Learning" (Ed.vol.) Asian South Pacific Bureau of Adult Education.

Vasudeva Rao B.S., Viswanadha Gupta P. and Srinivasa Rao G. (2005) "Akshara Bharathi Programme: Volunteers' Perceptions", Journal of Adult Education and Extension, Dept. of Adult and Continuing Education, Sri Venkateswara University, Tirupati, Vol. 1, No. 2, July-Dec.

Vasudeva Rao B.S., (1988) "National Adult Education Programme in Visakhapatnam District", Himalaya Publication House, Mumbai.

Vasudeva Rao B.S. and Viswanadha Gupta P. (2006) "Low Female Literacy: Factors and Strategies", Australian Journal of Adult Learning, Australia, Volume No. 46, No. 1, pp. 84-95,

Vasudeva Rao, B.S., (1999) "Evaluation of Total Literacy Campaign in Nellore District of Andhra Pradesh" Indian Journal of Adult Education, New Delhi.

Vasudeva Rao, B.S. and Viswanadha Gupta, P. (2008) Multi-Dimensional Approaches to Literacy Development, Associated Publishers, Ambala Cannt.

Vasudeva Rao, B.S., (2004), "Rural Development: Rural Development: Bureaucratic Culture vis-a-vis Education" Article Published in "Empowerment of People (Ed), Kanishka Publications, New Delhi.

Vasudeva Rao, B.S. & Sekhar K., (2003) "Evaluation Studies", The Associated Publishers Ambala Cantt.

Vasudeva Rao B.S. 2007 Rural Development Strategies and Role of Institutions Issues, Innovations and Initiatives (Ed.Vol) - The Associated Publishers, Ambala Cantt.

Vasudeva Rao B.S & Rajani Kanth G. (2007) Rural Development Initiatives and Empowerment of Weaker Sections Practices, Promotion and Programmes (Ed. Vol) - The Associated Publishers, Ambala Cantt.

Vasudeva Rao B.S & Rajani Kanth G. 2007 Rural Resources and Development Initiatives Structural Issues and Development.

Interventions (Ed. Vol) – The Associated Publishers, Ambala Cantt.

Venkata Ravi. R., .Narayana Reddy, N., (2004) "Empowerment of People Grassroots Strategies and Issues". (Ed.) Kanishka Publishers, Distributors, New Delhi, pp. 123, 153, 203 and 262.

Vijaya Kumar, S., (2000). "Human Development: An Overview" (Ed.) Atlantic Publishers and Distributors, New Delhi. pp. 16.

Viswanadha Gupta P (2008) "Literacy Attainment of Continuing Education Beneficiaries" Literacy and Development, Journal of Society for Promotion of Adult Continuing Education (SPACE), pp. 42-54, Issue No. 1.

Viswanadha Gupta P (2008) "Reproductive Health Needs of the Tribal Women", International Research Journal of Social Sciences, Puducherry, India, Volume No. 1, No. 2, pp. 165-175.

Viswanadha Gupta, P, (2006) "Functioning of Continuing Education Committees: A Case Study" (Ed) Published in Current Trends in Adult Education, Sarup & Sons, New Delhi. p. 313.

Viswanadha Gupta, P., Adinarayana Reddy P and Vasudeva Rao B S (2006) "A Study of the Functioning of Continuing Education Centres as Perceived by Continuing Education Committee Members", Jana Saksharatha, Journal of SRC for Adult Education, Indore, Vol. 7, No. 2, June.

Rajanikanth G. (1998) A Study of Mass Campaign for Total Literacy in Chittoor District, Andhra Pradesh Unpublished Dissertation Submitted to Andhra University.

Viswanadha Gupta, P., and Vasudeva Rao, B S., (2004) "Continuing Education Programme: Problems and Perspectives" Journal of Jana Saksharatha, Indore.

Umamaheswara Rao C. "Role of Capacity Building and Institutional Arrangement in Rural Development: 2011 With Special Focus on Natural Resources Management and Employment Generation Programmes in Andhra Pradesh" Ph.D (Unpublished), Andhra University, Visakhapatnam.

Radhakrishna Murthy Ch.(1996). A Comparative Study of Implementation of National Adult Education Programme by Government and Voluntary Agencies in Srikakulam District of Andhra Pradesh", Unpublished Ph.D Thesis Submitted to Andhra University.

Viswanadha Gupta P.(2007)."Continuing Education Programme in Vizianagaram District: A Study of Stakeholders and Learners" Unpublished Ph.D. Dissertation Submitted to Andhra University.

Srinivasa Rao G. (2007)"Attitude of the Preraks' Towards Continuing Education Programme in Vizianagaram District", Unpublished M.Phil Dissertation Submitted to Andhra University.

Workshop Proceedings (1999) on Integrated Rural Development Through Participatory Approach Organized by Sri Krishnadevaraya University, Anantapur on 30th & 31st January, 1999.

Index